STUDY GUIDE

John W. Hoopes
University of Kansas
James H. Mielke
University of Kansas

Second Edition

ANTHROPOLOGY
A GLOBAL PERSPECTIVE

Raymond Scupin
Lindenwood College
Christopher R. DeCorse
Syracuse University

PRENTICE HALL, *Englewood Cliffs, New Jersey 07632*

For
Lauren and Alexandra Hoopes
Diane, Evan, and Jessica Mielke

©1995 by PRENTICE-HALL, INC.
A Simon and Schuster Company
Englewood Cliffs, New Jersey 07632

10 9 8 7 6 5 4 3 2 1

ISBN 0-13-301581-5
Printed in the United States of America

CONTENTS

Preface

This study guide has been prepared as a supplement to the textbook, *Cultural Anthropology: A Global Perspective* (2nd edition), by Raymond Scupin and Christopher DeCorse. It is intended to help students review material in the text and study for examinations in a course for which the textbook is required reading.

The principal features of the study guide are:

1) **outlines of individual chapters to help students review major topics.**
2) **chapter highlights that summarize the most important points made in the text,**
3) **lists of terms, cultures, people, and places with which students should be familiar after having read the chapters,**
4) **questions to think about that integrate and emphasize concepts and theories, and**
5) **practice examinations that consist of true/false and multiple choice questions on the material in each chapter.**

To the Student:

Nothing can take the place of a careful reading of the textbook. However, using this study guide in conjunction with your reading will help you to evaluate how much of the reading you have understood and determine which materials you need to review more carefully. No one understands everything on the first reading, and your understanding of the subject matter will be much better if you concentrate on studying what you don't know, rather than what you know already. This study guide can help you to determine your weaknesses - "holes" in your knowledge that need to be filled if you are to do well on examinations.

One way to determine how much of the text you have understood is to review the contents of each chapter. The **Chapter Outline** will help you to scan the topics that have been covered. While you look over the outline, ask yourself whether you have a good understanding of what was discussed under each heading. If not, use the outlines as a guide to going back and doing a more careful reading of the sections that are least familiar.

Another way to review the contents of the text is with the **Chapter Highlights**. These have been written as brief summaries of the contents of each chapter. Terms and concepts that are important are in bold type for quick identification. We recommend that you read the Chapter Highlights over more than once so you have a general feeling for each chapter. You should also read the summaries in your textbook to see what the authors consider as the salient points of each chapter. You might even consider outlining each chapter and then looking over the Chapter Highlights in this workbook to see if the two correspond. If not, add information where it is missing.

The **Terms and Concepts, People, and Cultures** sections list words and names which are important for a clear understanding of each topic and chapter. We suggest that you define each of the words in the space provided. Writing something down helps in studying and retaining the information much better than simply reading. Also, spend time reviewing the definitions you have written.

The **Thinking About What You Have Read** sections of this guide are designed to make you think about the material presented in the text and put it into a larger perspective. You might even consider these to be essay questions to be answered. Again, writing something down always seems to make it stay with one longer.

A **Practice Examination**, based on each chapter, will help determine your strengths while at the same time pointing out areas where you need to focus your studying. Both True-False and Multiple-Choice questions have been included to give you a variety. An **Answer Key With Page Numbers** is provided at the end. If you make a mistake, figure out why your answer was incorrect, that is, learn by your mistakes.

A list of **Suggested Readings** is provided if you want to explore topics in more depth. You can also use this list as a starting point for research on specific topics of interest.

We hope you find this study guide useful in your exploration of anthropology.

In some cases we have used and updated material found in the *Study Guide* that was prepared for the first edition of the textbook. In this regard, we would like to acknowledge the earlier work, insights, and expertise of Charles O. Ellenbaum and Gail B. Ellenbaum.

We thank Sharon Chambliss, Associate Editor Sociology/Anthropology, for her guidance, patience, hard work, and humor during the process of producing this guide..

CHAPTER 1

INTRODUCTION TO ANTHROPOLOGY

Chapter Outline

Anthropology: The Four Subfields
  Physical Anthropology
  Archaeology
  Linguistic Anthropology
  Ethnology
Holistic Anthropology, Interdisciplinary Research, and the Global Perspective
Applied Anthropology
Anthropology and Science
  The Scientific Method
  Limits of Science
Anthropology and the Humanities
Why Study Anthropology?

Chapter Highlights

Chapter one sets the stage for your study of anthropology by introducing you to the anthropological perspective, its major fields and general goals. You will be introduced to a new way of viewing the world and its people, sort of like putting on a new pair of colored glasses and looking at the world anew. This outlook may seem confusing at times; this is natural since you will be learning a new **paradigm** (a set of assumptions, beliefs, methods, ideals, and research strategies that shape the observations and conclusions within a particular discipline). As you begin to learn the anthropological paradigm, a new world of explanation and understanding will hopefully start to unfold in front of you. You will be introduced to many different cultures and peoples in your reading and class discussions. This will expose you to international, cross-cultural, and global viewpoints. You will probably have to deal with contradictory claims and native viewpoints that may seem illogical and wrong to you. It is natural and okay to feel confused. You will also need to remember that your views, values, and actions may be considered as odd to people from other cultures. There are "insider viewpoints" (native) and "outsider viewpoints." These views may be radically different, yet both can be correct in describing a particular culture or event. They simply show differing perspectives. As a student anthropologist, you will be exposed to and learn the native viewpoint or perspective. Only then can you start to analyze and solve problems or ask questions that make sense within the context of the culture being examined. All native viewpoints are valid within the context of their own culture. All of you have valid cultural and cross-cultural viewpoints.

Your text opens with an imaginary encounter, the "first contact", with extraterrestrials. If you were among the space travelers, what types of questions would ask the extraterrestrials (assuming you could communicate)? How would you respond to these beings? What types of things would you look for while observing these creatures? These are also the types of questions you will probably ask as you engage in your "first contact" with worldly cultures you have not heard of before. At the same time, you should be cognizant of the fact that for the peoples being studied by the anthropologist that this might be their "first contact" with strange peoples and odd ideas and behaviors. The anthropologist may also experience "**culture shock**" (a psychological reaction that ranges from mild to severe when we experience a different culture from what we are used to) during this first contact, or after returning home after a prolonged stay in the other culture.

We can define **anthropology** as the systematic study of humanity in all of its facets. Two major goals of anthropology are to (1) understand the uniqueness and diversity of human behavior and human societies across the world and (2) to elucidate the similarities that link humans together as a single species. In order to meet these goals, anthropologists ideally employ a **holistic perspective** that encompasses the interaction of the four subfields of anthropology: physical anthropology, archaeology, linguistic anthropology, and ethnology or cultural anthropology.

Physical anthropology focuses on two areas: (1) human evolution and (2) human variation. The study of human evolution through the analysis of **fossils** is called **paleoanthropology**. Other physical anthropologists study human evolution by examining living primates (**primatology**) to ascertain the similarities and differences among these living forms, humans, and extinct primates. Other physical anthropologists focus on contemporary human variation through the study of genetics, physiology, biological adaptation, microevolution, demography, and disease and health. Some physical anthropologists use their knowledge and expertise to help solve problems that face societies today (this is called **applied anthropology**). One such specialty is **forensic anthropology** or the identification of human skeletal remains for legal purposes.

Archaeology is that branch of anthropology that seeks to learn more about the lifestyles, history, and evolution of past societies. Archaeologists use **artifacts**, the material products left by former societies, as clues to understanding the cultural dynamics of these extinct cultures. **Prehistoric archaeologists** are concerned with that period of time before written history. **Historical archaeologists**, on the other hand, study our past since the development of written history. **Classical archaeologists**, working in collaboration with historians, are interested in ancient civilizations found in such areas as Egypt, Greece, and Rome. The three major goals of these archaeologists are to (1) construct cultural chronologies (i.e., answer the questions of *when* and *where*?), (2) reconstruct past lifeways (i.e, *what* happened?), and (3) study culture process (the *how* and *why* questions of science).

Linguistic anthropology is the study of language, languages, and the relationship between language and culture. **Historical linguists** study grammatical structures and sounds in different languages in order to ascertain historical links among the languages and to reconstruct protolanguages. **Structural linguists** focus on the sounds, words, sentence structure, and meaning in different languages. The connection between language and social behavior is also of interest to anthropologists. This branch of linguistics is called **sociolinguistics**. Anthropological linguistics are also interested in such topics as the origin of language, non-human primate communication, non-verbal communication, and language learning or acquisition of children.

Ethnology (or **cultural anthropology**) is the study of contemporary peoples and cultures. Using a unique research strategy called **participant observation**, cultural anthropologists learn as much as they can about specific cultures. Participant observation involves learning the language and culture of the group being studied and taking part in the group's daily activities. Through key informants, participant observation, unstructured interviews, and structured interviews, anthropologists gain an increasingly complete picture of a people and their culture. Cultural anthropologists work with both quantitative and qualitative data. Both are necessary to create a full and complete **ethnography**, or a description of a specific culture. An ethnography asks three basic questions: What do these people do? How do they do it? Why do they do it that way?

Most anthropologists are committed to a **holistic (holism)** approach to understanding human behavior. The holistic perspective is one that is multi-faceted, taking into consideration all of the parts of the system and how those parts are related. This approach encompasses both biological and cultural phenomena. Anthropological explanations or the anthropological perspective entail data gleaned from fieldwork situations, participant observation, and the comparative method. These findings are then combined with the concept of culture and the holistic approach to produce a unique understanding of humankind.

Applied anthropology is emerging today as the major fifth subdiscipline of anthropology. Applied anthropology is the use of anthropological data and theories to offer practical solutions to problems within society.

The **scientific method** is a particular way of providing orderly and supported explanations. It is a logical system used to evaluate data that are obtained by systematic observation. It is not a panacea that solves all problems, nor is it without error. In fact, science theories are falsifiable since scientific explanations are testable, tentative, and subject to change. The scientific method rests on the faith that the universe possesses order and this order can be discerned and interpreted. There are two ways of generating testable propositions or what are called **hypotheses**: the **inductive method** and the **deductive method**. The inductive method begins with specific observations from which you then draw conclusions or make generalizations. The deductive method begins with a generalization or theory and from it you predict specific observations, actions, or applications.

Eric Wolf has called anthropology "the most scientific of the humanities and the most humanist of the sciences." In addition to conducting research that would be classified within the natural and social sciences, anthropologists investigate the creative dimensions of humankind including poetry, art, music, theater, literature, and mythology.

Why study anthropology? Anthropology provides a perspective that is different from other disciplines that study humans. It creates a deep appreciation for humanity past and present. It focuses on similarities and differences among peoples and cultures, giving us a better understanding of the human entity and the human experience. We can learn more about ourselves and our behavior by exploring the diversity of lifeways found across the world.

Terms and Concepts You Should Know

anthropology (3):

physical anthropology (3-4):

fossil (3):

paleoanthropology (3):

primatology (3):

forensic anthropology (3):

archaeology (4):

artifact (4):

midden (4):

prehistoric archaeology (5):

classical archaeology (5):

historical archaeology (5):

site (6):

"Garbage Project" (6):

linguistic anthropology (6):

culture (7):

historical linguistics (7):

structural linguistics (7):

sociolinguistics (7):

ethnology or cultural anthropology (7):

participant observation (7):

ethnographer or ethnologist (7):

ethnography (9):

holistic [holism] (9):

applied anthropology (11):

scientific method (11):

inductive method (12):

deductive method (12):

hypothesis (12):

theory (12);

paradigm (13):

ethnomusicology (14):

People to Know About

Clyde Snow (1):

Patty Jo Watson (6):

Bambi B. Schieffelin (8):

Napoleon Chagnon (10):

Cultures to Know About

Yanomamö (10):

Thinking About What You Have Read

The following questions or problems may be of help to you in studying the material presented in both the text and in your class. You may want to write out the answers to these questions (writing something down always seems to help solidify it in one's mind) or just think about them.

1. What are the major goals of anthropology? How can they be achieved?

2. What is anthropology? What distinguishes it from other academic fields that study humankind? What are the major subdivisions, and what does each one study? Do you think that the anthropological perspective and anthropological information can be applied to your career field?

3. What is physical anthropology? What do physical anthropologists (or biological anthropologists) study? What are the major subfields? How could physical anthropology be applied to your career field?

4. What is archaeology? What do archaeologists study? What are the major subfields within archaeology? How could archaeology be applied to your career field?

5. Who are the following anthropologists: Clyde Snow, Patty Jo Watson, Bambi B. Schieffelin, and Napoleon Chagnon? What did you learn about them and their areas of expertise?

6. What is anthropological linguistics? What do linguists study? What are the major subfields? Can anthropological linguistics be applied to your career field?

7. What is cultural anthropology or ethnology? What does it study? What are the major subfields? How could cultural anthropology be applied to your career field?

8. What is applied anthropology?

9. What is an ethnography? Compare and contrast ethnography and ethnology. What are the primary goals of ethnography and ethnology?

10. What is the scientific method? Make sure your understand the following terms and how they fit into the process of the scientific method: inductive and deductive methods, variable, hypothesis, and theory.

11. How is anthropology related to other disciplines that fall within the natural sciences, social and behavioral sciences, and humanities? Does anthropology have any connections with art, music, theater, law, engineering, business, or architecture?

12. Why study anthropology? How will it help you to become more broadly educated and successful in your chosen career?

CHECKING YOUR UNDERSTANDING: A PRACTICE EXAMINATION

We suggest that you take this practice exam and then check your answers against the key provided at the end of this section. Use the questions that you got wrong as a guide for further study. Try to learn why specific answers are right and wrong. You may even want to take the practice exam a second time to review what you have learned.

True-False Questions

1. According to your text, the four subfields of anthropology are archaeology, physical anthropology, classical archaeology, and anthropological linguistics.

2. In legal proceedings and trials that involve human skeletons the courts may rely upon the expertise of forensic anthropologists.

7

3. The term *anthropo* means "primate", while the term *logia* translates as "the study of", hence, anthropology is defined as the study of primates.

4. Primatology is the study of primitive cultures and mores.

5. The branch of anthropology that studies human evolution and variation is known as physical anthropology.

6. The study of past cultures and lifestyles is the goal of ethnologists.

7. Artifacts are the material products of former societies that give clues to the lifeways of an extinct peoples.

8. Patty Jo Watson is famous for her anthropological study of drug addiction and the Medellín drug cartel.

9. Sociolinguistics is the study of grammatical patterns and other linguistic structures in contemporary languages.

10. Ethnology is another word for cultural anthropology.

11. Classical archaeologists conduct research on ancient civilizations of Rome and Greece.

12. The study of language is called linguistics.

13. Most of the research conducted by Bambi Schiefflein could be categorized as ethnomusicology.

14. Anthropologists often employ a research strategy called participant observation that involves learning the language and culture of a people by engaging in the group's daily activities and lives.

15. An applied anthropologist might study the genetic differences among gorillas, chimpanzees, and humans to determine how similar they are to one another.

16. The use of anthropological data to offer practical solutions to contemporary problems within society is called applied anthropology.

17. The core of the scientific method is testability.

18. In the deductive method, the scientist first makes observations and collects data and then develops a hypothesis about the data.

19. A set of beliefs, assumptions, techniques, and research strategies that shape the questions asked, the observations made, and the conclusions that are drawn is called an ethnography.

20. According to the authors of your text, the study of anthropology will provide you with a deep appreciation of humanity and a global awareness.

Multiple Choice Questions

21. One of the first problems encountered when studying an existing society is
    A. investigating the physical characteristics of the people
    B. communicating with the people
    C. investigating the technology
    D. observing the behavior

22. According to your text, the two major goals of anthropology are to
    A. study human evolution and culture change
    B. understand the diversity of human behavior and discover the fundamental similarities that link all humans
    C. discovery new cultures and societies and understand the basis of human behavior
    D. study cultural and biological diversity and try to implement cultural change
    E. study exotic cultures before they disappear and discover the biological basis of human behavior

23. The study of human evolution through the study of fossils is called
    A. archaeology
    B. primatology
    C. forensic anthropology
    D. paleoanthropology
    E. ethnology

24. A forensic anthropologist who applied his skills to such problems as the assassination of John F. Kennedy and the identification of Argentina's "disappeared" is
    A. Bambi Schieffelin
    B. Napoleon Chagnon
    C. Raymond Scupin
    D. Clyde Snow
    E. Eric Clapton

25. The comparison and classification of different languages to explore the historical links among languages is called:
    A. structural linguistics
    B. sociolinguistics
    C. historical linguistics
    D. paleolinguistics
    E. ethnology

26. Archaeology can be BEST defined as:
    A. the study of fossilized bones and teeth
    B. the study of material products of past human societies
    C. 8the study of dinosaurs and other prehistoric life
    D. the study of ancient civilizations

27. The systematic study of language use in various social settings in order to explore the links between language and social behavior is called:
    A. structural linguistics
    B. sociolinguistics
    C. ethical linguistics
    D. normative linguistics
    E. kin-structured linguistics

28. A holistic perspective
    A. allows one to look for missing parts of a problem, theory, or hypothesis
    B. is a broad, comprehensive account that draws on all four subfields of anthropology
    C. allows anthropologists to "blow holes" in theories or hypotheses in order to disprove them
    D. most anthropologists ignore this perspective because it is usually not very fruitful
    E. is used only by physical anthropologists examining forensic cases

29. Anthropologist Napoleon Chagnon
    A. worked on the problem of racial assimilation in Haiti.
    B. is known for his work excavating the archaeological site of Troy.
    C. studied the Yanomamö in the Orinoco River Valley in Venezuela and Brazil
    D. is famous for his sociolinguistic study of the Hopi.

30. A testable proposition concerning the relationship between a particular set of variables is called a
    A. paradigm
    B. hypothesis
    C. theory
    D. deduction

31. In the _____ method of doing research the scientist first makes observations and collects data. The scientist then develops hypotheses about the data; and if a hypothesis is not falisified, it may be connected to other hypotheses to form a theory.
    A. paradigm
    B. inductive
    C. reactionary
    D. deductive
    E. opposition

32. If research begins with a general theory that is followed by hypothesis testing, this scientist is using the
    A. variable method
    B. deductive method
    C. inductive method
    D. applied method

33. A scientist's personal beliefs, values, and biases are known collectively as
    A. viewpoints
    B. subjective knowledge
    C. objective knowledge
    D. reductive knowledge

34. When scientists in a particular field of study share a common set of beliefs, assumptions, and methods that guide their research and the evaluation of its merits, this is referred to as a/n:
    A. induction
    B. objective knowledge
    C. paradigm
    D. theory

35. Knowledge that is beyond a scientist's personal beliefs, values, and biases is called:
    A. scientific knowledge
    B. common knowledge
    C. subjective knowledge
    D. objective knowledge

Suggested Readings

AGAR, MICHAEL H. 1980. *The Professional Stranger: An Informal Introduction to Ethnography*. New York, NY: Academic Press.

ASHMORE, WENDY AND ROBERT J. SHARER. 1988. *Discovering Our Past: A Brief Introduction to Archaeology*. Mountain View, CA: Mayfield.

BINFORD, LEWIS R. 1983. *In Pursuit of the Past: Decoding the Archaeological Record*. New York, NY: Thames and Hudson.

CHAGNON, NAPOLEON. 1974. *Studying the Yanomamö*. New York, NY: Holt, Rinehart & Winston.

EDDY, FRANK W. 1991. *Archaeology: A Cultural-Evolutionary Approach*. Englewood Cliffs, NJ: Prentice Hall.

FAGAN, BRIAN M. 1989. *People of the Earth: An Introduction to World Prehistory.* Glenview, IL: Scott-Foresman and Company.

_____. 1991. *In the Beginning: An Introduction to Archaeology.* New York, NY: Harper Collins.

_____. 1991. *Archaeology: A Brief Introduction.* Glenview, IL: Scott, Foresman.

FEDER, KENNETH L. 1990. *Frauds, Myths, and Mysteries: Science and Pseudoscience in Archaeology.* Mountain View, CA: Mayfield.

HICKERSON, NANCY P. 1980. *Linguistic Anthropology.* New York, NY: Holt, Rinehart & Winston.

LEWIN, ROGER. 1987. *Bones of Contention: Controversies in the Search for Human Origins.* New York, NY: Simon and Schuster.

JURMAIN, ROBERT AND HARRY NELSON. 1994. *Introduction to Physical Anthropology.* St. Paul, MN: West Publishing Company.

POIRER, FRANK W.; WILLIAM A. STINI; AND KATHY B. WREDEN. 1990. *In Search of Ourselves: An Introduction to Physical Anthropology.* Englewood Cliffs, NJ: Prentice Hall.

RELETHFORD, JOHN H. *The Human Species: An Introduction to Biological Anthropology.* Mountain View, CA: Mayfield.

_____. 1994. *Fundamentals of Biological Anthropology.* Mountain View, CA: Mayfield.

RENFREW, COLIN AND PAUL BAHN. 1991. *Archaeology: Theories, Methods, and Practice.* New York, NY: Thames and Hudson.

POWDERMAKER, HORTENSE. 1966. *Stranger and Friend: The Way of an Anthropologist.* New York, NY: Norton.

THOMAS, DAVID H. 1989. *Archaeology.* New York, NY: Holt, Rinehart & Winston.

WEISS, MARK L. AND ALAN E. MANN. 1990. *Human Biology and Behavior: An Anthropological Perspective.* Glenview, IL: Scott, Foresman/Little, Brown.

Answer Key with Page Numbers

1. F 3	13. F 8	25. C 7
2. T 3	14. T 9	26. B 7
3. F 3	15. F 11	27. B 7
4. F 3	16. T 11	28. B 9
5. T 3	17. T 11	29. C 10
6. F 4	18. F 12	30. B 12
7. T 4	19. F 13	31. B 12
8. F 6	20. T 16	32. B 12
9. F 7	21. B 1	33. B 13
10. T 7	22. B 3	34. C 13
11. T 7	23. D 3	35. D 13
12. T 7	24. D 5	

CHAPTER 2

EVOLUTION

Chapter Outline

Cosmologies and Human Origins
Western Stories of Origin
The Scientific Revolution
Catastrophism versus Uniformitarianism
CATASTROPHISM
UNIFORMITARIANISM
Theories of Evolution
Lamarck: Acquired Traits
Darwin, Wallace, and Natural Selection
Examples of Natural Selection
Principles of Inheritance
Mendel and Modern Genetics
MENDEL'S EXPERIMENTS
Dominant and Recessive Traits
Genes and Heredity
Principle of Segregation
Molecular Genetics
THE ROLE OF DNA
Population Genetics and Evolution
Mutations
Gene Flow
Genetic Drift
Natural Selection
How Does Evolution Occur?
Speciation
Punctuated Equilibrium
Adaptive Radiation
The Evolution of Life
Analogy and Homology
Plate Tectonics and Continental Drift
Blood Chemistry and DNA
Paleontological Record
THE PRECAMBRIAN AND PALEOZOIC ERAS
THE MESOZOIC ERA
THE CENOZOIC ERA
Scientific Creationism and Evolution
The Shortcomings of Creationism

Chapter Highlights

Humans worldwide have apparently always asked questions such as: "Where did I come from? Where am I going? What is my place and role in the world? Most cultures have explanations that provide answers to these basic questions. **Cosmologies** are the conceptual frameworks that provide answers to these questions and more. Imbedded within cosmologies are cultural explanations of origin, or what are called **origin myths**. Although origin myths differ in detail, they tend to explain the "why" more than the "how" of creation. They bring order and structure to apparent chaos. Often humans are the climax or pinnacle of creation. The origin myths embody the **worldview** of the people. Worldviews are the central conceptions of peoples, providing explanations of why and how things are and how they got there. Worldviews provide psychological support during times of crisis (e.g., death, sickness) and high anxiety or elation (e.g., birth, marriage). They also provide an integration to life by systematizing reality into an organized structure. Worldviews are adaptive because they can be modified or changed as life conditions or cultures change. An origin myth provides important insights into a people's worldview.

Early explanations of origins in the Western world often invoked a creator who placed all living things on the earth in perfect harmony with their environment. There was a Great Chain of Being (*scala naturae*), a hierarchical, unilineal graded sequence from the simplest to the most complex of organisms (with humans at the pinnacle). The world was static (non-evolving) and guided by a divine hand. Species were fixed entities that did not evolve or change. Early scholars sought to detect natural laws and provide a glimpse of the creator's flawlessness and genius. The world was thought to be young. Using the Bible as their base, both **James Ussher** and John Lightfoot calculated that the world began in October, 4004 B.C. The view of a static world with unchanging species posed some problems for naturalists who were studying geological formations and fossils. One of these scientists, **George Cuvier** suggested that the discontinuities in the strata and fossil record showed that species had disappeared because catastrophes (floods, earthquakes) had occurred. After the catastrophe, the areas were repopulated with organisms from surrounding regions. This view, called **catastrophism**, was challenged by other naturalists such as **Buffon** who theorized that the earth changed through gradual, natural processes and was at least 168,000 years old. As more information accumulated this **uniformitarian** view became articulated in the geological works of both **James Hutton** and **Charles Lyell**.

One early comprehensive theory of evolutionary change was proposed by **Jean Baptiste de Lamarck**, who unveiled his ideas in 1800 and later articulated them in full form in 1809 in *Philosophie Zoologique*. Lamarck combined two concepts, **use and disuse** and the **inheritance of acquired characteristics**, to explain evolutionary change in organisms. For Lamarck, the environment was dynamic and organisms adapted to changing conditions. Today we know that Lamarck's explanation was incorrect, but he should be credited for his perspective of a dynamic, interacting ecosystem.

The concept of a static, created world was finally shattered by the work of two naturalists, **Charles Darwin** and **Alfred Russel Wallace**, who theorized that evolutionary change occurred by a process called **natural selection**. In the struggle for existence, survival is not random, but depends on the hereditary makeup of the organisms. That is, there is differential survival (in the struggle for existence, the elimination process was selective) and differential fertility (differential production of offspring). Evolution is then a gradual change in the hereditary makeup of the species.

Our initial understanding of genetics and the inheritance of characteristics can be traced back to the work of **Johan Gregor Mendel**. Mendel, using peas, showed that, (1) inheritance is particulate and that (2) the particles (what we now call **alleles**) occur in pairs and separate (segregate) in the formation of the sex cells or gametes (called the **Principle of Segregation**. Mendel, working with more that one trait at a time, then developed the **Principle of Independent Assortment**. Today, we know that this principle only works if the characteristics (genes) are not linked (that is, the traits are located on different chromosomes). Modern geneticists now often focus their work at the molecular level (**DNA**) of the gene in attempts to locate and map all of the genes in the human genome.

Anthropologists are often concerned with the extent of variation and changes that occur in the genetic structure of populations over time. **Evolution** (microevolution) is defined as a change in the genetic composition of a population over time (or a change in gene frequencies over time). There are four mechanisms of evolutionary change: **mutation, gene flow, genetic drift,** and **natural selection**. These forces interact to introduce, mix, increase, and decrease genetic variation within and between populations.

Evolutionary change above the species level (macroevolution) is also of interest to anthropologists. The **gradualist** (Darwinian) view of **speciation** suggests that when gene flow is interrupted and populations become genetically isolated, new species can arise. Thus, speciation is a slow and gradual process taking many years. On the other hand, the theory of **punctuated equilibrium (Stephen Jay Gould** and **Nile Eldredge)** posits that speciation occurs rapidly and then species are characterized by a long period when little evolution occurs (a period of stasis) during which natural selection acts to keep the population adapted to the environment. There are times in the fossil record that numerous new species come into being in a short span of time. This rapid diversification, or **adaptive radiation**, is often associated with environmental changes. This type of speciation occurred after the demise of the dinosaurs about 65 million years ago and during the colonization of Madagascar by lemurs.

Evolutionary relationships among species are often studied by examining the similarities and differences among fossil forms. **Analogous** traits are those that have a similar function in two species but are different in structure and origin. The different structures do not reflect evolutionary relationships, but arise by **convergent evolution**. **Homologous** traits are those that have a similar structure but may or may not show a similar function. The correspondence between the traits is due to the fact that they have been derived from a common ancestor.

The concept of **continental drift** is important for anthropological interpretations of the beginnings of the **Primate** order about 65 million years ago and the separation and divergence of the **Old World monkeys** and **New World monkeys**.

16

Evolutionary relationships are not only studied by observing the fossil record, but inferences can be made by examining the molecular similarities and differences among living organisms. This technique, called **molecular dating** (or the **molecular clock**), uses nuclear DNA and mitochondrial DNA to elucidate evolutionary relationships and time of divergence of species and higher taxonomic levels.

Cosmological explanations often involve *supernatural* or divine forces that cannot be observed. We accept the explanations as true, that is, we believe in them or have faith that they are correct. On the other hand, scientific explanations (hypotheses, theories) of origins and evolution are based on the idea that the universe operates according to regular, *natural* processes that can be observed. Scientific explanations involving origins and evolution are tentative and falsifiable just like other scientific explanations (i.e., the scientist could be wrong). Thus, these two types of explanations are based on different views of the world, use different methods, have different premises, and should not be directed compared or be competitive. **"Scientific creationism,"** as the text discusses, is *not science*, but religion. In the debate of "scientific creationism" versus evolution, the question one must ask is <u>not</u> which explanation is correct, but what is science and what is non-science?

Be sure that you familiarize yourself with the geological time scale presented on page 34 of the text, especially the Cenozoic era and its seven epochs. The order and timing of the epochs are important for discussions that follow.

<u>Terms and Concepts You Should Know</u>

cosmology [cosmologies] (18)

catastrophism (20)

uniformitarianism (20-21)

evolution (21)

inheritance of acquired characteristics (21)

industrial melanism [Peppered moths] (23-24)

hybrid (24)

dominant (25)

recessive (25)

gene (25)

allele (25)

homozygous (25)

heterozygous (25)

genotype (25)

phenotype (25)

Principle of Segregation (26)

Principle of Independent Assortment (26)

somatic cells (27)

gametes (27)

chromosome (27)

mitosis (27)

meiosis (28)

recombination (28)

DNA [deoxyribonucleic acid] (28)

double helix (28)

DNA bases (29)

amino acids (29)

codons (29)

population (29)

gene pool (29)

evolution (29)

mutation (29)

gene flow (30)

genetic drift (30)

founder effect (30)

natural selection (22, 30-31)

adaptation (31)

ecological niche (31)

speciation (31)

species (31)

gradualism [gradualistic theory] (31-32)

punctuated equilibrium (32)

adaptive radiation (32)

era (32, 34)

epoch (32, 34)

periods (32, 34)

Nemesis theory (33)

analogy (33)

convergent evolution (33)

homology (33)

plate tectonics (35)

continental drift (35)

Pangaea (35)

Gondwana (36)

Laurasia (36)

molecular dating/molecular clock (36-37)

DNA hybridization (36-37)

Cenozoic Era (37)

Tertiary Period (37)

Quaternary Period (37)

scientific creationism (37-38)

People to Know About

James Ussher (20)

George Cuvier (20)

Comte Georges Loius Leclerc de Buffon (20)

James Hutton (21)

Charles Lyell (21)

Jean Baptiste de Lamarck (21)

Charles Darwin (22)

Alfred Russel Wallace (22)

Thomas Malthus (22)

Gregor Johan Mendel (24)

Stephen Jay Gould (32)

Niles Eldredge (32)

Vincent Sarich (36-37)

Allan Wilson (36-37)

Thinking About What You Have Read

The following questions or problems may be of help to you in studying the material presented in both the text and in your class. You may want to write out the answers to these questions (writing something down always seems to help solidify it in one's mind) or just think about them.

1. Define cosmology and origin myth. What are the Navajo and the Greek origin myths? What is your origin myth? Why do you believe that it is true?

2. Briefly describe the scientific contributions of James Ussher, Georges Cuvier, Georges Buffon, James Hutton, Charles Lyell, and Thomas Malthus.

3. What is the difference between catastrophism and uniformitarianism?

4. What contribution did Lamarck make to our understanding of evolutionary change? What is *use and disuse* and the *inheritance of acquired characteristics*? What is wrong with these two ideas given our current understanding of inheritance and genetics?

5. What were the specific contributions of Charles Darwin and Alfred Russel Wallace? How did they develop their thinking on evolution?

6. What is natural selection? Can you think of some examples of natural selection? How does natural selection operate?

7. What did Johan Gregor Mendel discover when he bred pea plants? What is particulate inheritance? What is the Principle of Segregation and Principle of Independent Assortment? Does the Principle of Independent Assortment always hold true? If not, why not?

8. What is the structure of DNA? What role does it play?

9. How do populations evolve? What are the four mechanisms of evolution and how do they operate? Give examples.

10. How do the effects of genetic drift differ from those of gene flow? [*Hint*: Explain what happens within a population and among a group of populations.]

11. How is gene flow influenced by cultural factors such as religion, language, socioeconomic status, and ethnicity?

12. Molecular dating is based on two key assumptions. What are these assumptions, and do you think they are reasonable ones? How reliable is this technique?

13. What is speciation? What are the differences between the gradualist theory and punctuated equilibrium? Which theory do you think is correct? Could they both be operating at different times? Could there be other explanations?

14. What is continental drift and why is it important for anthropology?

15. What is *Scientific Creationism*? Is it science? What is the difference between **science** and **non-science**? What is science? What is religion?

CHECKING YOUR UNDERSTANDING: A PRACTICE EXAMINATION

We suggest that you take this practice exam and then check your answers against the key provided at the end of this section. Use the questions that you got wrong as a guide to further study. Try to learn why specific answers are right and wrong. You may even want to take the practice exam a second time to review what you have learned.

True-False Questions

1. Cosmological explanations frequently involve divine or supernatural forces, while scientific explanations rely on natural processes, observation, and testing.

2. The changes in the peppered moths (*Biston betularia*) of England provide a graphic example of the inheritance of acquired characteristics.

3. In order to propose the theory of evolution by natural selection, Charles Darwin had to clearly understand the concept of heredity or how specific traits were passed on from one generation to the next.

4. Somatic cells are sex cells, while gametes are body cells.

5. Mitosis is cell division.

6. Evolution can be defined as the process of change in allele frequencies between one generation and the next.

7. An individual's genetic makeup evolves as the person grows older and matures.

8. Most, if not all, genetic mutations are beneficial to the organism.

9. Mutations that occur in the somatic cells are heritable changes in the genetic structure of an organism.

10. Gene flow is not influenced by cultural influences such as religious practices, socioeconomic status, and ethnicity.

11. The specific environmental conditions to which a species is adapted is referred to as its ecological niche.

12. Natural selection molds the genetic variation found in the gene pool of a population.

13. Mutation is the ultimate source of new genetic variants.

14. Charles Darwin postulated that speciation was a gradual process of evolution that occurred slowly as different populations became isolated from one another.

15. Analogy refers to similarities in organisms that have no genetic relationship.

16. The Nemesis theory is an untestable proposition that cannot be evaluated by scientists.

17. Homology refers to traits that have a common genetic origin but may differ in form and function.

18. Plate tectonics is the complex geological process that brings about the drift of continents.

19. The Cenozoic era was characterized by the dominance and adaptive radiation of the dinosaurs.

20. Scientific creationism is a scientifically valid alternative to Darwinian evolution.

Multiple Choice Questions

21. Most cultures have developed explanations that provide answers to fundamental questions about human origins, the nature of the universe, and the place and role of humans in the universe. The conceptual frameworks that account for these things are called
    A. empirical explanations
    B. cosmologies
    C. legends
    D. explanatory tales

22. The geological concept that the world was not subjected to repeated catastrophes but was shaped by gradual, natural processes is known as
    A. uniformitarianism
    B. simplism
    C. natural theology
    D. gradualism

23. The geological theory known as catastrophism was espoused by
    A. James Hutton
    B. Charles Lyell
    C. George Cuvier
    D. James Ussher

24. The Inheritance of Acquire Characteristics is often equated with the work of
    A. Charles Lyell
    B. Jean Baptiste de Lamarck
    C. James Hutton
    D. Charles Darwin

25. The theory of evolution by natural selection was proposed by
    A. James Hutton
    B. Charles Darwin and Alfred Russel Wallace
    C. George Cuvier and Charles Lyell
    D. Watson and Crick

26. The observation that organisms produce more offspring than can generally be expected to survive and reproduce is credited to
    A. Charles Darwin
    B. Alfred Russel Wallace
    C. Thomas Malthus
    D. Gregor Mendel

27. By crossbreeding pea plants, _____ was able to demonstrate that traits were inherited in a particulate manner, not by the blending of parental substances.
    A. Charles Darwin
    B. Johan Gregor Mendel
    C. James Hutton
    D. Francis Crick

28. A discrete unit of hereditary information that determines specific characteristics of an organism is called a
    A. genotype
    B. phenogram
    C. gene
    D. segregation unit

29. Alternate forms of the same gene are known as
    A. segregation units
    B. alleles
    C. genotypes
    D. phenotypes
    E. heterozygotes

30. When an organism has two different alleles for a trait (e.g., Tt), the organism is _____ for that gene.
    A. recessive
    B. homozygous
    C. heterozygous
    D. agenic
    E. phenotypically mute

31. The actual genetic constitution of an organism is referred to as the _____, while the outward appearance of the organism is called the _____.
    A. homozygote / heterozygote
    B. allele / gene
    C. genotype / phenotype
    D. recessive / dominant

32. The particles are present in pairs which separate in the formation of the sex cells (or gametes). This is known as the
    A. principle of segregation
    B. principle of independent assortment
    C. law of alleles
    D. principle of gametes

33. Humans have _____ pairs of chromosomes.
    A. 46
    B. 48
    C. 12
    D. 23
    E. 25

34. Cell division is known as _____, while the production of gametes is called _____.
    A. replication / duplication
    B. duplication / replication
    C. mitosis / meiosis
    D. meiosis / mitosis
    E. generation / degeneration

35. DNA (Deoxyribonucleic acid) bases are arranged in sequences of three, called
    A. codons
    B. genes
    C. alleles
    D. nucleics
    E. amino acids

36. The assortment of genes found within a population is called the
    A. codon group
    B. drift potential
    C. gene pool
    D. gamete pond
    E. allelic stream

37. The process of change in allele frequencies between one generation and the next is
    A. gene flow
    B. evolution
    C. natural selection
    D. gene pool effect

38. Alterations in the genetic material at the cellular level that occur randomly are known as
    A. genetic drifts
    B. mutations
    C. gene flushes
    D. gene flows
    E. gene shifts

39. Mutations
    A. occur when needed to allow individuals to survive environmental changes such as shifts in the climate or the onslaught of a new disease.
    B. are always beneficial, making the organism better adapted.
    C. are very important from an evolutionary perspective because they introduce new variation (new alleles) into the gene pool.
    D. are goal directed, non-random changes in the DNA of an organism.

40. Change loss of genetic material (alleles) is known as
    A. gene flow
    B. genetic flux
    C. genetic drift
    D. mutation
    E. natural selection

41. Founder effect occurs when
    A. lost genes are recovered by a population through directed mutation.
    B. is a type of genetic drift that results when only a small number of individuals from a larger population start a new population.
    C. is a form of gene flow in which mutated genes are recovered by genetic induction.
    D. is a subset of natural selection, complementing differential fertility.

42. Natural selection
    A. is change in the genetic structure of a population due to differential reproductive success of certain individuals.
    B. introduces new alleles into a population.
    C. increases the genetic variation within a population by adding new genes to the gene pool by differential mortality.
    D. occurs when genes are exchanged between at least two populations.

43. A group of organisms that have similar morphological characteristics and can potentially interbreed and produce viable, fertile offspring is called a(an)
    A. analogy
    B. homology
    C. species
    D. niche group

44. The two proponents of the theory known as punctuated equilibrium are
    A. Charles Darwin and Alfred Russel Wallace
    B. George Cuvier and Charles Lyell
    C. John Pangaea and William Laurasia
    D. Stephen Jay Gould and Niles Eldredge

45. _____ is the theory that new species, rather than gradually emerging through geographic isolation, evolve rapidly. The population then maintains its adaptation for many generations before experiencing rapid speciation again.
    A. Darwinian evolution
    B. Lamarckian evolution
    C. Punctuated equilibrium
    D. Interrupted stasis
    E. Plate tectonics

46. The rapid diversification and adaptation of an evolving population into new ecological niches is known as
    A. adaptive radiation
    B. gene flow
    C. genetic drift
    D. homology
    E. epoch flux

47. The _____ theory suggests that extraterrestrial forces are partly responsible for the pace and direction of the evolution of life on the earth.
   A. Alien
   B. Nemesis
   C. Exotic
   D. Catastrophic
   E. Outer Limits

48. Analogous forms result from convergent evolution while _____ traits have a common genetic origin even though they may differ in form and function.
   A. homologous
   B. homogeneous
   C. equivalent
   D. hybridization

49. _____ has helped paleontologists and other scientists understand the geographical distribution of different plant and animal species. This process has, for example, provided clues for the interpretation of the differences between the Old and New World monkeys.
   A. Scientific creationism
   B. Continental drift
   C. Punctuated equilibrium
   D. Nemesis theory

50. Genetic material of living animals can be used to estimate when different species diverged. This technique involves comparing the DNA sequences (DNA hybridization) and amino acid sequences of different species. This technique is known as
   A. DNA cloning
   B. molecular dating
   C. punctuated dating
   D. equilibrium dating
   E. genetic aging

Suggested Readings

BOORSTIN, D. 1983. *The Discoverers.* New York, NY: Random House.

CAVALLI-SFORZA, L.L. and W.F. BODMER. 1971. *The Genetics of Human Populations.* San Francisco, CA: W.H. Freeman.

CUMMINGS, M.R. 1991. *Human Heredity: Principles and Issues.* St. Paul, MN: West Publishing Company.

EDEY, M.A. and D.C. JOHANSON. 1989. *Blueprints: Solving the Mystery of Evolution.* Boston, MA: Little, Brown.

ELDREDGE, NILES. 1985. *Time Frames: The Rethinking of Darwinian Evolution and the Theory of Punctuated Equilibrium.* New York: Simon & Schuster.

FUTUYMA, D.J. 1986. *Evolutionary Biology.* Sunderland, MA: Sinauer.

_____. 1983. *Science on Trial: The Case for Evolution.* New York, NY: Pantheon Books.

GJERTSON, D. 1989. *Science and Philosophy: Past and Present.* London, Penguin.

GODFREY, L.G. (Ed.). 1983. *Scientists Confront Creationism.* New York, NY: W.W. Norton.

GOULD, S.J. 1977. *Ever Since Darwin.* New York, NY: W.W. Norton.

_____. 1980. *The Panda's Thumb.* New York, NY: W.W. Norton.

_____. 1983. *Hen's Teeth and Horse's Toes.* New York, NY: W.W. Norton.

_____. 1985. *The Flamingo's Smile.* New York, NY: W.W. Norton.

_____. 1991. *Bully for Brontosaurus.* New York, NY: W.W. Norton

_____. 1993. *Eight Little Piggies.* New York, NY: W.W. Norton.

GRIBBEN, J. 1985. *In Search of the Double Helix: Quantum Physics and Life.* New York, NY: McGraw-Hill.

GREENE, J.C. 1959. *The Death of Adam.* Ames, IA: Iowa State University Press.

HARTL, D.L. 1991. *Basic Genetics.* Boston, MA: Jones and Bartlett Publishers.

JURMAIN, R. and H. NELSON. 1994. *Introduction to Physical Anthropology.* Minneapolis/St. Paul, MN: West Publishing Company.

MAYR, E. 1982. *The Growth of Biological Thought.* Cambridge, MA: Harvard University Press.

MORRIS, L.N. 1971. *Human Populations, Genetic Variation, and Evolution.* San Francisco, CA: Chandler.

POIRIER, F, W.A. STINI, and K.B. WREDEN. 1994. *In Search of Ourselves: An Introduction to Physical Anthropology.* Englewood Cliffs, NJ: Prentice Hall.

RELETHFORD, J.H. 1994. *The Human Species: An Introduction to Biological Anthropology.* Mountain View, CA: Mayfield Publishing Company.

STASKI, E. and J. MARKS. 1992. *Evolutionary Anthropology: An Introduction to Physical Anthropology and Archaeology.* Fort Worth, TX: Harcourt Brace Jovanovich College Publishers.

UNDERWOOD, J.H. 1979. *Human Variation and Human Microevolution.* Englewood Cliffs, NJ: Prentice Hall.

WEISS, M.L. and A.E. MANN. 1990. *Human Biology and Behavior: An Anthropological Perspective.* Glenview, IL: Scott, Foresman/Little, Brown Higher Education.

WOODWARD, V. 1992. *Human Heredity and Society.* St. Paul, MN: West Publishing Company.

Answer Key with Page Numbers

1. T 20	18. T 35	35. A 29
2. F 23	19. F 37	36. C 29
3. F 24	20. F 38	37. B 29
4. F 27	21. B 18	38. B 29
5. T 28	22. A 20-21	39. C 29
6. T 29	23. C 20	40. C 30
7. F 29	24. B 21	41. B 30
8. F 29	25. B 22	42. A 30
9. F 29	26. C 22	43. C 31
10. F 30	27. B 24	44. D 32
11. T 31	28. C 25	45. C 32
12. T 31	29. B 25	46. A 32
13. T 31	30. C 25	47. B 33
14. T 32	31. C 25	48. A 34-35
15. T 33	32. A 26	49. B 36
16. F 33	33. D 27	50. B 36
17. T 33,35	34. C 28	

CHAPTER 3

THE RECORD OF THE PAST

Chapter Outline

Chapter Highlights

This chapter introduces several concepts that are important for understanding the methods used by anthropologists to study the human past. Several subdisciplines of anthropology, such as historical linguistics, are concerned with aspects of the past. However, **paleoanthropology** and **archaeology** stand out as the two that deal specifically with material remains of the human experience. Paleoanthropology, which focuses on early **human evolution**, is concerned with fossils of ancient humans and human ancestors. Archaeology is concerned with elements of **material culture**, such as tools, structures, burials, and food remains.

Fossils are remains of ancient plants, animals, and humans that have survived as a result of geological processes. Examples would be impressions of leaves left in mudstone or shells preserved in limestone. The replacement of organic tissues by minerals can produce materials like petrified wood or bones. The latter include fossilized skulls, teeth, and skeletal parts of ancient humans that were formed millions of years ago. These are found at **fossil localities** whose age can be determined by techniques such as **faunal succession** or **potassium-argon dating** (see below).

The **archaeological record** may include fossils, but it also includes fossilized evidence of human activity in the form of sites, features, and artifacts. A **site** is any location where there are physical traces of past human activity. Sites can be caves, ruins, or even scatters of stone tools. **Features** are defined as any "unmoveable" evidence of past human activity. Examples of features would be hearths, storage pits, house foundations, or graves. **Artifacts** are moveable objects that were either made by humans or bear traces of human modification. They can range from chipped stone projectile points or pottery vessels to bronze daggers and gold masks. Waste flakes and bones with butchering marks are also referred to as artifacts. Artifacts are interpreted by means of their **context**, the situation in which they were found (such as in a tomb, in the ruins of a house, or lying next to other artifacts on the ground.) Knowing the context, for example, can help one to know the age of the artifact, the way that it was used, and the specific culture or person to whom it belonged. Much information is lost when artifacts are removed from their contexts by nonarchaeologists.

Archaeology began with **antiquaries**, individuals who seek artifacts for private collections or museums. However, it has developed from simple looting into a careful, problem-oriented science. Questions about the past are addressed through the formulation of a research design that makes clear the project's objectives, hypotheses, and methodology.

There are several ways that archaeologists investigate the past. **Historical archaeology** combines the methods of history with those of archaeology, supplementing research on material remains with written documents. Historical archaeology can provide information not available from documents, such as details about everyday life and the experiences of women, minorities, and other members of society who were marginalized in historical records. It can also be used to check the reliabilty of historical sources. One example of the application of historical archaeology is **Elizabeth Brumfiel**'s study of women's contributions to the economic practices of the **Aztecs**. **Ethnoarchaeology** refers to the use of archaeological methods to study living societies. Its specific objective is understanding material culture in a living context. Examples of ethnoarchaeology would be studies of how animals are butchered with stone tools, how houses are constructed or abandoned, or how pottery is made and distributed.

Archaeologists use a variety of methods to find archaeological sites. Accidental discovery is most valuable when trained specialists can be informed immediately of the find. The intentional search for sites in a given region is known as a survey. **Unsystematic surveys** rely upon the archaeologist's intuition and chance discovery. **Systematic surveys** use a specific method, such as a **grid** or **transect**, to be sure all of a given area is investigated. Surveys are most successful when remains can be seen on the surface. **Subsurface testing** can be used to find buried features. Techniques range from simple **shovel tests** or drilled **auger holes** to the use of a **proton magnetometer** or **electrical resistivity**. These latter measure subtle variations in electromagnetic fields to reveal buried features such as walls, ditches, or tombs. Remote sensing refers to the gathering of data without directly touching archaeological remains. It includes the use of aerial photos or satellite images to find features such as structures, roads, or irrigation systems.

Excavation is used to reveal three-dimensional relationships between features and artifacts at an archaeological site. It is also used to retrieve artifacts and samples of soil, bones, or other materials for further analysis. A **grid** is used to maintain spatial control during excavation. Among the most useful deposits to excavate are **middens**, or ancient refuse dumps, and **tells**, mounds of accumulated construction debris. These usually contain high densities of artifacts and features. Excavation is a destructive process—a deposit or feature cannot be excavated twice—so archaeologists are careful to record as much information as possible.

The age of archaeological sites, features, and artifacts can be determined by means of relative and absolute dating. **Relative dating** establishes relationships in terms of "older" or "younger." **Absolute dating** is used to assign a specific date or period in time. The **law of superposition** states that materials are deposited through time from bottom to top, and is used to assign relative dates through **stratigraphy**. **Faunal succession** makes use of changes in animal populations over time for the same purpose. Another technique of relative dating looks at changes in the elements fluorine, uranium, and nitrogen (the **FUN trio**). **Seriation**, placing objects in order according to their style or technology, is a third technique of relative dating. Absolute dating can be accomplished by measuring **radioactive isotopes** in objects with devices such as the **mass spectrometer**. These isotopes change at a predictable rate, known as a **half-life**, through **radioactive decay**.

Radiocarbon dating makes use of the half-life of **carbon-14** (5,730 years) to determine the amount of radioactive carbon left in organic objects. Because living things only absorb carbon when they are alive, there will be less carbon-14 in something that is old than something that died recently. This technique can be used to date wood, bone, or shell, but not rocks or minerals. It is useful back as far as about 50,000 years, before which the amounts of carbon-14 are too small for reliable dates. **Potassium-argon dating** uses the decay of **potassium-40** to determine the age of volcanic rocks. It can be used to date materials as much as 4.5 billion years old. **Dendrochronology**, or tree-ring dating, makes use of counts of growth rings to determine the age of wooden beams in ancient structures. Radiocarbon dates on tree rings have helped to **calibrate** radiocarbon dates and make them more accurate.

The reconstruction of the human past from material remains is a complicated process, similar to trying to determine the contents of a book when most of the pages are missing. Because preservation limits the survival of sites, features, fossils, and artifacts and because only a small part of the remains that survive can be recovered using archaeological techniques, our view of the past will always be incomplete. Anthropologists are forced to reconstruct the past from a fragmentary record. The distant past is of intense interest to humans living today. However, it is important to recognize that reconstructions containing speculations about missing information will be influenced more by beliefs in the present than by the actual events of the past. For this reason, archaeology and paleoanthropology are self-critical disciplines that work from the known to the unknown. Understanding past cultures requires a good understanding of human culture in general, which is why the various subdisciplines of anthropology are interdependent.

Terms and Concepts You Should Know

interdisciplinary research (41):

fossil (41):

site (43):

artifact (43):

feature (43):

context (43):

preservation (43):

antiquary (44):

research design (45):

historical archaeology (45):

ethnoarchaeology (45):

direct historical approach (47):

underwater archaeology (47):

survey (49):

systematic/unsystematic surveys (49):

transect (49):

subsurface testing (49):

shovel test (49):

proton magnetometer (49):

resistivity (49):

remote sensing (49):

aerial photography (49):

excavation (50):

datum point (50):

midden (50):

tell (52):

settlement mound (52):

relative dating (52):

law of superposition (52):

faunal succession (52):

faunal correlation (53):

palynology (53):

FUN trio (54):

absolute dating (54):

radioactive decay (54):

half-life (54):

mass spectrometer (54):

radiocarbon dating (54):

potassium-argon dating (55):

fission-track dating (55):

dendrochronology (55):

independent evaluation (56):

calibration (56):

seriation (56):

People to Know About

Elizabeth Brumfiel (46):

Fray Bernardino de Sahagun (46):

Nicholas Steno (52):

William Smith (52):

Arthur Keith (54):

Willard Libby (54):

James Deetz (56):

Gustav Kossina (57):

Places to Know About

Tenochtitlan (46):

Port Royal (48):

Lascaux (48):

Cultures to Know About

Aztecs (46):

Thinking About What You Have Read

The following questions or problems may be of help to you in studying the material presented in both the text and in your class. You may want to write out the answers to these questions (writing something down always seems to help solidify it in one's mind) or just think about them.

1. What are the main differences between archaeology, paleoanthropology, and the disciplines of anthropology that concentrate on living peoples and cultures? What can ethnographers study that archaeologists working on the past cultures cannot? What information can archaeologists obtain that can't be learned from ethnography?

2. Under what situations and in what kinds of environments are fossils likely to form? What are the processes that will help or hinder the formation of fossils? If you were looking for fossils of early humans, what kinds of geological deposits would be most useful? Why?

3. Define the difference between a site and a feature. Define the difference between a fossil and an artifact. What are some examples of specific contexts in which sites, features, fossils, and artifacts might be found?

4. What kind of information can an anthropologist learn from an object's context that is lost if the object is removed from an archaeological site without any information about its context being recorded?

5. What kinds of archaeological materials are preserved for the longest periods of time? What kinds of materials are preserved for the shortest periods of time? What are some of the special circumstances under which perishable materials can be preserved?

6. If you were to put together an archaeological research design, what would be its most important elements?

7. Given what you know about history, provide an example of how historical archaeology might help to answer questions that written documents cannot.

8. If you were an ethnoarchaeologist, what kinds of cultural phenomena would you choose to investigate and why? What would be some of the methods you would use?

9. How was Elizabeth Brumfiel able to use different sources of information to answer questions about the roles of women in Aztec society? What were the hypotheses she chose to investigate? What were her conclusions?

10. As an archaeologist investigating prehistoric settlements around the town or city in which you live, what are some of the techniques you would use to locate archaeological sites? What methods could you use to detect subsurface features?

11. Why do archaeologists use grids when they excavate?

12. What are the principal methods that could be used to date fossil localities with remains of early humans (ca. 2 million years ago)? What are the principal methods that could be used to date an Egyptian tomb and the objects found inside it? Would these methods provide relative or absolute dates?

13. What are the principal problems faced by archaeologists and paleoanthropologists in trying to reconstruct past human behavior? How can information from other types of anthropologists be used to solve these problems?

14. What are the principal stages that you would include in an archaeological research plan? What are the activities that you would undertake first? What are the most important parts of a field project? What do you do with your results?

15. Who would be the principal non-anthropologists with whom an archaeologist would plan a research project or consult for additional information on the interpretation of remains? Why?

CHECKING YOUR UNDERSTANDING: A PRACTICE EXAMINATION

We suggest that you take this practice exam and then check your answers against the key provided at the end of this section. Use the questions that you got wrong as a guide to further study. Try to learn why specific answers are right and wrong. You may even want to take the practice exam a second time to review what you have learned.

True-False Questions

1. Paleoanthropologists often work with archaeologists to locate and excavate fossil sites.

2. Organic remains altered by natural processes such as gnawing by scavengers can still become fossils.

3. A cave in which leopards drop the bones of their prey has the potential to become a fossil locality.

4. The locations where past human activity is preserved are known as artifacts.

5. Pottery and glass artifacts are more likely to be preserved than objects made of cotton or wool.

6. Archaeologists can record every piece of information about each artifact they recover.

7. Ethnoarchaeologists focus on material culture and how it is currently used.

8. Elizabeth Brumfiel's research on Aztec society indicates that the production of cloth by women was an important element of their tribute-based economy.

9. Underwater sites are immune to the continued disturbances associated with human activity typical of most land sites.

10. Buried house foundations and roads can be located by measuring the electrical resistivity of the surrounding soil.

11. The distribution of sites on the landscape can provide information about the political organization of an ancient culture.

12. Relative dates are more precise than absolute dates.

13. Scientists were able to assign relative dates to layers of rock based on differences in the fossils they contained several decades before the publication of Darwin's theory of evolution.

14. Fossils of both plants and animals can be used to reconstruct the environments in which human ancestors lived.

15. The amounts of fluorine, uranium, and nitrogen in fossils can be used to obtain absolute dates.

16. Radioactive decay occurs at a set rate regardless of environmental conditions.

17. Fission-track dating is based on the decay of a radioactive isotope of uranium.

18. Patterns of thick and thin rings in trees have been used to build up a master sequence for the American Southwest that extends to almost 9,000 years ago.

19. Archaeology, because it produces scientific information, cannot be used to support specific political agenda.

20. Interpretations of the past have little influence on the present.

Multiple Choice Questions

21. The paleoanthropologist is a physical anthropologist specializing in the:
    A. recovery of artifacts from buried deposits
    B. interpretation of fossil remains of humans and their ancestors
    C. investigation of human cultures (their lifestyles, technology, and social systems)
    D. extraction and analysis of ancient DNA

22. Fossils are:
    A. remains, impressions, or traces of living creatures that are preserved by geological processes
    B. stones and other materials that have been modified by past human activity
    C. theoretical reconstructions of ancient species, such as dinosaurs and Neanderthals
    D. geological formations that imitate the shapes of living creatures

23. Nonmoveable artifacts, such as hearths, pits, or walls, are referred to by archaeologists as:
     A. fossil localities
     B. strata
     C. middens
     D. features

24. The context of an artifact is important for an archaeologist to know because:
     A. it can reveal valuable information about the artifact's use, age, and relationship to other artifacts and features
     B. artifacts must always remain in the context in which they were found
     C. if the context of an artifact is unknown, the artifact has no value for scientific investigation
     D. objects cannot be preserved if they are taken out of their archaeological context

25. The main reason why stone tools and pottery are so important for understanding the human past is that:
     A. they were the most valuable posessions of ancient peoples
     B. spear points and ceramic vessels are usually placed in burials
     C. these materials last much longer than bone, wood, leather, or other organic materials
     D. they are the only artifacts that can be associated with clear archaeological contexts

26. "Antiquarianism" refers to the:
     A. practice of collecting ancient objects
     B. preservation of an ancient way of life
     C. belief that the world is no more than 5000 years old
     D. rejection of evolution and scientific archaeology

27. One of the main reasons for conducting historical archaeology is that:
     A. there is more widespread interest in historic times
     B. historical records usually present biased accounts of what happened in the past
     C. art objects from Greece, Rome, and Egypt often depict known historic personages
     D. there are more historic sites than prehistoric ones

28. Ethnoarchaeology refers to the practice of:
    A. investigating the practices of living cultures with an archaeological perspective
    B. studying the archaeology of a particular ethnic group
    C. training natives or indigenous peoples in archaeological methods
    D. reconstructing the evolution of a single human race from sites, features, and artifacts

29. Archaeologist Elizabeth Brumfiel has used records of the Aztec culture of Mexico to study the:
    A. importance of human sacrifice in Aztec religion
    B. relationships between the Aztecs and ancient Egyptians
    C. political expansion of the Aztec empire
    D. role of women in Aztec economic systems

30. An example of an underwater site would be:
    A. Tenochtitlan, Mexico
    B. Lascaux, France
    C. Port Royal, Jamaica
    D. Urumqui, China

31. An archaeological survey usually begins with:
    A. the careful analysis of aerial photographs and satellite imagery
    B. a study of previous descriptions or maps and interviews with people who live in the area
    C. use of a proton magnetometer
    D. shovel tests placed at regular intervals across the area in which a site is located

32. Which of the following would NOT be an example of subsurface testing?
    A. proton magnetometry
    B. electrical resistivity survey
    C. auger holes and shovel tests
    D. transect survey

33. Which of the following is most likely to be evident in an aerial photograph?
    A. scatters of stone flakes
    B. an ancient hearth
    C. prehistorical irrigation systems
    D. burials and tombs

34. The first steps undertaken in most archaeological excavations are:
    A. establishment of a datum and a grid
    B. using heavy machinery to strip off modern vegetation and expose a vertical profile through the archaeological deposit
    C. reassembling the archaeological site from field notes and photographs
    D. dating artifacts and features using radioactive carbon

35. "Tells" are:
    A. gatherings at which archaeologists describe what they have found
    B. special instruments used for excavating small bones and other delicate archaeological deposits
    C. large mounds in the Near East that are composed of settlement debris accumulated over several centuries
    D. fossilized artifacts from mesobotanical deposits at sites in occidental Africa

36. One example of relative dating in archaeology would be:
    A. going out with your cousin for pizza and a movie
    B. placing artifacts in chronological order based on their different depths in an archaeological excavation
    C. using potassium-argon dating to figure out the age of a fossil locality
    D. using dendrochronology to determine the construction dates of a prehistoric pueblo

37. Palynology is the study of:
    A. faunal correlation
    B. pollen grains
    C. radioactive artifacts
    D. fluorine, uranium, and nitrogen in bones

38. The term "FUN trio" refers to:
    A. Moe, Larry, and Curly
    B. the practice of finding, unearthing, and naming a site
    C. fluorine, uranium, and nitrogen in bones
    D. the three steps of Fossil Unit Nomenclature

39. Absolute dating techniques such as radiocarbon and potassium-argon dating are based on the fact that:
    A. radioactive isotopes decay at a known rate
    B. certain isotopes become more radioactive over time
    C. the level of radioactivity is a constant
    D. carbon 14 is present in all geological sediments

40. The interval of time required for one-half of a full gram of carbon 14 to decay into a stable isotope of nitrogen is:
    A. 2,865 years
    B. 5,730 years
    C. 11,460 years
    D. 22,920 years

41. Which of the following materials could NOT be dated directly using measurements of carbon 14?
    A. a wooden boat
    B. animal bones
    C. flint projectile points
    D. textile mummy wrappings

42. Potassium-argon dating is used to determine the age of:
    A. any organic materials
    B. bones, antlers, or ivory
    C. volcanic rocks
    D. trees and wooden objects

43. The age of minerals that contain a radioactive isotope of uranium can be determined using:
    A. potassium-argon dating
    B. dendrochronology
    C. radiocarbon dating
    D. fission-track dating

44. Dendrochronology is a technique that makes use of:
    A. radioactive decay
    B. changes in fauna over time
    C. the law of superposition
    D. variation in the growth rings of trees

45. One of the most important contributions of dendrochronology is that it has improved the accuracy of _____ through the independent dating of samples.
    A. potassium-argon dates
    B. radiocarbon dates
    C. palynology
    D. measurements of isotopic decay

46. Seriation is a technique for dating archaeological materials that is based on the assumption that:
    A. the relative frequency of certain artifacts, attributes, or styles changed over time in recognizable patterns
    B. most primitive technologies used in the distant past have survived to the present day
    C. archaeological excavation will reveal the relationships between artifacts and features in three dimensions
    D. dating techniques that use radioactive decay will always be subject to a certain degree of laboratory error

47. The change in patterns on gravestones from New England cemeteries noted by archaeologist James Deetz illustrates how:
    A. social status is reflected in gravestone design
    B. foreign designs are integrated into local traditions
    C. artifact styles increase and decrease in popularity
    D. urn-and-willow motifs give way to Death's-head patterns

48. Recent archaeological research in South Africa has demonstrated that the ancestors of black South Africans:
    A. were not present in the region until around the same time as the arrival of white settlers
    B. occupied the region some 1,500 years before the initial European settlement
    C. came from the north as migrating, Bantu-speaking farmers in the latter half of the eighteenth century
    D. are most closely related to the Australian aborigines

49. In archaeology, the validity of a particular interpretation is strengthened by:
    A. the political convictions of the researcher
    B. its relevance to current philosophies and concerns
    C. confirmation through independent lines of evidence
    D. its acceptance by the leading authorities in the field

50. Historically, archaeological theory in the United States has been most heavily influenced by:
    A. linguistic anthropology
    B. physical anthropology
    C. ancient history
    D. cultural anthropology

Suggested Readings:

ASHMORE, WENDY, AND ROBERT J. SHARER. 1988. *Discovering Our Past: A Brief Introductionto Archaeology*. Mountain View, CA: Mayfield Publishing Company.

BASS, GEORGE. 1966. *Archaeology Underwater*. New York: Praeger.

BRAY, WARWICK, AND DAVID TRUMP. 1970. *A Dictionary of Archaeology*. London: Penguin Press.

BUTZER, KARL. 1982. *Archaeology as Human Ecology*. Cambridge: Cambridge University Press.

DANIEL, GLYN. 1981. *A Short History of Archaeology*. New York: Thames & Hudson.

DEETZ, JAMES. 1977. *In Small Things Forgotten: The Archaeology of Early American Life*. New York: Anchor Books.

FAGAN, BRIAN M. 1994. *Archaeology: A Brief Introduction* (5th ed.). New York: Harper Collins.

PROTHERO, DONALD R. 1989. *Interpreting the Stratigraphic Record*. New York: W. H. Freeman.

RENFREW, COLIN, AND PAUL BAHN. 1991. *Archaeology: Theories, Methods, and Practice*. New York: Thames & Hudson.

SCARRE, CHRIS, ED. 1988. *Past Worlds: The Times Atlas of Archaeology*. London: Times Books.

TAYLOR, R.E. 1987. *Radiocarbon Dating: An Archaeological Perspective*. Orlando: Academic Press.

THOMAS, DAVID HURST. 1991. *Archaeology: Down to Earth*. New York: Holt, Rinehart, and Winston, Inc.

THROCKMORTON, PETER, ED. 1987. *The Sea Remembers: Shipwrecks and Archaeology from Homer's Greece to the Rediscovery of the Titanic*. New York: Weidenfeld & Nicholson.

TRIGGER, BRUCE G. 1989. *A History of Archaeological Thought*. Cambridge: Cambridge University Press.

WILLEY, GORDON R., AND JEREMY A. SABLOFF. 1993. *A History of American Archaeology*, 3rd ed. New York: W. H. Freeman.

Answer Key with Page Numbers

1. T 41	18. T 56	35. B 52
2. T 42	19. F 57	36. B 52
3. T 43	20. F 57	37. B 53
4. F 43	21. B 41	38. C 54
5. T 44	22. A 41	39. A 54
6. F 45	23. D 43	40. B 54
7. T 46	24. A 43	41. C 54
8. T 47	25. C 44	42. C 55
9. F 48	26. A 44	43. D 55
10. T 49	27. B 45	44. D 55
11. T 50	28. A 46	45. B 56
12. F 52	29. D 47	46. A 56
13. T 52	30. C 48	47. C 57
14. T 53	31. B 49	48. B 57
15. F 54	32. D 49	49. C 57
16. T 54	33. C 50	50. D 57
17. T 55	34. A 50	

CHAPTER 4

THE PRIMATES

Chapter Outline

Primate Characteristics
    Dentition, Eyesight, and Brain Size
    Reproduction and Maturation
Classification of Primates
    Primate Subdivisions
    Classification of Fossil Primates
The Evolution of the Primate Order
    Primate Origins
    Fossil Prosimians
    Modern Prosimians
    Evolution of the Anthropoids
        EVOLUTION OF THE PLATYRRHINES
        MODERN MONKEYS OF THE AMERICAS
        EVOLUTION OF THE CATARRHINES
            Parapithecids
            Cercopithecoids
        MODERN PRIMATES OF EUROPE, ASIA, AND AFRICA
    Emergence of the Hominoids
        HOMINOID EVOLUTION
            Proconsul
        ANCESTORS OF MODERN HOMINOIDS
            Origins of the Hylobatids
            Evolution of the Orangutan
            Gigantopithecus
        AFRICAN PONGIDS AND HOMINIDS
        THE EXTINCTION OF MOST MIOCENE APES
    Modern Apes
        THE GIBBON AND SIAMANG
        THE ORANGUTAN
        THE GORILLA
        THE CHIMPANZEE
Primate Behavior
    Primate Social Groups
        DOMINANCE HIERARCHY
        PRIMATE AGGRESSION
        PRIMATE SEXUAL BEHAVIOR
The Human Primate

Chapter Highlights

Since human beings are members of the **Order Primates**, it is important that anthropologists study both **extinct** and **extant** primates. In doing so, anthropologists learn a great deal about our closest relatives, while at the same time we learn more about human behavior, genetics, adaptation, variation, and morphology. We share an evolutionary heritage with all living primates, but the popular view that we are descended from living monkeys and apes is false.

No single trait distinguishes primates from other mammals; rather, they share a group of features that make the order unique. Some of these features are evolutionarily related to **arboreal** adaptations, while others are probably related to feeding behaviors. These "primate" characteristics include: a generalized skeletal structure, mobile digits (**prehensile, pentadactyly, opposable thumbs**), flatten nails, depth perception (**stereoscopic and binocular vision**), foreshortened snout and reduced **olfactory sense**, expanded and elaborated brain, long period of **gestation** and infancy, dependency on learned behavior, and a tendency toward erectness.

Taxonomies provide scientists with convenient and accepted ways of classifying and referring to living and extinct organisms. As an example of a hierarchical classification, humans are placed in the Order **Primates**, Suborder **Anthropoidea**, Infraorder **Catarrhini**, Superfamily **Hominoidea**, Family **Hominidea**, Genus *Homo*, and species *sapiens*.

The order Primates is divided into two suborders: **Prosimii (prosimians)** and **Anthropoidea (anthropoids)**. The prosimians include the modern day **lemurs, lorises,** and **tarsiers**. The anthropoids include all the **monkeys, apes,** and **humans** (both extinct and extant). Anthropoids are further divided into the New World Monkeys (**Platyrrhini**) and Old World Monkeys, apes, and humans (**Catarrhini**). Apes and humans are grouped as **hominoids**, while the lesser apes (gibbons and siamangs) are classified as **hylobates**, the great apes (gorilla, chimpanzee, and orangutan) as **pongids**. and humans as **hominids**.

Forerunners to the primates probably appeared during the **Paleocene** about 65 million years ago. An early possible ancestor, *Purgatorius*, is known from the late Cretaceous and Paleocene deposits in Montana. These were probably small, nocturnal, arboreal, insect (**insectivores**) eaters. A group of animals known collectively as the **plesiadapiforms** were once thought to be early primates, but they are now considered by most authorities to be related to colugos and not primates. Numerous fossil prosimians appear during the **Eocene** (55-38 mya) in both North America and Europe. These forms have been called "Primates of the Modern Aspect", because they resemble modern-day primates. An example of these "true primates" is the 50 million year old prosimian found in Wyoming called *Tetonius*. Modern day prosimians include the lemurs (Madagascar), the lorises (tropical Southeast Asia and Africa), and the tarsiers (Southeast Asia).

Many of the prosimians became extinct at the close of the Eocene as climatic changes (general hemispheric cooling) brought about a southward movement of some prosimian groups. There is little or no fossil evidence of primates during the **Oligocene** (38-22 mya) from North America or northern Europe. New primate forms (the first **anthropoids**) arise in the tropical forests of the Old World. Most of the Old World fossil evidence comes from the **Fayum** in Egypt. During the Oligocene the Fayum was a lush tropical forest, ideal for primate habitation. One of the most interesting Oligocene anthropoids is the form called *Aegyptopithecus* (about 33 million years ago). Scientists think that these primates were the first apes because of the structure of the teeth (**dentition**), even though the skeleton is very monkey-like.

The earliest fossil record for the New World Monkeys (Platyrrhini) is sparse and fragmentary. Currently, it is theorized that the New World Monkeys evolved from the African anthropoid primates. It is suggested that they migrated from Africa to South America by "rafting" (floating on large clumps of vegetation that were carried out to sea after violent storms) when the continents were much closer together. This hypothesis is strengthened by the fact that there is no fossil evidence for Eocene or Oligocene anthropoids in North America. This origin would also explain the similarities found between the Old and New World primates. We would also expect some differences since the two groups evolved over a period of about 40-50 million years without contact.

The **Miocene epoch** (22-5 mya) has been characterized as the epoch of hominoid (ape) adaptive radiation. One of the well-known fossil forms from this time is ***Proconsul*** which lived in Africa from about 23 to 17 million years ago. *Proconsul* was adapted to a forest environment and probably primarily ate fruits. Another Miocene form, ***Sivapithecus***, live in Europe and Asia from about 14 to 7 million years ago. This was a diversified group, possibly consisting of six species. It is considered by many researchers to be an ancestor to the orangutan. A very interesting fossil form, called ***Gigantopithecus***, ("giant ape") is known from jaws and teeth recovered in India, Vietnam, and China. The Indian finds date between about 9-5 mya while the Chinese fossils may be as late as 500,000 years ago. It is suggested that this primate may have reached a height of 6 to 9 feet, weighing up to 600 pounds. The dentition resemble those of *Sivapithecus* (thick enamel with low, flat cusps). Most paleontologists think that this animal was probably a very highly specialized hominoid that became extinct about 1 million years ago. Most apes disappear from the fossil record during the late Miocene (10-5 mya).

The modern apes are descended from the Miocene hominoids. These modern forms include the **Hylobates** (gibbon and siamang) and **Pongids** (orangutan, gorilla, and chimpanzee). The gibbons and siamangs live in monogamous family units throughout Southeast Asia. They are known for their locomotor behavior known as **brachiation**. The orangutan is the only Asian great ape alive today, living in Borneo and Sumatra. Males are solitary creatures that do most of their long distance traveling on the ground. They have been studied extensively by Biruté Galdikas(-Brindamour). The gorilla, the largest African ape, has been the focus of study by the late Dian Fossey (You may have seen the film, *Gorillas in the Mist*, which depicted Fossey's work). Our most detailed knowledge of chimpanzee behavior comes from the work of Jane Goodall who has studied the chimpanzees of the Gombe since 1960.

Research on modern primate behavior includes inquiries into such aspects as **mother-infant relations**, social learning, tool use, communication, **troop behavior and composition, social grooming, displays, dominance hierarchies**, aggression, and sexual behavior.

Terms and Concepts You Should Know

Primates (61)

arboreal (61)

opposable thumb (62)

dentition (62)

omnivorous (62)

olfaction (62)

binocular vision (63)

stereoscopic vision (63)

gestation period (63)

taxonomy (63)

taxa (63)

Platyrrhini (64-65, 69-70)

Catarrhini (65, 70)

Hominoids (65, 72-73)

Pongids (65, 76-77)

Hominids (65, 76-77)

cranium (65)

Tetonius (68)

Parapithecids (70)

Apidium (70)

Victoriapithecus (70)

Aegyptopithecus (72)

Proconsul africanus (73)

Ramapithecus (76)

Sivapithecus (76)

Gigantopithecus (76)

brachiaton (78)

knuckle walking (78)

social grooming (82)

dominance hierarchy (82)

People to Know About

Jane Goodall (79-82)

Dian Fossey (80-81)

Thinking About What You Have Read

2The following questions or problems may be of help to you in studying the material presented in both the text and in your class. You may wish to write out the answers to these questions (writing something down always seems to help solidify it in one's mind) or just think about them.

1. What is a primate? What characteristics do primates share?

2. Why are anthropologists interested in studying primates? What can the study of non-human primates tell us about human morphology, behavior, physiology, and genetics?

3. When did the primate order arise? What fossils have been recovered from the Paleocene and Eocene?

4. What are the anthropoids? When and where did they develop (discuss both New and Old World monkey origins)?

5. What are some of the characteristics that distinguish New World monkeys from Old World monkeys?

6. Describe and explain the significance of the following fossil forms: *Apidium, Victoriapithecus,* and *Aegyptopithecus.*

7. How does the fragmentary nature of the fossil evidence affect the validity of interpretations? What cautions should be taken?

8. What types of evidence are missing from the fossil record that would contribute to our understanding of extinct groups? How could these data be used?

9. Describe the Fayum region of Egypt and the fossils that have been recovered from that area.

10. What is the significance of the following forms: *Proconsul africanus, Sivapithecus,* and *Gigantopithecus*?

11. What role do social groups play in primate lives? That is, what are the advantages of being a member of a group?

12. Who are Jane Goodall and Dian Fossey? What did they do?

13. What is the purpose of social grooming in primate groups?

14. Discuss primate dominance hierarchies and primate aggression.

15. How are humans similar to and different from the other (non-human) primates?

CHECKING YOUR UNDERSTANDING: A PRACTICE EXAMINATION

We suggest that you take this practice exam and then check your answers against the key provided at the end of this section. Use the questions that you got wrong as a guide to further study. Try to learn why specific answers are right and wrong. You may even want to take the practice exam a second time to review what you have learned.

True-False Questions

1. According to paleontological evidence, human beings are descended from modern day chimpanzees.

2. Primates have very specialized skeletal structures.

3. Primates are more dependent upon olfaction for survival than on vision.

4. Primates have enhance depth perception because of both binocular and stereoscopic vision.

5. Humans are classified as prosimians.

6. Interestingly, there is no disagreement among primatologists about how particular species are related to one another and how they should be classified.

7. Classification of extant (living) species is much more difficult than the classification of extinct species.

8. *Altialasius koulchii* is a 60 million year old fossil that was recovered near the Atlas mountains of Morocco that lends support to the idea that the early primates emerged in Africa.

9. Lemurs are the most geographically diverse group of prosimians, inhabiting most of Africa and southern Asia.

10. The divergent evolution of the higher primates is closely tied to plate tectonics and continental drift.

11. The fossil record of the monkeys in the Americas is abundant, diverse and one of the most complete of the fossil records for any known lineage of animals.

12. Many New World monkeys have prehensile tails.

13. Primate species where competition for sexual mates is limited exhibit little sexual dimorphism, whereas species characterized by intense competition display the most dramatic dimorphism.

14. *Aegyptopithecus* is a good candidate as the ancestor to all living New World monkeys.

15. Modern gorillas and chimpanzees are directed related to the Miocene fossil known as *Proconsul*.

16. Modern apes, descendants of the Miocene hominoids, are found only in Africa.

17. Male orangutans lead solitary lives, interacting with females only for reproductive purposes.

18. Social grooming not only promotes hygiene but also reduces conflict and friction between males and females within a troop.

19. Dominance hierarchies in primate troops are fixed, static entities that are inherited from ones parents.

20. Interestingly, chimpanzees never fight, quarrel, or harm one another.

Multiple-Choice Questions

21. As members of the animal kingdom, humans are classified as:
   A. Mollusca
   B. Rodentia
   C. Arthropods
   D. Primates

22. A diet made up of a variety of foods (fruits, plants, nuts, seeds, meat, insects) is known as what type of diet?
   A. opposable
   B. carnivorous
   C. omnivorous
   D. diurnal
   E. gestational

23. In contrast to most other animals, primates produce few offspring, and these undergo long periods of growth and development. The length of time that the young remains in the mother's womb is also longer. This time is called the
    A. gestation period
    B. growth spurt period
    C. omnivorous period
    D. uterus period

24. Modern taxonomy is based on the early work of which Swedish naturalist?
    A. Johansson
    B. Buffon
    C. Linnaeus
    D. Marx
    E. Goodall

25. Humans and their immediate ancestors are classified in the family
    A. Prosimii
    B. Hominidea
    C. Platyrrhini
    D. Primates

26. Monkeys that inhabit the Americas are classified (infraorder) as
    A. Platyrrhini
    B. Catarrhini
    C. Prosimii
    D. Hominidea

27. Scientists speculate that the first mammals related to the primates appeared during the Paleocene about _____ million years ago.
    A. 20
    B. 65
    C. 10
    D. 150

28. The earliest recognizable primates ("Primates of the Modern Aspect") appear in the fossil record during the
    A. Paleocene
    B. Pleistocene
    C. Pliocene
    D. Eocene

29. One of the earliest possible primate ancestors comes from a number of sites in North America. These small animals lived during the Paleocene and were probably insect eaters. These fossils are called
    A. *Gigantopithecus*
    B. *Homo paleocenecus*
    C. *Purgatorius*
    D. *Aegyptopithecus*

30. Animals, such as the 50 million year old fossil form called *Tetonius*, were probably active during the night or what is called _____.
    A. diurnal
    B. crepuscular
    C. nocturnal
    D. arboreal

31. All living prosimians have nails instead of claws on their digits, but some species retain modified nails called _____ on their hind feet that are used for hygiene.
    A. brachiators
    B. grooming claws
    C. hygiene brushes
    D. cuticle combs

32. The most likely origin of the platyrrhines is
    A. Europe
    B. Southeast Asia
    C. Africa
    D. the Middle East

33. Grasping or prehensile tails are characteristics of many
    A. Old World monkeys
    B. great apes
    C. prosimians
    D. New World monkeys

34. One of the most prolific sites for fossil catarrhines is the
    A. Las Chapas region in Boliva
    B. Fayum Depression in Egypt
    C. Red River Valley in central Asia
    D. Lepuchican Rift in Africa

35. An early potential ancestor of the monkeys of Europe, Asia, and Africa is the fossil from the middle Miocene of Kenya called
    A. *Kenyapithecus*
    B. *Victoriapithecus*
    C. *Africanipithecus*
    D. *Miocenepithecus*

36. This 33-10 million year old fossil form, from the Fayum, resembles both primitive monkeys and apes in certain morphological features.
    A. *Purgatorius*
    B. *Aegyptopithecus*
    C. *Gigantopithecus*
    D. *Apidium*

37. The best known Miocene protoape, called _____, exhibited both monkey and ape characteristics.
    A. *Proconsul*
    B. *Apidium*
    C. *Purgatorius*
    D. *Pan troglodytes*

38. The only existing hominoid (a member of the family Pongidae) whose evolutionary history is comparatively well known is the
    A. lemur
    B. orangutan
    C. loris
    D. baboon

39. The largest primate fossil ever found belongs to the genus
    A. *Bigapithecus*
    B. *Gigantopithecus*
    C. *Superpithecus*
    D. *Jumbopithecus*

40. Apes species were very abundant (adaptive radiation of the apes) during the early part of which epoch?
    A. Paleocene
    B. Oligocene
    C. Eocene
    D. Miocene

41. The primary mode of locomotion of the gibbon and siamang is
    A. knuckle walking
    B. bipedality
    C. vertical clinging and leaping
    D. brachiation

42. Gibbons and siamangs live
    A. in large troops
    B. in male dominated harem units
    C. in monogamous family groups
    D. a solitary life

43. Gorillas thrive in social groups that average about twelve animals. These groups are dominated by an older male or _____.
    A. *noyau*
    B. consort
    C. silverback
    D. brachiator

44. From a genetic standpoint, chimpanzees and humans are almost _____ percent identical.
    A. 20
    B. 99
    C. 10
    D. less than 1

45. A temporary "sexual" bond that is established between an estrus female and an adult male chimpanzee is called a
    A. consortship
    B. fleeting bond
    C. sexual tryst
    D. nocturnal union

46. The primatologist who has studied chimpanzee behavior for over 30 years is
    A. Dian Fossey
    B. Jane Goodall
    C. Louis Leakey
    D. Margaret Mead

47. An important behavior common to the primates is the
    A. mother-infant attachment
    B. sibling rivalry pattern
    C. use of tools to achieve desired goals
    D. establishment of a monogamous relationship

48. Many primates congregate in social groups known as
    A. clans
    B. hordes
    C. troops
    D. gaggles

49. The relative social status or rank of a primate, which is determined by its ability to successfully compete with its peers for objectives of value such as food and sexual partners, is known as the
    A. aggressive ranking
    B. dominance hierarchy
    C. brachiation factor
    D. social listing

50. What characteristics make humans unique among the primates?
    A. the ability to brachiate
    B. habitual bipedal locomotion.
    C. a nocturnal lifestyle
    D. an enhanced olfactory sense

Suggested Readings

ANKEL-SIMONS, FRIDERUN. 1983. *A Survey of Living Primates and their Anatomy.* New York, NY: MacMillan Publishing Co.

BRAMBLETT, C.A. 1976. *Patterns of Primate Behavior.* Mountain View, CA: Mayfield.

CIORCHAN, R. and A CHIARELLI (eds.). 1980. *Evolutionary Biology of the New World Monkeys and Continental Drift.* New York, NY: Plenum.

CONROY, G. 1990. *Primate Evolution.* New York, NY: W.W. Norton.

DUNBAR, R. 1988. *Primate Social Systems.* New York, NY: Cornell University Press.

FEDIGAN, L.M. 1982. *Primate Paradigms: Sex Roles and Social Bonds.* Montreal, Canada: Eden Press.

FLEAGLE, J.G. 1988. *Primate Adaptation and Evolution.* San Diego, CA: Academic Press.

FOSSEY, D. 1983. *Gorillas in the Mist.* Boston, MA: Houghton Mifflin.

GOODALL, JANE. 1986. *The Chimpanzees of the Gombe: Patterns of Behavior.* Cambridge, MA: Harvard U2niversity Press.

HAMBURG, D. and E. MCCOWN (eds.). 1979. *The Great Apes*. Menlo Park, CA: Benjamin/Cummings.

HRDY, S.B. 1981. *The Woman that Never Evolved*. Cambridge, MA: Harvard University Press.

JOLLY, A. 1985. *The Evolution of Primate Behavior*. New York, NY: Macmillan.

KANO, T. 1992. *The Last Ape: Pygmy Chimpanzee Behavior and Ecology*. Stanford, CA: Stanford University Press.

KINZEY, W. (ed.). 1987. *The Evolution of Human Behavior: Primate Models*. Albany, NY: State University of New York Press.

LANCASTER, J.B. 1975. *Primate Behavior and the Emergence of Human Culture*. New York, NY: Holt, Rinehart and Winston.

LAWICK-GOODALL, JANE. 1971. *In the Shadow of Man*. New York, NY: Dell Publishing.

LEWIN, R. 1987. *Bones of Contention: Controversies in the Search for Human Origins*. New York, NY: Simon & Schuster.

LINDEN, E. 1981. *Apes, Men, and Language*. Middlesex, England: Penguin.

MCGREW, W.C. 1992. *Chimpanzee Material Culture: Implications for Human Evolution*. Cambridge: Cambridge University Press.

PASSINGHAM, R. 1982. *The Human Primate*. San Francisco, CA: W.H. Freeman.

PATTERSON, F. and E. LINDEN. 1981. *The Education of Koko*. New York, NY: Holt, Rinehart and Winston.

PREUSCHOFT, H.; D. CHIVERS; W. BROCKELMAN; and N. CREEL (eds.). 1984. *The Lesser Apes: Evolutionary and Behavioral Biology*. Edinburgh: Edinburgh University Press.

QUIATT, DUANE (ed.). 1972. *Primates on Primates: Approaches to the Analysis of Nonhuman Primate Social Behavior*. Minneapolis, MN: Burgess Publishing Company.

RICHARD, A.F. 1985. *Primates in Nature*. New York, NY: W.H. Freeman.

ROSEN, S.I. 1974. *Introduction to the Primates*. Englewood Cliffs, NJ: Prentice Hall.

SMUTS, B.B. 1985. *Sex and Friendship in Baboons*. Chicago, IL: Aldine.

SMUTS, B.B.; D.L. CHENEY; R.M. SEYFARTH; R.W. WRANGHAM; and T.T. STRUHSAKER (eds.). 1987. *Primate Societies.* Chicago, IL: University of Chicago Press.

SUSMAN, R.W. (ed.). 1979. *Primate Ecology: Problem-Oriented Field Studies.* New York, NY: John Wiley.

_____. 1984. *The Pygmy Chimpanzee: Evolutionary Morphology and Behavior.* New York, NY: Plenum.

SZALAY, F. and E. DELSON. 1978. *Evolutionary History of Primates.* New York, NY: Academic Press.

TERRACE, H.S. 1979. *Nim: A Chimpanzee Who Learned Sign Language.* New York, NY: Alfred A. Knopf.

WOOD, B.; L. MARTIN; and P. ANDREWS (eds.). 1986. *Major Topics in Primate and Human Evolution.* Cambridge, England: Cambridge University Press.

Answer Key With Page Numbers

1. F 61		18. T 82		35. B 70	
2. F 61		19. F 82		36. B 72	
3. F 62		20. F 82		37. A 73	
4. T 63		21. D 61		38. B 76	
5. F 64		22. C 62		39. B 76	
6. F 63		23. A 63		40. D 76-77	
7. F 65		24. C 63		41. D 78	
8. T 67		25. B 64		42. C 78	
9. F 68		26. A 64-65		43. C 79	
10. T 68		27. B 65		44. B 79	
11. F 69		28. D 65,67		45. A 79	
12. T 70		29. C 65,67		46. A 79	
13. T 72		30. C 68		47. A 80	
14. F 72		31. B 68		48. C 81	
15. F 76		32. C 69		49. B 82	
16. F 78		33. D 70		50. B 83	
17. T 78		34. B 70			

CHAPTER 5

HOMINID EVOLUTION

Chapter Outline

Trends in Hominid Evolution
   Bipedalism
      ADAPTIVE ASPECTS OF BIPEDALISM
         Tool Use
         Transport of Food and Offspring
   Reduction of the Face, Teeth, and Jaws
   Increase in Cranial Capacity
   Other Physical Changes
Fossil Evidence for Hominid Evolution
   Java Man: The "First" Homo erectus
   Peking Man and other Homo erectus
      RECENT DISCOVERIES
   The Piltdown Fraud
   Taung Child: A South African Australopithecine
   Other South African Australopithecines
   Australopithecus boisei: The "Nutcracker Man"
      DATING *AUSTRALOPITHECUS BOISEI*
   Homo habilis: The "Handyman"
   The Oldest Australopithecines: Australopithecus afarensis
      THE LAETOLI FOOTPRINTS
   Australopithecus aethiopicus*: The "Black" Skull*
Interpreting the Fossil Record
   Australopithecus africanus*: An Ancestor*
   Australopithecus afarensis*: An Ancestor*
   Revised Models
   Missing Pieces in the Fossil Record?
   Molecular-Dating Evidence for Hominid Evolution
From *Homo erectus* to *Homo sapiens*
   Transitional Forms
The Evolution of *Homo sapiens*
   Multiregional Evolutionary Model
   Replacement Model
   Mitochondrial DNA Research
Archaic *Homo sapiens*
   Homo sapiens neanderthalensis
      NEANDERTALS AND MODERN HUMANS

Chapter Highlights

Sometime during the Miocene epoch (25 -5 million years ago) a new form of primate emerged. These primates, **hominids**, probably gave rise to the later forms of hominids and eventually human beings. The period from about 8-4 million years ago is not represented by many fossil primates thus the timing and details of this transition are not well documented. However, it was reported in the September 22, 1994 , issue of *Nature* (Tim D. White, Gen Suwa, & Berhane Asfaw, Vol. 371, pp. 306-312) that a new species of early hominid (*Australopithecus ramidus*) had been found in Aramis, Ethiopia, dating to about 4.4 million years. The primitive morphology and early date suggests that the fossils may represent a "root species" for the hominids. This chapter documents major fossils finds that are important in the evolution of the family **Hominidae**.

Hominids have evolved distinctive characteristics. The first feature to evolve (sometime between 10 and 4 million years ago) that makes hominids different from the other primates is habitual bipedal locomotion or **bipedalism**. Numerous theories have been suggested to account for this phenomenon, ranging from energetic efficiency in scavenging and migration, to enhancing vision on the open savanna, to freeing the hands for transport of objects and food, and to making of tools. Other trends in hominid evolution include: an increase in **cranial capacity**; a reduction in the face, teeth, and jaws (reduced robusticity); an increasing reliance on cultural adaptations, and an adjustment to a terrestrial habitat.

The first fossil hominids to be found were the **neandertals** (*Homo sapiens neanderthalensis*). Even though the first neandertal was found in 1848 in Gibraltar, these forms were not recognized as ancient "humans" until the discovery in Germany in 1856 of a skull cap from the Neander Valley (near Düsseldorf) and later finds from Spy, Belgium. Then in 1891 **Eugene Dubois** reported the discovery of *Pithecanthropus erectus* from Java (now classified as *Homo erectus*). Then in the 1920s, work at the site of **Zhoukoudian,** near Beijing, China (Peking), uncovered fossils that were named *Sinanthropus pekinensis* (now classified as *Homo erectus*). These fossils date to between about 460,000 and 230,000 years ago. Recent finds of *Homo erectus* in Africa date between 1.6 million and 400,000 years ago. Among these is the find called the "Turkana Boy" (**Nariokotome site**).

In 1912 Charles Dawson "discovered" a fossil that would become known as the **"Piltdown Man"** or *Eoanthropus dawsoni*. The fossil consisted of what looked like a modern human skull with an apelike jaw -- the perfect "missing link." It was found that the jaw was actually that of a juvenile female orangutan that had been dyed and the teeth filed down in order to match the human cranium. This fossil would eventually be unmasked as a hoax.

In 1924 a skull was discovered at a limestone quarry near the town of **Taung** in South Africa. The skull was given to **Raymond Dart** who reported in 1925 that a fossil, intermediate between living anthropoids and humans (a "man-like ape") had been found. Dart named the fossil *Australopithecus africanus*. During the 1940s similar fossils were unearthed in South Africa by Dart and **Robert Broom.** The fossils from the sites of **Sterkfontein** and **Makapansgat** were also classified as *Australopithecus africanus*. A more robust form was found in neighboring sites of **Kromdraai** and **Swartkrans**. These forms were designated *Australopithecus robustus*. Dating of these finds is a problem, but they probably range from about 2 to 1 million years ago.

Excavations at the site of **Olduvai Gorge** in Tanzania by Louis and Mary Leakey have produced numerous hominid fossils. One of the first to be discovered was the fossil known as **"Zinj"** (*Zinjanthropus boisei*). This fossil, along with other "hyper-robust" forms from Olduvai and the Lake Turkana region have been classified as *Australopithecus boisei*. Excavations at Olduvai also revealed a very different looking hominid with a cranial capacity of about 640 cc. This form was given the name *Homo habilis*. Excavations by Richard Leakey (Louis and Mary's son) and coworkers along the eastern shores of Lake Turkana have produced other fossils that have been classified as *Homo habilis* that date from about 2.2 to 1.6 million years ago. Olduvai has also produced *Homo erectus* material.

In 1974 a joint American-French team of paleoanthropologists lead by **Donald Johanson** and **Maurice Taieb** discovered, in the Hadar region of Ethiopia, the fossil form that has become known as "Lucy" or *Australopithecus afarensis*. These hominids date from about 4 to 3 million years. Then in 1978 Mary Leakey uncovered fossil footprints at the site of **Laetoli** (northern Tanzania) that confirmed that hominids were fully bipedal by at least 3.5 million years ago.

In 1985 **Alan Walker** found fragments of a robust australopithecine that were dated to about 2.5 million years. This find, called the **"Black Skull"** or *Australopithecus aethiopicus* has a cranial capacity of only 410 cm^3, the smallest brain volume of any known hominid. The skull has primitive traits resembling *A. afarensis* coupled with robust features similar to those of *A. boisei*.

As more and more fossil material is unearthed it becomes a challenge to interpret the material and provide evolutionary scenarios for these hominid forms. There are numerous ideas and competing phylogenies (family trees). Some individuals like to *lump* the material, while others are known as *splitters*. Your text presents a number of different phylogenies that have been proposed by various researchers. You should examine these with a critical eye, looking for similarities and differences.

Some anthropologists have suggested alternative phylogenies and timing of events that are not based on the fossil material itself, but on **molecular data** derived from living primates. The first of these suggestions placed the hominid-pongid split sometime between about 7 and 5 million years. Many paleoanthropologists now feel that this date is more reasonable than the an early one of 10 to 20 million years. Recent work with **mtDNA (mitochondrial DNA)** has suggested that modern *Homo sapiens* arose in Africa about 200,000 years ago and then spread to the rest of the world, replacing all of the indigenous hominid forms. This controversy is encapsulated in two competing theories: (1) the **multiregional hypothesis** and (2) the **replacement model**. Proponents of the multiregional hypothesis suggest that there was a gradual transition from *Homo erectus* to modern *Homo sapiens* in different parts of the world. The proponents of the replacement model argue that modern *Homo sapiens* arose once in one part of the world (Africa) and then spread out from there replacing the other hominids throughout the world.

Terms, Concepts, Sites, and Fossils You Should Know

hominid (86)

bipedalism (86)

foramen magnum (87)

prognathic (89)

sagittal crest (89)

cranial capacity (89-90)

Zhoukoudian (90)

Pithecanthropus erectus ["Java Man"] (90)

Sinanthropus pekinensis ["Peking Man"] (91)

Homo erectus (90-92)

"Turkana Boy" [Nariokotome] (92)

Piltdown (92-93)

Eoanthropus dawsoni (92-93)

Taung (93-94)

Australopithecus africanus (93-95)

Makapansgat (93)

Sterkfontein (93)

Kromdraai (93)

Australopithecus robustus (94-95)

Swartkrans (93-94)

Australopithecus boisei [*Zinjanthropus*] (95-96)

Olduvai Gorge (95)

Homo habilis (96)

Australopithecus afarensis (96-97)

"Lucy" (96)

"First Family" (96)

Laetoli (97)

Australopithecus aethiopicus (98)

"Black Skull" (98)

Australopithecus afarensis (100)

molecular dating (102)

transitional forms (103)

postorbital constriction (103)

multiregional model (103-104)

replacement model (104-105)

mitochondrial DNA [mtDNA] (105)

archaic *Homo sapiens* (105)

anatomically modern *Homo sapiens* (105)

Homo sapiens neanderthalensis [neandertals] (106-107)

People to Know About

Owen Lovejoy (88)

Eugene Dubois (90)

W.C. Pei (90)

Davidson Black (91)

Franz Weidenreich (91)

G.H.R. von Koenigswald (91)

Charles Dawson (92)

Raymond Dart (93)

Robert Broom (93)

Mary, Louis, and Richard Leakey (95-96)

Donald Johanson (96,99)

Thinking About What You Have Read

The following questions or problems may be of help to you in studying the material presented in both the text and in your class. You may want to write out the answers to these questions (writing something down always seems to help solidify it in one's mind) or just think about them.

1. Discuss the transition from quadrupedal locomotion to upright bipedalism. What are some of the theories that have been proposed to account for this shift in behavior? What is the fossil evidence for the change? Why did this transformation take place? What are the advantages and disadvantages of bipedal locomotion?

2. When did the cranial capacity in hominids increase? What are some of the implications of an increasing cranial capacity?

3. Describe and discuss the fossil material named *Homo erectus*. When was the first fossil found? Where was it found? Who found it? What is the geographical distribution of *Homo erectus* finds?

4. What was the Piltdown hoax?

5. What are austalopithecines? When were they first discovered? Who was responsible? How many species of australopithecines are there and where are they found?

6. What is *Homo habilis*? What is the "Black Skull"? Who is "Lucy"?

75

7. What are some of the problems involved in interpreting the fossil record?

8. Many interpretations of hominid evolution have been advanced over the years. Discuss at least three phylogenies and the proponents of each.

9. How is molecular data used to help interpret the fossil record? What is mtDNA, and how is it used to study hominid evolution?

10. It is now clear that Neandertals were an extinct sidebranch of hominid evolution. Discuss this statement

11. What are archaic *Homo sapiens* and anatomically modern *Homo sapiens*? What are the differences. Give fossil examples of each.

CHECKING YOUR UNDERSTANDING - A PRACTICE EXAMINATION

We suggest that you take this practice exam and then check your answers against the key provided at the end of this section. Use the questions that you got wrong as a guide to further study. Try to learn why specific answers are right and wrong. You may even want to take the practice exam a second time to review what you have learned.

True-False Questions

1. Three trends characterize hominid evolution: the development of bipedalism; a reduction in the face, jaw, and anterior teeth; and an increase and elaboration in brain size.

2. During the evolution of the hominids, the brain increased in size first, followed by the development of bipedal locomotion.

3. Bipedalism occurred by at least 4 million years ago.

4. It has been shown conclusively that bipedalism arose as a result of the need for tool use among early hominids.

5. *Pithecanthropus erectus* is now classified as *Homo erectus*.

6. *Sinanthropus pekinensis* was found by Eugene Dubois in Java in 1891.

7. All of the original fossil material recovered at Zhoukoudian was lost during World War II.

8. *Eoanthropus dawsoni* is a 1.8 million year old *Homo erectus* fossil from the Lake Turkana region in Africa.

9. Piltdown man has now been reclassified as an early *Homo erectus* fossil from England.

10. *Australopithecus africanus* and *Australopithecus robustus* fossils have been found in Southeast Asia.

11. The Taung child was discovered by Donald Johanson while he was excavating the material that is known as "Lucy."

12. *Australopithecus afarensis* has been dated to between 1 and 2 million years ago.

13. The earliest known hominid is *Australopithecus afarensis*.

14. It is now clear that the *Australopithecus africanus* evolved into *Homo erectus* which evolved into *Homo sapiens*.

15. With the discovery of the "Black Skull" interpretations of the course of hominid evolution became clear and easy to trace.

16. Hominid remains from the period between about 400,000 and 200,000 years ago are difficult to classify because they exhibit physical traits characteristic of both *Homo erectus* and *Homo sapiens*.

17. The multiregional model of hominid evolution would predict that one would expect to find a great deal of regional morphological (genetic) continuity between *Homo erectus* and *Homo sapiens* fossils from the same region.

18. One of the best-known examples of archaic *Homo sapiens* is Neandertal.

19. Using mtDNA, anthropologists have demonstrated that *Australopithecus afarensis* is ancestral to both *Homo habilis* and *Australopithecus africanus*.

20. Anthropologists have determined conclusively that Neandertals are clearly an extinct side branch of hominid evolution.

Multiple Choice Questions

21. The earliest and most important trend in hominid evolution is
    A. tool use
    B. bipedalism
    C. meat eating
    D. increase in cranial capacity

22. The earliest stone tools date to
    A. 10,000 years ago
    B. 2.4 million years ago
    C. 8 million years ago
    D. 500,000 years ago

23. Faces that protrude are called
    A. nocturnal
    B. prognathic
    C. foramen magnums
    D. sagittals

24. A bony ridge on the top of the skull that anchors large muscles that are used for chewing is called the
    A. foramen magnum
    B. mastication ridge
    C. sagittal crest
    D. gracile anchor

25. The first *Homo erectus* was found in 1891 by
    A. Louis Leakey
    B. Mary Leakey
    C. Eugene Dubois
    D. Charles Darwin

26. The first *Pithecanthropus erectus* fossil was found in
    A. South Africa
    B. East Africa
    C. India
    D. Java

27. In 1929 a team of Chinese researchers, led by W.C. Pei, started to excavate hominid fossil at the site of
    A. Yellow River
    B. Two River Falls
    C. Zhoukoudian
    D. Mao

28. The fossil material called *Sinanthropus pekinensis* spans the time period from about
    A. 4 to 2 million years ago
    B. 460,000 to 230,000 years ago
    C. 30,000 to 10,000 years ago
    D. 2 to 1 million years ago

29. *Homo erectus* fossils date from between
    A. 4 and 5 million years ago
    B. 4 and 2 million years ago
    C. 40,000 and 10,000 years ago
    D. 1.6 million and 400,000 years ago

30. Fossils known as *Homo erectus* have been found in
    A. Asia and Africa
    B. Europe and North America
    C. Africa and Europe
    D. Africa and South America

31. One of the oldest and most complete fossil finds classified as *Homo erectus* comes from the Nariokotome site in Kenya. This form is known by the nickname
    A. "Olduvai Old Man"
    B. "Turkana Boy"
    C. "Piltdown Man"
    D. "Lucy"

32. Piltdown, discovered near Sussex, England, in 1912, is now considered
    A. an early Australopithecus afarensis
    B. a hoax
    C. a late neandertal
    D. a European form of Homo habilis

33. The first australopithecine was found at _____ in South Africa.
    A. Taung
    B. Makapansgat
    C. Olduvai Gorge
    D. Lake Turkana

34. Who "found" the first *Australopithecus africanus* in 1924?
    A. Raymond Dart
    B. Robert Broom
    C. Eugene Dubois
    D. Louis and Mary Leakey

35. There are two forms of *Australopithecus* from South Africa:
    A. *Australopithecus africanus* and *Homo habilis*
    B. *Australopithecus africanus* and *Australopithecus robustus*
    C. *Australopithecus africanus* and *Australopithecus afarensis*
    D. *Zinjanthropus boisei* and *Australopithecus robustus*

36. The Leakeys are known for their work at which site?
    A. Taung
    B. Swartkrans
    C. Olduvai Gorge
    D. Zhoukoudian

37. The hyper-robust australopithecine from Olduvai Gorge is known as
    A. *Sinanthropus pekinensis*
    B. *Homo habilis*
    C. *Australopithecus afarensis*
    D. *Australopithecus boisei*

38. *Australopithecus afarensis* ("Lucy") was found in 1974 by
    A. Louis Leakey
    B. Richard Leakey
    C. Donald Johanson
    D. Raymond Dart

39. *Australopithecus afarensis* has been dated between
    A. 1 and 2 million years ago
    B. 1 million and 500,000 years ago
    C. 3 to 4 million years ago
    D. 8 to 10 million years ago

40. Mary Leakey found _____ at the site of Laetoli that are dated to about 3.5 million years.
    A. fossilized bows and arrows
    B. footprints
    C. stone tools
    D. ancient houses

41. The "Black Skull", also known as _____ was found west of Lake Turkana in 1985 by Alan Walker. This skull is dated to about 2.5 million years and resembles *Australopithecus boisei*.
    A. *Homo erectus*
    B. *Homo habilis*
    C. *Australopithecus aethiopicus*
    D. *Australopithecus robustus*

42. Some scientists, known as _____, argue that the current categories of fossil hominids do not reflect all the species represented. In fact, they argue that *A. afarensis* does not constitute a single, sexually dimorphic species, but rather at least two distinct species.
   A. reclassifiers
   B. deconstructionists
   C. splitters
   D. taxonophils

43. In the 1970s Donald Johanson and Timothy White proposed a new interpretation of hominid evolution that placed which fossil form at the base of hominid evolution at 3-4 million years ago?
   A. *A. africanus*
   B. *A. boisei*
   C. *A. aethiopicus*
   D. *A. afarensis*

44. At the molecular level, humans and chimps are about _____ different.
   A. 50%
   B. 25%
   C. 2%
   D. 80%

45. In addition to using the actual fossil evidence to interpret and time events in hominid evolution, anthropologists also use what other type of data?
   A. molecular (genetic) data obtained from living primates
   B. physiological data
   C. clones of fossil data
   D. there are no other data that can be used to interpret or understand the fossil record except the actual fossils themselves

46. The consensus among scientists is that *Homo erectus* evolved in
   A. Europe
   B. Africa
   C. Asia
   D. Java

47. According to the _____ model, the gradual evolution of Homo erectus into modern *Homo sapiens* took place in many areas of Africa, Asia, and Europe at about the same time.
   A. replacement
   B. transitional
   C. sapienization
   D. multiregional

48. The replacement model or single-source model of Stringer and Andrews holds that *Homo sapiens* evolved in _____ first and then migrated to all the other parts of the world.
    A. Europe
    B. Asia
    C. Africa
    D. Java

49. Using _____, Allan Wilson, Rebecca Cann, and Mark Stoneking suggested that a common ancestor (dubbed "*Eve*" in the popular press) to all humans can be traced back to about 200,000 years ago in Africa.
    A. fossil dentition
    B. fossil skulls
    C. mitochondrial DNA
    D. stone tools and other artifacts

50. Neandertal fossils data from about
    A. 2 - 1 million years ago
    B. 3 - 4 million years ago
    C. 130,000 - 35,000 years ago
    D. 20,000 - 10,000 years ago

Suggested Readings

ANDREWS, P. and J.L. FRANZEN (eds.) 1984. *The Evolution of Early Man*. Frankfurt: Cour. Forsch.-Inst. Seckenberg.

BEHRENSMEYER, A.K. and A.P. HILL. 1980. *Fossils in the Making: Vertebrate Taphonomy and Paleoecology*. Chicago, IL: University of Chicago Press.

BRAIN, C. 1981. *The Hunters or the Hunted? An Introduction to African Cave Taphonomy*. Chicago, IL: University of Chicago Press.

CANN, R.L.; M. STONEKING; and A.C. WILSON. 1987. "Mitochondrial DNA and Human Evolution". *Nature* 325:31-36.

CIOCHON, R.L. and A.B. CHIARELLI (eds.) 1983. *New Interpretations of Ape and Human Ancestry*. New York, NY: Plenum Press.

CIOCHON, R.L. and J.G. FLEAGLE. 1993. *The Human Evolution Source Book*. Englewood Cliffs, NJ: Prentice Hall.

CONROY, G. 1990. *Primate Evolution*. New York, NY: W.W. Norton.

DART, R. 1959. *Adventures with the Missing Link.* New York, NY: Harper & Brothers.

DAY, M.H. 1986 *Guide to Fossil Man.* Chicago, IL: University of Chicago Press.

FALK, D. 1992. *Braindance.* New York, NY: Henry Holt.

GRINE, F. (ed.). 1988. *Evolutionary History of the "Robust" Australopithecines.* Hawthrone, NY: Aldine de Gruyter.

JANUS, C.J. and W. BRASHER. 1975. *The Search for Peking Man.*

JIA, L. 1975. *The Cave Home of Peking Man.* Peking: Foreign Language Press.

JIA, L. and H. WEIWEN. 1990. *The Story of Peking Man.* New York, NY: Oxford University Press.

JOHANSON, D.C. and M.A. EDEY. 1981. *Lucy: The Beginnings of Humankind.* New York, NY: Simon & Schuster.

KLEIN, R.G. 1989. *The Human Career: Human Biological and Cultural Origins.* Chicago, IL: University of Chicago Press.

LEWIN, R. 1987. *Bones of Contention: Controversies in the Search for Human Origins.* New York, NY: Simon & Schuster.

LOCK, A. and PETERS, C. (eds.) 1991. *Handbook of Human Symbolic Evolution.* Oxford, England: Oxford University Press.

MELLARS, P. and STRINGER, C. (eds.). 1989. *The Human Revolution.* Princeton, NJ: Princeton University Press.

PFEIFFER, J.E. 1982. *The Creative Explosion.* New York, NY: Harper and Row.

RAK, Y. 1983. *The Australopithecine Face.* New York, NY: Academic Press.

SMITH, F. H. and F. SPENCER (eds.) 1984. *The Origins of Modern Humans.* New York, NY: Alan R. Liss, Inc.

SOLECKI, R. 1971. *Shanidar: The First Flower People.* New York, NY: Alfred A. Knopf.

TATTERSAL, I.; E. DELSON; and J. VAN COUVERING. 1988. *Encyclopedia of Human Evolution and Prehistory.* New York, NY: Garland Publishing.

THORNE, A.G. and M.H. WOLPOFF. 1992. "The multiregional evolution of humans". *Scientific American*, 266(4):76-83. (April).

TOBIAS, P. 1971. *The Brain in Hominid Evolution.* New York, NY: Columbia University Press.

TRINKAUS, E. 1983. *The Shandar Neanderthals.* New York, NY: Academic Press.

_____ (ed.). 1989. *The Emergence of Modern Humans: Biocultural Adaptation in the Later Pleistocene.* Cambridge: Cambridge University Press.

TRINKAUS, E. and P. SHIPMAN. 1994. *The Neandertals: Of Skeletons, Scientists, and Scandal.* New York, NY: Vintage Books.

WALKER, A. and R.E. LEAKEY. 1993. *The Nariokotome Homo erectus Skeleton.* Cambridge, MA: Harvard University Press.

WEINER, J.S. 1955. *The Piltdown Forgery.* London: Oxford University Press.

WOLPOFF, M.H. 1980. *Paleoanthropology.* New York, NY: Knopf.

WOOD, B.; L. MARTIN; and ANDREWS, P. (eds.). 1986. *Major Topics in Primate and Human Evolution.* Cambridge, England: Cambridge University Press.

Answer Key with Page Numbers

1. T 86-87	18. T 106	35. B. 94-95
2. F 87	19. F 105	36. C 95-96
3. T 88	20. F 106-107	37. D 95
4. F 87-89	21. B 87	38. C 96
5. T 90	22. B 87	39. C 97
6. F 90	23. B 89	40. B 97
7. T 91	24. C 89	41. C 98
8. F 92	25. C 90	42. C 98
9. F 92-93	26. D 90	43. D 100
10. F 93-96	27. C 90	44. C 102
11. F 93	28. B 91	45. A 102
12. F 96	29. D. 92	46. B 102
13. T 97	30. A 92	47. D 103
14. F 98	31. B 92	48. C 104
15. F 100	32. B 92	49. C 105
16. T 103	33. A 93	50. C 106
17. T 103-104	34. A 93	

CHAPTER 6

HUMAN VARIATION

Chapter Outline

Chapter Highlights

Physical anthropologists have long been interested in understanding contemporary **human variation** and **adaptation**. Realizing that the variation is the result of the interaction of numerous factors, anthropologists have often employed a **holistic** perspective or approach. In order to understand the variation and adaptation three factors are often explored: (1) **evolutionary processes** that maintain, decrease, or introduce the genetic diversity within and among populations; (2) the physical **environment**; and (3) **culture** (behaviors, beliefs, practices).

The total complement of genes possessed by a population is referred to as the **gene pool**. Within a population many genetic systems are **polymorphic** (more than one allele) providing the variation one sees expressed in individuals. Variation is introduced, maintained, lost, and shaped by the four mechanisms of evolution: **mutation, gene flow, genetic drift**, and **natural selection**. These mechanisms do not operate in isolation but are influenced by cultural practices. For example, marriage patterns such as **endogamy** restrict the amount of gene flow that occurs between populations, and linguistic differences between societies may impede gene flow and enhance the potential for genetic drift. The physical environment interacts with the genetic endowment of individuals, molding the phenotypes during growth and development. Variation thus occurs through developmental **acclimatization**, which is the adjustment of the body during the growth period to specific environments.

Early attempts to study human variation often simply constituted classifying groups (or individuals) based on certain outward phenotypic traits (most often skin color). These classifications, sometimes called **folk taxonomies**, lumped humans into categories that later became known as **racial groups** or **races**. Sometimes physical characteristics were correlated to cultural differences which, in turn, were then related to behavior. In the eighteenth and nineteenth centuries naturalists and others began to apply "scientific" principles to categorize human groups. One of these early classifiers was **Carolus Linnaeus** who grouped humans into four races based on skin color and other traits: Europeans (white), Asiatics (yellow), Africans (black), and North American Indians (red). Then in 1781 **Johann Blumenbach** modified Linnaeus' classification and proposed that there were five races. Other similar classifications followed, all being typological and relying on a few traits such as skin color, hair form, hair color, and facial features. These classifications were non-dynamic and typological in nature.

In 1950 William Boyd employed genetic characteristics (e.g., ABO blood groups) to group humans into six races: European, African, Asiatic, American Indian, Australoid, and a hypothetical Early European. The traits that Boyd chose were thought to be non-adaptive (not subject to natural selection). We now know that the traits he used are molded by the mechanisms of evolution and are not non-adaptive. Other classifications followed, such as **Stanley Garn's** (1961) hierarchical classification of humans into **geographical races, local races**, and **microraces**. These later attempts incorporated the idea that a group of populations share some biological characteristics, and that they also differ from each other in selected traits. In 1977 Alice Brues provided the following as a biological definition of race, ". . . a division of a species that differs from other divisions by the frequency with which certain hereditary traits appear among its members."

From a biological standpoint, the race concept is fraught with problems. As Relethford (1994:167) states, "Biological variation is real; the order we impose on this variation by using the concept of race is not." Scientists are not able to agree on the number of races. How many traits should be used when classifying humans into racial units: 3, 10, 25, 100, 400? What happens if some of traits are shared between groups? Since much of the variation is **continuous** in nature, it is difficult to create discrete categories or units. Traits are not concordant, that is, they are not linked to one another -- possessing light skin pigmentation does not automatically mean that the person also B blood, is Rh negative, and has brown hair. Also, a number of continuous traits are difficult to measure with an accuracy. The concept of race minimizes variation within the group while emphasizing differences between groups. This approach contradicts studies that have shown that there is much more variation *within* (94%) large continental groups (Africa, Europe, Asia, etc.), than *between* groups (only 6% of the variation). So, from a biological perspective the race concept is basically useless as a scientifically valid tool or approach to studying human variation. Also, categorizing people is not very interesting exercise, and it does not involve any really interesting questions such as: Why is there variation, how is that variation maintained, and how is the variation lost and modified?

Alternative approaches to the race concept involve actually trying to explain the biological variation that exits in human populations. One approach is to plot traits over a geographical area (**clines**) to see if there is any spatial variation. Then the anthropologist attempts to determine if the observed variation can be related to environmental factors such as climatic differences, latitude changes, altitude differences, specific habitat differences, and temperature differences. Often a **multivariate approach** is taken that examines the interrelationships among a number of different traits. Some of these studies focus on the **adaptive aspects** of the variation. These approaches have been used to examine traits such as **skin color, body build, cranial and facial features**, selected **biochemical traits, sickle cell anemia**, and **lactose intolerance**.

There are a number of hypotheses that have been put forth to explain the varying degrees of skin pigmentation found throughout the world's populations. There is a clear clinal distribution of skin color grading from dark to light as one moves away from the equator. Using this as a guide, anthropologists have proposed that skin color is an adaptive trait that is molded by natural selection. It has been suggested that there is a relationship between skin color and the amount and intensity of solar radiation. Factors that may be important include: heat gain and dissipation, **vitamin-D synthesis** (prevention of **rickets** and osteomalacia), skin cancer, frostbite, nutrient photolysis, and tropical diseases.

Body build also appears to be subject to, and influenced by, environmental factors. Human body size and shape generally conforms to both **Bergmann's** and **Allen's Rules**, which relate to heat retention and dissipation. The cranium and face also respond to climatic factors as do many biochemical traits. For example, the **ABO blood group system** has been influenced and molded by various diseases, including smallpox, bubonic plague, and typhoid fever. The relationship between **Sickle cell** and **falciparum malaria** is the best documented association between a disease and a genetic trait. In areas where malaria is endemic the **heterozygote (Hb^AHb^S)** is at a selective advantage, leading to a condition known as a **balanced polymorphism**. Some populations have a high frequency of individuals who are able, as adults, to digest **lactose** (milk sugar) because they maintain high levels of **lactase** in their systems. This is a genetic trait that appears to be related to either pastoralism or enhanced calcium absorption.

Other human characteristics are affected by the environment during growth and development. This type of adaptation is known as **developmental acclimatization.** As an example of this type of phenotypic plasticity, humans adjust to the stresses of high altitude **(hypoxic stress)** by developing larger lungs, larger hearts (right ventricle), and more red blood cells. These changes facilitate the transfer of oxygen within the human body.

Culture also influences human variation. Such things as the shift from hunting and gathering to agriculture placed new and varied stresses on human groups. The rise of civilization and urbanization have affected human variability. Physical anthropologists must be cognizant of many culture features when studying the genetic and physiological diversity of populations. Genetics, environment and culture influence such traits as intelligence, body size and build, and skin color. Human features such as these are difficult to study and there is much controversy concerning the amount of variation that is genetic, environmental, or cultural.

Relethford, John H., 1994, *The Human Species*, Mayfield Publishing Company.

Terms and Concepts You Should Know

polymorphism (110)

polytypic (111)

endogamy (111)

acclimatization (111)

race (112-

folk taxonomy (112)

continuous variation (114)

racism (115)

geographic races (115)

clinal distribution [cline] (116-117)

multivariate analysis (117)

melanin (118)

vitamin D (119)

Bergmann's Rule (120)

Allen's Rule (120)

sickle-cell anemia (121-122)

malaria (121-122)

balanced polymorphism (122)

lactase deficiency (122-123)

pastoralism (123)

hypoxia (123)

intelligence quotient (125)

People To Know About

Linnaeus (113-114)

Blumenbach (113-114)

Stanley Garn (115)

R.C. Lewontin (117-118)

Thinking About What You Have Read

The following questions or problems may be of help to you in studying the material presented in both the text and in your class. You may want to write out the answers to these questions (writing something down always seems to help solidify it in one's mind) or just think about them.

1. How does culture affect the genetic structure of a population?

2. Discuss the history of racial classification.

3. Is race a biologically meaningful unit?

4. Are there any alternatives to racial classifications?

5. Explain how clinal distributions are used to study human variation. Does this approach seem to be a viable alternative to racial classifications?

6. The geographic distribution of skin color suggests that natural selection has played a role in molding this trait. What are some of the selective agents that are thought to be responsible for the varying degrees of pigmentation seen in populations across the globe?

7. Do humans generally follow both Bergmann's and Allen's rules?

8. Does head shape and nose form vary in any systematic way with climate?

9. Discuss the relationship between malaria and sickle cell.

10. What are lactose and lactase? Why do some populations have high frequencies of lactose-tolerant adults while others do not?

11. How do humans adapt to varying environments?

12. Discuss the relationship (or lack of) among heredity, intelligence, and race.

CHECKING YOUR UNDERSTANDING: A PRACTICE EXAMINATION

We suggest that you take this practice exam and then check your answers against the key provided at the end of this section. Use the questions that you got wrong as a guide to further study. Try to learn why specific answers are right and wrong. You may even want to take the practice exam a second time to review what you have learned.

True-False Questions

1. Modern humans are grouped into three distinct species.

2. Cultural practices affect genetic and physical variation by influencing gene flow or altering the environment.

3. The genetic variation present in human populations is the product of four fundamental processes of evolution: mutation, gene flow, genetic drift, and natural selection.

4. Anthropologists speculate that Paleolithic populations consisted of small bands (30-100 individuals) in which genetic drift may have been an important factor.

5. Culture may influence human genetic variation through religious beliefs, social organization, marriage practices, and social prejudices.

6. Cultural factors can affect people's health and, as a consequence, their growth and development.

7. Although the diversity of human populations is undeniable, the problems involved in delineating specific races has little practical or scientific value in studying human variation.

8. Early racial classification correlated physical characteristics with cultural differences often assuming that populations that shared certain physical traits also exhibited similar behaviors.

9. Racist beliefs have no basis in biological fact: human groups never fit into neat categories.

10. Many physical anthropologists avoid making racial classifications and instead focus on explaining why there is variation in human groups.

11. Anthropologists have found that almost 94% of human variation occurs within each of the major geographic (continental) racial groups, while only 6% of the variation is attributable to differences among these racial groups.

12. Darkly pigmented individuals may be more susceptible to frostbite than lightly pigmented individuals.

13. Anthropologists have found that people living in cold climates tend to have round heads and long, narrow noses.

14. Allen's rule maintains that individuals living in cold areas generally have shorter, stockier limbs.

15. A balanced polymorphism occurs when two alleles compete for the same genotype while mutating into different forms.

16. It has been surmised that populations that have a high frequency of lactose-tolerant individuals also have a history of pastoralism.

17. Individuals raised at high altitude experience hypoxic stress during their growth and development.

18. In the nineteenth century Count de Gobineau developed a theory of history based on race where he argued that each race had its own intellectual capabilities and that the Aryans were the superior race.

19. Using IQ tests, anthropologists have determined that some races are less intelligent than others, thus demonstrating that intelligence is highly heritable and a good indicator of one's racial classification.

20. Howard Gardner, using cross cultural research methods, concluded that intelligence does not constitute a single characteristic but rather amounts to a mix of many differing faculties.

Multiple Choice Questions

21. In order to understand human variation, anthropologists consider three primary causes. Which of the following is not one of these causes?
    A. evolutionary process
    B. environment
    C. race
    D. culture

22. The total complement of genes in a population is known as the
    A. genetic load
    B. gene pool
    C. population unit
    D. polymorphism group

23. Genes that have two or more alleles produce phenotypes that vary. This variation is known as a(n)
    A. induction
    B. polymorphism
    C. cloned unit
    D. genetic polyploidy

24. Species that are made up of populations that can be distinguished regionally on the basis of discrete physical traits are called
    A. polytypic
    B. incipient species
    C. genetic units
    D. acclimatization groups

25. The marriage to someone within one's own group or _____ acts to restrict gene flow.
    A. genetic drift
    B. acclimatization
    C. endogamy
    D. polymorphism

26. The physiological process of becoming accustomed or adjusted to a new environment is known as
    A. physiological induction
    B. polymorphic drive
    C. acclimatization
    D. clinal adaptation

27. Although difficult to assess the relative importance of each, there are three primary factors that contribute to human biological variation. Which of the following is not one of these factors?
    A. genetic factors
    B. environmental factors
    C. clinal factors
    D. cultural factors

28. According to your text, _____ constitute divisions within a species based on identifiable hereditary traits.
    A. families
    B. races
    C. polymorphisms
    D. taxonomic acclimatization

29. _____ were informal, unscientific racial classfications based on skin color.
    A. Teleologies
    B. Clines
    C. Folk taxonomies
    D. Genetic hybrids

30. One of the earliest scientific efforts to organize human variation into racial categories was attempted by _____. He constructed a taxonomy in 1758 that divided *Homo sapiens* into four races based on skin color.
    A. Gregor Mendel
    B. Carolus Linnaeus
    C. William Boyd
    D. Stanley Garn

31. A problem confronting early racial taxonomists such as Blumenbach was the fact that instead of falling into discrete divisions, many characteristics exhibited a spectrum from one extreme to another. This phenomenon is known as
    A. mongrelization
    B. balanced polymorphism
    C. continuous variation
    D. geographic acclimatization

32. The ideology that advocates the superiority of certain races and the inferiority of others, and leads to prejudice and discrimination is known as
    A. elitism
    B. racism
    C. mongrelism
    D. polymorphism

33. In 1961 anthropologist _____ examined race from a different perspective. Not relying on single, arbitrary characteristics, he focused on the impact that evolutionary forces may have had on geographically isolating human populations. He divided humans into geographical races, local races, and microraces.
    A. William Boyd
    B. Johann Blumenbach
    C. J. Deniker
    D. Stanley Garn

34. Because many human traits vary independently of one another, some anthropologists have found it useful to examine single traits as they vary over geographic space. This approach plots or maps the frequency of traits much like a topographic map depicts changing altitudes. If one plots human traits in this fashion it is called a
    A. clinal distribution
    B. genograph
    C. trait flow map
    D. morpho-map

35. The examination of the interrelationships among a number of different traits at the same time is known as a
    A. polymorphic study
    B. clinal study
    C. multivariate analysis
    D. polytypic exam

36. The dark pigment that is responsible for variations of tan, brown, and black skin color and which primarily determines the lightness or darkness of the skin is called
    A. hemoglobin
    B. carotene
    C. melanin
    D. rickets

37. Too little vitamin D during growth and development may cause a condition called
    A. rickets
    B. hemoglobin stunting
    C. anemia
    D. sickle cell

38. According to _____ rule, one would expect to find large, stocky individuals in cold climates and small individuals in warm climates.
    A. Allen's
    B. Garn's
    C. Birdsell's
    D. Bergmann's

39. The belief that a careful study of the bumps on the cranium could be used to "read" an individual's personality and mental abilities and even the future is called
    A. anthropometry
    B. craniometry
    C. phrenology
    D. bumpology

40. It has been hypothesized that the distribution of ABO antigens in various populations may be the result of natural selection acting to mold this genetic system. What are the selective agents involved?
    A. infectious diseases such as plague and smallpox
    B. humidity and temperature in the habitat
    C. hypoxia and nutrition
    D. malaria and lactose

41. What is the selective agent responsible for maintaining the sickle cell allele in some populations?
    A. rickets
    B. antigens
    C. malaria
    D. lactose

42. When the heterozygote is at a selective advantage in an environment, the condition that arises is called a
    A. lost allele syndrome
    B. balanced polymorphism
    C. cline
    D. genetic tolerance

43. Lactose tolerance in a population may be related to a long history of
    A. malaria
    B. smallpox
    C. pastoralism
    D. hypoxic stress

44. Adaptation to high altitude which involves a greater lung capacity, larger hearts, and more red blood cells is probably due to
    A. the genetic stress syndrome
    B. developmental acclimatization
    C. lactose and lactase intolerance
    D. genetic engineering

45. The intelligence quotient (IQ) test was invented by French psychologist
    A. Pierre Pandu
    B. Alfred Binet
    C. Jacques Kno
    D. Tina Lafondu

Suggested Readings

BAKER, P.T. and M.A. LITTLE (eds.). 1976. *Man in the Andes: A Multidisciplinary Study of High-Altitude Populations*. Stroudsburg, PA: Dowden, Hutchinson & Ross.

BRUES, A.M. 1993 *People and Races*. New York, NY: Macmillan.

CAMPBELL, B. 1983. *Human Ecology*. New York, NY: Aldine.

CLEGG, E.J. and J.P. GARLICK (eds.) 1980. *Disease and Urbanization*. Symposium for the Study of Human Biology, vol. 20. London, England: Taylor and Francis.

DEVOR, E. (ed.). 1993. *Molecular Applications in Biological Anthropology*. Cambridge, England: Cambridge University Press.

EDELSTEIN, S.J. 1986. *The Sickled Cell: From Myths to Molecules*. Cambridge, MA: Harvard University Press.

FALLOWS, J. 1989. *More Like Us*. Boston, MA: Houghton Mifflin.

FRISANCHO, A.R. 1979. *Human Adaptation: A Functional Interpretation*. St. Louis, MO: The C.V. Mosby Company.

GOULD, S.J. 1981. *The Mismeasure of Man*. New York, NY: W.W. Norton.

JURMAIN, R. and H. NELSON. 1994. *Introduction to Physical Anthropology*. Minn/St. Paul: MN: West Publishing Company.

LITTLE, M.A. and J.D. HAAS. 1989. *Human Population Biology: A Transdisciplinary Science*. New York, NY: Oxford University Press.

MASCIE-TAYLOR, C.G.N. 1993. *The Anthropology of Disease*. Oxford, England: Oxford University Press.

MCNEILL, W.H. 1976. *Plagues and People*. New York, NY: Anchor Press/Doubleday.

MOLNAR, S. 1992. *Human Variation: Races, Types, and Ethnic Groups*. Englewood Cliffs, NJ: Prentice Hall.

MONTAGU, A. 1964. *Man's Most Dangerous Myth: The Fallacy of Race*. Cleveland, OH: The World Publishing Company, Meridian Books.

MORAN, E.F. 1979. *Human Adaptability: An Introduction to Ecological Anthropology.* North Scituate, MA: Duxbury Press.

MOURANT, A.W. 1983. *Blood Relations: Blood Groups and Anthropology.* New York, NY: Oxford University Press.

ORTNER, D.J. 1983. *How Humans Adapt: A Biocultural Odyssey.* Washington, DC: Smithsonian Institution Press.

POIRIER, F.E.; W.A. STINI; and K.B. WREDEN. 1994. *In Search of Ourselves: An Introduction to Physical Anthropology.* Englewood Cliffs, NJ: Prentice Hall.

POLEDNAK, A.P. 1989. *Racial and Ethnic Differences in Disease.* New York, NY: Oxford University Press.

RELETHFORD, J.H. 1994. *The Human Species: An Introduction to Biological Anthropology.* Mountain View, CA: Mayfield.

ROBERTS, D.F. 1978. *Climate and Human Variability.* Menlo Park, CA: Cummings Publishing Company.

ROSE, M.R. 1991. *Evolutionary Biology of Aging.* New York, NY: Oxford University Press.

STASKI, E. and J. MARKS. 1992. *Evolutionary Anthropology.* Fort Worth, TX: Harcourt Brace Jovanovich College Publishers.

SWEDLUND, A.C. and G.J. ARMELAGOS. 1990. *Disease in Populations in Transition: Anthropological and Epidemological Perspectives.* New York, NY: Bergin and Garvey.

ULIJASZEK, S.J. and C.G.N. MASCIE-TAYLOR (eds.). 1993. *Anthropometry: The Individual and the Population.* Cambridge, England: Cambridge University Press.

WEISS, K.M. 1993. *Genetic Variation and Human Disease.* Cambridge, England: Cambridge University Press.

WEISS, M.L. and MANN, A.E. 1990. *Human Biology and Behavior.* Glenview, IL: Scott, Foresmans / Little, Brown Higher Education.

WILSON, E.O. 1978. *On Human Nature.* Cambridge, MA: Harvard University Press.

99

Answers With Page Numbers

1. F 110	16. T 123	31. C 114
2. T 110	17. T 123	32. B 115
3. T 111	18. T 124	33. D. 113, 115
4. T 111	19. F 125	34. A 116
5. T 111	20. T 125	35. C 117
6. T 112	21. C 110	36. C 118
7. T 112	22. B 110	37. A 119
8. T 114	23. B 110	38. D 120
9. T 115	24. A 111	39. C 120
10. T 116	25. C 111	40. A 121
11. T 118	26. C 111	41. C 121
12. T 119	27. C 111	42. B 122
13. T 120	28. B 112	43. C 123
14. T 120	29. C 112	44. C 123
15. F 122	30. B 113-114	45. B 125

CHAPTER 7

PALEOLITHIC CULTURES

Chapter Outline

Chapter Highlights

Although paleoanthropologists can use fossils to interpret the physical characteristics of early human ancestors, our understanding of the culture of ancient humans is derived primarily from the study of material remains of their activities, such as sites, features, and artifacts. Humans are distinguished from their ancestors by the use of stone tools, which—fortunately for archaeologists—can be preserved for millions of years. These changed over time, from the **Lower Paleolithic** (2.4 million to 200,000 years ago) to the **Middle Paleolithic** (200,000 to 40,000 years ago) to the **Upper Paleolithic** (40,000 to 10,000 years ago). The first of these periods corresponds to the time of *Homo habilis*, with **Oldowan** technology, and *Homo erectus*, with **Acheulian** technology. The second corresponds to the time of **archaic *Homo sapiens*** (**Neandertals**), with **Mousterian** and related technologies. The last corresponds to the time of **modern *Homo sapiens*** prior to the end of the Ice Age (**Pleistocene**), and is characterized by a wide variety of tool types in both the Old and New Worlds. It was during this last period that Australia became inhabited and the first Native Americans crossed the Bering Strait.

The earliest known stone tools were found at the site of **Olduvai Gorge** by **Louis and Mary Leakey**. These dated to around 2.4 million years ago and were associated with fossilized remains of *Homo habilis*. Called **Oldowan** tools, they consist of rounded river cobbles that have had chips removed via **percussion flaking** on one side (**unifacial**) or two sides (**bifacial**) to produce sharp edges. The first toolkits were simple, consisting of **choppers, hammer stones,** and **flakes**. Other objects of unknown use, called **manuports**, were carried to sites by humans. Archaeologists have investigated the way these objects were manufactured by doing **experimental studies** to test various ways of producing these objects. **Use-wear studies**, such as those performed on stone tools from **Koobi Fora**, can reveal patterns that show whether sharp edges were used to cut wood, meat, or other materials.

Large numbers of tools and bones found together in deposits at Olduvai Gorge have been interpreted as possible living floors, or surfaces upon which early hominids dwelt. These may represent **home bases**, to which individuals returned with food obtained through hunting, gathering, or scavenging. However, they may also represent deposits created by non-human activities, such as animal predators that hoarded bones. Although the nature of these features remains a topic of debate, paleoanthropologists like **Richard Potts** argue that early hominids still lived in social groups because: 1) social groups are common to higher primates, 2) tool use was probably learned in a social setting; 2) and activities resulting in archaeological sites included communal use of stone materials. Anthropologists studying early hominids have turned to investigations of other primates, such as baboons, chimpanzees, and gorillas, to gain insights into what *Homo habilis* society might have been like. They have learned that baboons, while aggressive, also maintain cooperative relationships. Chimpanzees use tools, share food, and even pass information from one generation to the next.

Around 1.65 million years ago, *Homo erectus* evolved from *H. habilis* and became the first hominid to migrate out of Africa. *H. erectus* sites have been found in Africa, Europe, the Middle East, and Asia. They were probably the inventors of the improved stone tools known as Developed Oldowan, although this style soon evolved into a distinctive technology referred to as the **Acheulian** industry. Acheulian tools, also made with percussion flaking, included **hand axes, cleavers,** and scrapers used to process meat. Unlike the Oldowan tools, more advanced Acheulian tools were made by using a **"soft hammer"** or **baton method** to remove flakes from a core of fine-grained stone. This resulted in greater control over the finished product, and is evidence of more careful planning in tool manufacture. In addition to an improved stone tool technology, *Homo erectus* had a more elaborate material culture than earlier populations as evidenced by sites like **Zhoukoudien.** These were the first people to make fire. At **Terra Amata**, in southern France, people with an Acheulian culture erected simple shelters made of stones and saplings and ate oysters, mussels, and a variety of large game animals around 300,000 years ago. Over time, *Homo erectus* evolved into the earliest (archaic) *Homo sapiens* and stone tools became even more efficient.

Modern humans evolved from **archaic *Homo sapiens*,** the earliest of which date to around 200,000 years ago. The **Middle Paleolithic** period, during which this transition occurred, saw the emergence of a tool-making strategy known as the **Levallois technique.** This was a method of shaping a core by removing flakes in a definite pattern in order to make a more efficient use of the fine-grained stone. The result of this strategy was a trend away from larger, cruder core tools to finer, more specialized flake tools. One variety of archaic *H. sapiens* was the **Neandertal,** found in Europe and the Middle East between 130,000 and 35,000 years ago. Neandertals lived in very harsh, **Ice Age** climates, in caves, rock shelters, and occasional open sites. Their **Mousterian** technology consisted of a wide variety of **flake tools** made using the Levallois technique. Neandertals are the earliest humans for whom we have evidence of ritual activity. This includes sites like **Drachenlock Cave,** Switzerland, which was reported to contain cave bear skulls arranged within a "shrine" of stone slabs. Other sites, like **Shanidar Cave** in Iraq, have evidence for both intentional burials and the long-term care of disabled individuals. Neanderthals were eventually replaced by modern *Homo sapiens* as stone tools became more refined with the production of finer and more sophisticated tools made of special flakes called **blades.**

During the **Upper Paleolithic** period, modern humans continued to live in groups of hunters and gatherers. In Europe, their stone tool technology was highly varied through time and space. The most distinctive chracteristic of this period is the use of long, narrow stone **blades** and a new technique called **pressure flaking** in which fine flakes were removed by applying pressure to the edge of a blade with pieces of bone, antler, or wood. This allowed for the production of fine spear points as well as tools like **borers** and **burins.** Burins, tools with sharp points, made it possible to carve bone or ivory into harpoon barbs, needles, or even figurines. Other tools improved the working of leather and wood. Upper Paleolithic people lived in caves and simple shelters, some made of mammoth bones. Variation in tools and dwellings through time and space has allowed us to define many distinct **archaeological cultures** for this period. Perhaps the most dramatic evidence from this time period is the world's first art, in the form of **"Venus" figurines,** carved bones, and elaborate **cave paintings** such as those at the site of **Lascaux.**

The Upper Paleolithic, which came to an end with the close of the last Ice Age, also saw the migration of the first humans from northeast Asia across the Bering Strait into North America. These **Paleo-Indians**, who lived as nomadic bands that hunted large game, were the ancestors of modern Native Americans in North, Central, and South America. At present, archaeologists are divided over the interpretation of evidence for when the first humans arrived in the Americas. There is abundant evidence for the widespread presence of mammoth hunters using distinctive **Clovis spear points** between about 11,200 and 10,900 years ago. These **fluted points**, so named because of a characteristic **channel flake**, were made by pressure flaking. Because this is the earliest recognized stone tool industry in North America, advocates of the **Clovis-first hypothesis** favor a date of around 12,000 years ago for the first Paleo-Indians. Advocates of the **pre-Clovis hypothesis**, who cite evidence from sites like **Meadowcroft Rock Shelter** and **Monte Verde**, claim that the first populations could have arrived much earlier. However, pre-Clovis sites are rare and more highly problematic than Clovis sites.

The Upper Paleolithic period also saw the first migrations to the continent of Australia. Archaeological evidence suggests that the first humans arrived sometime after 50,000 years ago and spread over most of Australia between 35,000 and 40,000 years ago. The current hypotheses, based on skeletal remains from sites like **Lake Mungo** and **Kow Swamp**, suggest two waves of immigrants to the island.

Terms and Concepts You Should Know

Lower Paleolithic (128)

hammerstone (129)

flakes (129)

percussion flaking (129)

unifacial tools (129)

bifacial tools (129)

pebble tools (129)

choppers (129)

manuports (129)

People to Know About

Louis and Mary Leakey (128)

Glynn Isaac (130)

Lewis Binford (130)

Richard Potts (130)

Jane Goodall (131)

Dian Fossey (131)

Henri de Lumley (133)

Joseph Greenberg (140)

James Adovasio (141)

Tom Dillehay (142)

Places to Know About

Olduvai Gorge (128)

Torralba and Ambrona (133)

Terra Amata (133)

Howieson's Poort (134)

Drachenloch (135)

Shanidar Cave (135)

Cultures to Know About

Thinking About What You Have Read

The following questions or problems may be of help to you in studying the material presented in both the text and in your class. You may want to write out the answers to these questions (writing something down always seems to help solidify it in one's mind) or just think about them.

1. Discuss the specific changes in stone tool manufacture that corresponded to the appearance of the following human species: *Homo habilis*, *Homo erectus*, Neandertals, Cro-Magnon. What do you think were the principal factors influencing the types of tools that humans were able to make?

2. What are some of the types of research that anthropologists can do to help them to understand the uses of ancient stone tools and the methods used to manufacture them?

3. Compare and contrast the multiregional and the replacement models for the spread of modern *Homo sapiens*. How would an anthropologist go about testing the specific implications of each model?

4. Who were the Neandertals? When and where did they live? What do we know about their belief systems?

5. What did the people of the Upper Paleolithic period eat and how did they obtain their food? What were the conditions that affected the types of foods available to them?

6. How did the culture of the Upper Paleolithic differ from that of earlier humans? Was life easier or harder? What are some of the things invented during the Upper Paleolithic that are still important for modern humans?

7. What made *Homo erectus* different from *Homo habilis*?

8. What are the differences between "archaic" and "modern" *Homo sapiens* in terms of material culture? Why do you think these differences existed?

9. What do the changes in stone tools over time reveal about changes in the humans who were making them? How were the styles of tools and their methods of manufacture affected by changes in human behavior?

10. What are the specific differences between the following technologies: Oldowan, Acheulian, Mousterian, Solutrean? What generalizations can you make about trends in stone tool manufacture over time?

11. When did humans begin to create works of art? What were the first art objects made? How can we interpret who made them, why they were made, and why they were important to the artists who made them?

12. What does the evidence about early humans reveal any information about the origins of religious traditions? What are some of your own hypotheses about the reasons for "ritual" activity by early humans? How could these hypotheses be tested?

13. Describe the processes by which the entire globe, including regions as far apart as Australia and Siberia, came to be occupied by human beings. What were the principal reasons behind human migration? When and where did the most significant migrations of early humans occur?

14. What are the principal arguments for and against the idea of a pre-Clovis migration to the New World? What is the nature of the archaeological evidence that supports or refutes the pre-Clovis hypothesis?

15. Discuss the dating of the earliest populations in Australia, naming specific sites that have yielded both stone tools and human remains. What are some of the current theories regarding the nature of the initial colonization of Australia?

CHECKING YOUR UNDERSTANDING - A PRACTICE EXAMINATION

We suggest that you take this practice exam and then check your answers against the key provided at the end of this section. Use the questions that you got wrong as a guide to further study. Try to learn why specific answers are right and wrong. You may even want to take the practice exam a second time to review what you have learned.

True - False Questions

1. The beginnings of human culture can be studied by looking at the fossilized remains of ancient human skeletons.

2. Humans are the only primates to use tools.

3. Scientific evidence indicates that the first humans were making chopper tools and hammerstones.

4. Archaeologists have trouble understanding the manufacture of ancient stone tools because they are unable to do experiments that will reveal how they were made.

5. Baboons have been documented to forge cooperative ties and friendships as well as acting out aggressive tendencies.

6. Chimpanzees are the only apes that regularly use tools to crack nuts and extract insects from nests.

7. *Homo erectus* had a cranial capacity equal to that of modern humans.

8. Humans were building shelters on the French Riviera approximately 300,000 years ago.

9. Among the foods enjoyed by *Homo erectus* were oysters, mussels, and meat from the wild ox.

10. During the Middle Paleolithic period in Africa, styles of stone tools changed much more rapidly than during the Lower Paleolithic.

11. Modern *Homo sapiens* was the first hominid species to intentionally bury their dead.

12. Neandertals probably cared for individuals with disabilities.

13. Burins are special projectile points for hunting large game like mammoths.

14. The harpoon was invented by people with an Upper Paleolithic technology.

15. Upper Paleolithic artisans made stone tools in distinctive styles that vary from region to region.

16. Compared to the Middle Paleolithic, the Upper Paleolithic had more nonutilitarian objects.

17. Paleolithic hunters and gatherers lived mostly in marginal areas, such as dry desert region.

18. Cro-Magnon people had the technology to start a fire whenever one was needed.

19. Upper Paleolithic peoples of Europe produced ivory sculptures and mural paintings.

20. During the Upper Paleolithic, modern *Homo sapiens* migrated throughout the world, including North and South America and Australia.

Multiple Choice Questions

21. The term "Paleolithic" also means:
    - A. "Old Stone Age"
    - B. "ancient knowledge"
    - C. "before Adam"
    - D. "cave people"

22. Oldowan tools were manufactured by:
    - A. breaking chips of stone from a cobble with a hammerstone
    - B. applying continuous pressure to flint with a piece of bone or antler
    - C. carving pieces of mammoth tusk or bone
    - D. combining two or more different materials

23. When an archaeologist examines the polish or residue found on the edges of an ancient stone tool, she is doing a:
    - A. palynological study
    - B. trace element analysis
    - C. use-wear study
    - D. pressure-flake analysis

24. Archaeologists Glynn Isaac and Louis Leakey have suggested that sites like those at Olduvai Gorge, where thousands of bones and artifacts were found together, represent:
    - A. cemeteries where funeral rituals were practiced
    - B. the remains of primitive warfare
    - C. home bases to which male hunters brought food
    - D. small villages, with populations of fewer than 100 people

25. Lewis Binford has suggested that much of the bone found at hominid sites represents the remains of:
    - A. animals killed by other predators but scavenged by humans
    - B. animals that were killed by female hunters
    - C. individuals who died all at once as a result of natural disasters
    - D. feasts that accompanied large social gatherings

26. Which of the following has NOT been suggested by Richard Potts as a key factor suggesting that hominids lived in social groups?
    - A. social groups are a general part of higher primate life
    - B. tool use and manufacture were learned in a social setting
    - C. the construction of shelters was critical to survival
    - D. sites were created by the communal use of stone materials

27. Nancy Tanner has suggested that early hominids may have been similar to chimpanzees with respect to:
    A. mothers rewarding daughters for learning how to use tools
    B. competition, aggression, and dominance among females
    C. the simple cultivation of various types of wild seeds
    D. methods for modifying stone pebbles into unifacial tools

28. The Acheulian stone tool technology is associated with which early hominid?
    A. Neandertals
    B. *Australopithecus robustus*
    C. *Homo habilis*
    D. *Homo erectus*

29. One of the principal innovations of Acheulian technology was the use of:
    A. bifacial stone tools
    B. bone or antler hammers to strike off flakes
    C. pressure flaking to produce projectile points
    D. a core-and-blade technique

30. The first hominid to take advantage of the controlled usage of fire was:
    A. *Homo sapiens*
    B. *Australopithecus afarensis*
    C. *Homo erectus*
    D. *Homo habilis*

31. A shelter of stones and saplings was built by people who used Acheulian tools at the site of:
    A. Zhoukoudien
    B. Terra Amata
    C. Olduvai Gorge
    D. Cro-Magnon

32. The Levalloisian technique refers to a:
    A. method of excavation used by Henri de Lumley at Terra Amata
    B. precise means of identifying archaeological strate at Paleolithic sites
    C. method of excavation used to uncover Neandertal burials at Shanidar
    D. method of preparing a stone so that it will provide useful flakes

33. The Howieson's Poort industry of southern Africa indicates a trend during the Middle Stone Age of:
    A. larger, cruder tools than were made in earlier periods
    B. using finer-grained stones to make more carefully flaked tools
    C. going from bifacial implements to unifacial ones
    D. smaller and more dispersed settlements than in earlier periods

34. Neandertals are also known as:
    A. archaic *Homo erectus*
    B. modern *Homo erectus*
    C. archaic *Homo sapiens*
    D. modern *Homo sapiens*

35. At Drachenlock Cave in Switzerland, the discovery of _____ was interpreted as a crude shrine used by Neandertals. Unfortunately, this find was not well documented.
    A. mummified bodies of heavily-built men and women
    B. a colorful painting of bison, horses, and elephants
    C. twenty cave bear skulls in an arrangement of stone slabs
    D. skeletons of thirty-three penguins surrounded by bone flutes

36. The first hominids to practice intentional burial of their dead were
    A. modern *Homo sapiens*
    B. *Homo erectus*
    C. Neandertals
    D. *Homo habilis*

37. The most important technological development in stone tool production for the Upper Paleolithic period was the ability to make:
    A. sharpened cores
    B. long, narrow blades
    C. scraping tools
    D. hand axes

38. Solutrean projectile points are impressive artifacts because they are so:
    A. delicate
    B. massive
    C. versatile
    D. simple

39. A burin is a:
    A. spear thrower
    B. harpoon
    C. long, thin blade of stone
    D. chisel-like tool for working bone or ivory

40. The Upper Paleolithic, which dates from about 40,000 to 10,000 years ago, was characterized by all of the following except
    A. modern *Homo sapiens*
    B. blade tools of many traditions
    C. first evidence for the controlled usage of fire
    D. ivory figurines and cave art

41. Upper Paleolithic hunters increased the power and accuracy of their projectiles by using:
    A. slingshots
    B. spear throwers
    C. bows and arrows
    D. stone projectile points

42. At the 15,000 year-old site at Mezirich in the Ukraine, archaeologists have excavated the remains of five shelters made from:
    A. rough stone slabs
    B. blocks of marble
    C. tree trunks
    D. mammoth bones

43. The term "archaeological culture" refers to:
    A. what archaeologists do to investigate the past
    B. expressions of ethnic identity in material remains
    C. variation in Upper Paleolithic technologies
    D. prehistoric sculpture and cave painting

44. An archaeologist who wanted to understand the lifestyle and social organization of Upper Paleolithic peoples would get the most useful information by studying:
    A. the habits of bears, elephants, and other animals they hunted
    B. ethnicity in modern European populations that are descended from them
    C. the characteristics of modern hunting and gathering peoples
    D. mechanical properties of stone used for making tools

45. Colorful paintings of bison, deer, and other animals in caves were made by:
    A. Neandertals
    B. *Homo erectus*
    C. modern *Homo sapiens*
    D. archaic *Homo sapiens*

46. In addition to archaeology, support for the origin of Native Americans has been provided by both _____ anthropology and _____ anthropology.
    A. forensic/applied
    B. cultural/biological
    C. physical/linguistic
    D. economic/political

47. Although most anthropologists agree on where Native Americans originated, they disagree about:
    A. whether the first populations were hunter-gatherers or farmers
    B. when the population migrations actually took place
    C. the particular subspecies (archaic or modern *Homo sapiens*)
    D. the types of boats or canoes that would have been utilized

48. Critics of the pre-Clovis hypothesis interpret the archaeological evidence to indicate that the first humans to populate the Americas arrived:
    A. approximately 12,000 years ago or later
    B. from Greenland by means of wooden and skin canoes
    C. prior to about 30,000 years ago
    D. without any distinctive stone tool tradition

49. Monte Verde has provided evidence that some Paleo-Indian people:
    A. made and used distinctive fluted projectile points
    B. hunted extinct species of giraffe and rhinoceros
    C. were of a physical type very similar to the Neandertals
    D. lived in huts made of wooden frames covered by hides

50. Archaeological evidence suggests that most of the continent of Australia was populated by:
    A. 120,000 years ago
    B. 70,000 to 85,000 years ago
    C. 35,000 to 40,000 years ago
    D. 12,000 years ago

Suggested Readings

BORDES, FRANCOIS. 1968. *The Old Stone Age*. New York: McGraw-Hill.

DIBBLE, H., AND A. MONTET-WHITE, EDS. 1988. *Upper Pleistocene Prehistory*. Philadelphia: University of Pennsylvania Press.

DILLEHAY, THOMAS. 1989. *Monte Verde: A Late Pleistocene Settlement in Chile*. Washington: Smithsonian Institution Press.

FAGAN, BRIAN. 1990. *The Journey from Eden: The Peopling of Our World*. New York: Thames & Hudson.

_____. 1987. *The Great Journey: The Peopling of Ancient America*. New York: Thames & Hudson.

GOWLETT, J.A.J. 1984. *Ascent to Civilization: The Archaeology of Early Man*. New York: Knopf.

ISAAC, GLYNN. 1984. *The Archaeology of Human Origins: Studies of the Lower Pleistocene in East Africa, 1971-1981*. Advances in World Archaeology 3:1-87.

LEAKEY, R., AND R. LEWIN. 1977. *Origins*. New York: Dutton.

LEE, R.B., AND I. DEVORE, EDS. 1968. *Man the Hunter*. Chicago: Aldine.

LEROI-GOURHAN, A. 1984. *The Dawn of European Art: An Introduction to Paleolithic Cave Paintings*. Cambridge: Cambridge University Press.

SACKETT, JAMES R. 1982. Approaches to Style in Lithic Archaeology. *Journal of Anthropological Archaeology* 1:59-112.

STRINGER, CHRISTOPHER B. 1990. The Emergence of Modern Humans. *Scientific American* 259(12):98-103.

TRINKHAUS, ERIK. 1989. *The Emergence of Modern Humans: Biocultural Adaptation in the Later Pleistocene*. New York: Cambridge University Press.

TRINKHAUS, E., AND W.W. HOWELLS. 1979. The Neanderthals. *Scientific American* 241:94-105.

WOLPOFF, MILFORD H. 1980. *Paleoanthropology*. New York: Knopf.

Answer Key with Page Numbers

1.	F 128	21.	A 128	41.	B 136
2.	F 128	22.	A 129	42.	D 137
3.	T 129	23.	C 129	43.	B 139
4.	F 129	24.	C 130	44.	C 139
5.	T 131	25.	A 130	45.	C 139
6.	T 131	26.	C 131	46.	C 140
7.	F 131	27.	A 131	47.	B 141
8.	T 133	28.	C 131	48.	A 141
9.	T 133	29.	B 132	49.	D 142
10.	T 134	30.	C 132	50.	C 143
11.	F 135	31.	B 133		
12.	T 135	32.	D 134		
13.	F 136	33.	B 134		
14.	T 136	34.	C 134		
15.	T 139	35.	C 135		
16.	T 139	36.	C 135		
17.	F 139	37.	B 136		
18.	T 139	38.	A 136		
19.	T 139	39.	D 136		
20.	T 140	40.	C 136		

CHAPTER 8

THE ORIGINS OF DOMESTICATION AND SETTLED LIFE

Consequences of Domestication
Population Growth
Health and Nutrition
Increasing Material Complexity
Increasing Social Stratification and Political Complexity

Chapter Highlights

One of the most significant changes in the human condition was brought about through the transition from a mobile way of life based on hunting and gathering to a **sedentary** lifestyle based on **food production**. This chapter discusses evidence for the origins of plant and animal **domestication** and the effects of agriculture on human populations.

The emergence of food production was a response to worldwide climatic changes at the end of the Pleistocene period. These resulted in a higher degree of **seasonality** and major changes in plant and animal resources. Forests began to replace grasslands and herds of **megafauna**, like mammoths and giant bison, gradually became extinct. As hunting resources changed, humans began to consume a wider variety of plants and animals. This change, known as **broad-spectrum collecting**, resulted in new strategies and technologies for food gathering and processing. The **Mesolithic** (Old World) and **Archaic** (New World) periods refer to these post-Pleistocene adaptations. They are characterized by the artifacts like fine, **pressure-flaked** projectile points, **microliths**, and **ground stone tools**. Microliths were used to make sickles for harvesting wild grains. Ground stone tools were used for pulverizing seeds, cutting down trees, and woodworking. Sites like **Star Carr** indicate that Mesolithic peoples made use of a wide variety of animal products, like hides, bones, and antlers.

The term "Neolithic" is used in the Old World to refer to the appearance of sedentary, agricultural villages around 10,000 years ago. It is characterized by the use of domesticated plants and animals. **Domestication** is defined as the genetic modification of wild species to make them more productive. It was accomplished over time through both natural and artificial selection. Domestication occurred in many different parts of the world at different times and under different circumstances. The wide variety of food products we consume today are a testament of these early developments.

The transition from hunting and gathering Mesolithic and Archaic populations to agricultural villages was a gradual process that can be investigated through archaeology. **Flotation** is used to recover ancient plant remains. Seeds and other remains survive in **coprolites**, or dried human feces. The use of microliths to cut seed-producing grasses is indicated by **silica gloss** left on the tools by the abrasion of plant stalks. Animal bones are an important class of information, and can reveal practices such as the **selective killing** of male sheep to increase herd structure. Other evidence includes the existence of **storage bins** and plant impressions on pottery sherds.

Paleoethnobotany is the the study of interrelationships between ancient human and plant populations. Archaeologists often seek evidence for the transition to agriculture in those areas where the wild ancestors of domesticated species are found. Wild wheat and barley are found in the foothills of Turkey and Iraq. *Bos primigenius*, the wild ancestor of cattle, was native to southeastern Europe. The wild ancestor of corn, **teosinte**, is known from the uplands of western Mexico. Because the transitions from wild species to domesticated ones can be gradual, it is often difficult to say specifically when and where they occurred.

There are several major theories as to why domestication happened. **V. Gordon Childe** suggested it was due to a drying trend that concentrated humans, plants, and animal populations around isolated fertile areas he called "oases." **Robert Braidwood** hypothesized that humans gradually became more familiar with the life cycles of useful species, and that domestication spread outward from "nuclear" zones where wild species were most abundant. Economist **Ester Boserup** emphasized the role of **population pressure** in encouraging human populations to adopt methods for intensifying food production. Population pressure was also identified as a factor by **Lewis Binford**, who suggested that rising sea levels at the end of the Pleistocene led to increases in the density of hunting and gathering populations. The resulting shortages of wild resources encouraged food production. **Mark Cohen**, who interpreted population growth as a constant process, also saw domestication as a response to food crises. The principal critique of population pressure hypotheses is that many hunting and gathering societies are successful at controlling growth through practices like **birth spacing** and **infanticide**. Food production is just one of many possible responses to population pressure.

There are many hypotheses as to how plants and animals were domesticated. **Kent Flannery** suggested that domestication resulted from human efforts to get species to thrive outside of their natural ecological ranges. **David Rindos**, on the other hand, stressed the role of natural selection and unintentional processes of plant and human **coevolution**. Human competition with seed-eating animals, weeding, the unconsious dispersal of seeds that would not normally germinate, or the storage of seeds, would have - over time - produced changes in both plant morphology and human behavior. Other researchers have pointed to the utility of ground seeds as **weaning foods** or social benefits of special food products as factors in plant domestication. They stress that beyond domestication, agriculture required a commitment to its continued use.

There are a number of cultures that help us to understand the process of domestication and the origins of agriculture in different parts of the world. In Southwest Asia (also known as the Middle East), the use of microlithic **sickle blades**, **grinding stones**, and simple storage bins permitted the **Natufians** to live in small villages of circular pit-houses at around 12,000 years ago. As the use of domesticated wheat, barley, legumes, sheep, and goats became more important, small Natufian settlements grew into Neolithic villages like **Jericho**, with mud-brick structures and stone walls at around 10,000 years ago. In the uplands of the **Fertile Crescent**, from which the Tigris and Euprates rivers flow, the herding of sheep and goats helped produce societies based on pastoralism. Over time, the use of irrigation canals for farming led to the settlement of **Mesopotamia**.

120

In Europe, agricultural systems based on barley, lentils, and sheepherding spread up river valleys from Southwest Asia and the Black Sea region of Southeastern Europe. Cattle were probably domesticated in this area. There was a persistence of Mesolithic patterns in northern areas, such Great Britain and Scandinavia, but by 4000 B.C. agriculture was found throughout Europe. Among the traces of these early farming cultures are **megalithic chambered tombs** and sites like **Stonehenge**, in southern England, that indicate growing social complexity and a sophisticated knowledge of the natural world.

In Southeast Asia, the earliest agriculture was probably based on the cultivation of root crops (**vegeculture**) in warm, tropical regions. Rice was most likely domesticated in the wetlands of areas like southern China or Thailand, where the site of **Khok Phanom Di** has rice husks dating to 7,000 years ago. In northern China, the most important domesticates were varieties of millet, grains cultivated in the Yellow River valley. The Neolithic culture of **Yangshao**, dating between 5000 and 3000 B.C., is characterized by large villages of pit-houses with specialized pottery vessels, sheep, goat, and other elements of settled village life.

The transition to agriculture in Africa began as early as 18,000 years ago, when people at sites like **Wadi Kubbaniyah** in the Upper Nile Valley were harvesting and processing wild grasses with microlithic tools and grinding stones. Wetter conditions in the Sahara around 8,000 years ago allowed for the expansion of populations utilizing a variety of plants and animals that were originally domesticated in Southwest Asia. In Sub-Saharan Africa, the process occurred much later. Yams may have been cultivated in West Africa as early as 7,000 years ago, but the evidence is ambiguous. Pastoralism based on cattle, goats, and sheep became a dominant pattern in much of sub-Saharan Africa around 4,000 years ago. Pottery with impressions of millet and sorghum dates to about 3,200 years ago.

The transition to agriculture has been documented in a number of areas throughout the Americas. In Mesoamerica, the best evidence comes from the **Tehuacan Valley** of Mexico, where grinding stones (known as *manos* and *metates*) were first used at around 10,000 years ago. The remains of pumpkins, chili peppers, avocados, and early **maize** found in dry caves there have been dated to about 7,000 years ago, although the first **pit-houses** do not appear until about 2,000 years later.

In South America, intensive use of wild plant species began around 10,000 years ago and the first domesticated varieties appeared between 8,000 and 5,000 years ago. Food plants, including tubers like **manioc** and potatoes, were domesticated in the tropical lowlands and Andean highlands, respectively. Maize was probably introduced at an early date via Central America. Other important food crops included chili peppers and peanuts. The first sedentary communities took advantage of rich marine resources along the Pacific coast of Peru. Among the earliest cultivated plants were gourds and cotton, grown for containers and fiber. A significant difference between South America and Mesoamerica was the importance of domesticated animals, especially **llamas** and **guinea pigs**.

North America had much lower population densities than either Mesoamerica and South America, with hunting and gathering patterns remaining predominant for a longer period of time. However, species like **sunflower, marsh elder, goosefoot,** and **amaranth** were probably used intensively by late Archaic peoples between 4,000 and 3,000 years ago. Maize, beans, and squash gradually diffused northward from Mexico beginning around 1000 B.C., but did not become widely cultivated in eastern North America until between A.D. 800 and 1100. By this time, groups like the **Hohokam** in the southwestern U.S. were using extensive irrigation systems to grow corn. After A.D. 1000, maize farming supported large and dense settlements like **Cahokia** in the Mississippi Valley.

The most significant consequence of food production was a dramatic rise in human populations. Agriculture increased the productivity of a given amount of land, allowing for greater **population density**. Domesticated foods together with sedentism brought about decreases in infant mortality and birth spacing, increasing life expectancy and population growth rates. The net result was a surge in world populations that has continued to the present day. Agriculture was not without its costs, however. Prehistoric farmers relied on a smaller variety of foods, reducing the quality of their overall **nutrition** and increasing the risks of periodic food shortages. The health of agriculturalists is poorer on the average than that of hunter-gatherers, but differences in population structure make these two groups hard to compare. Agricultural populations have more children and old people, and dense settlements increase the frequency of infectious diseases, but farmers also have higher life expectancies.

After population growth, another significant consequence of agriculture was increasing **social complexity**. Food storage and **surplus** permitted an increased **division of labor**, since not everyone in the society needed to be a food producer. Full-time craftspeople were able to increase and improve manufactured products. Property ownership and centralized decision making led to differences in social status. While hunting and gathering societies tend to be egalitarian, in that everyone has more-or-less equal access to basic resources, agricultural societies become **stratified** as a result of varying levels of access to land, water, and labor. The accumulation of wealth produced social ranking, with concurrent differences in power among families and individuals. Along with population growth, food-production resulted in greater disparity between the haves and the have-nots. Social and political complexity are direct results of the Neolithic transition.

Terms and Concepts You Should Know

subsistence (146)

nomadism (146)

food production (146)

tundra (146)

broad-spectrum collecting (147)

Mesolithic period (147)

Archaic period (147)

microlith (147)

ground stone tools (147)

adze (147)

midden (147)

Neolithic period (147)

cultivation (148)

artificial selection (148)

domestication (148)

rachis (148)

flotation (149)

coprolite (149)

Bos primigenius (150)

ethnobotany (151)

paleoethnobotany (151)

"Neolithic revolution" (151)

oasis hypothesis (151)

readiness hypothesis (152)

nuclear zones (152)

coevolution (153)

silica gloss (154)

obsidian (154)

tell (155)

pastoralism (155)

shaduf (157)

megaliths (158)

vegeculture (158)

pot irrigation (160)

imaging radar (160)

metate (161)

mano (161)

Cotton Preceramic (162)

Eastern Agricultural Complex (162)

fallow (163)

Harris lines (163)

enamel hypoplasias (163)

egalitarian societies (164)

stratified societies (164)

People to Know About

V. Gordon Childe (151)

Robert Braidwood (152)

Ester Boserup (152)

Lewis Binford (152)

Mark Cohen (152)

Carl Sauer (153)

Kent Flannery (153)

David Rindos (153)

Places to Know About

Starr Carr (147)

Fertile Crescent (154)

Jericho (154)

Ali Kosh (155)

Stonehenge (158)

Khok Phanom Di (158)

Wadi Kubbaniya (159)

Tehuacan Valley (161)

Cultures to Know About

Jomon (150)

Natufians (154)

Yangshao (159)

Thinking About What You Have Read

The following questions or problems may be of help to you in studying the material presented in both the text and in your class. You may want to write out the answers to these questions (writing something down always seems to help solidify it in one's mind) or just think about them.

1. What were the principal differences in climate, human subsistence strategies, and human population mobility between the late Pleistocene and the early Holocene epochs?

2. How is the Mesolithic period distinguished from the Upper Paleolithic period in terms of technology? How is Neolithic technology different from Mesolithic technology?

3. What is meant by the term "domestication?" In archaeological deposits, how can one tell that plant remains are from domesticated rather than wild species? How can one tell domesticated animals from their wild ancestors?

4. What are the main techniques used to recover archaeological information pertinent to research on the transition from hunting and gathering to food producing ways of life?

5. Describe at least two of the principal theories that have been offered for the origins of agriculture. What are their strong points? What are their weaknesses? Of the theories presented in your textbook, which do you find the most acceptable and why?

6. What is the relationship that scholars like Ester Boserup, Lewis Binford, and Marc Cohen have proposed between human populations and technological change? What are some of the implications of this relationship for archaeological remains? (That is, can their theories be tested? How?)

7. Discuss the notion of "coevolution" as presented by David Rindos. What are the specific implications of this theory? Do you think that coevolution is a process that is still underway? Why?

8. What is the principal evidence for the origins of food production in Southwest Asia? What were the first plant and animal domesticates in this region? What were the specific characteristics of the first farming villages here?

9. What were the main processes responsible for the origins of agriculture in Europe? Where did the earliest agricultural villages appear and what were the most important domesticates? What are some of the features one would expect to find in European Neolithic communities?

10. How did the origins of agriculture in Southeast Asia and China differ from the origins of agriculture in the Fertile Crescent? What were the principal domesticates? Describe a Neolithic community in China.

11. What were the differences between northern Africa and sub-Saharan Africa with respect to the appearance of domestication and sedentary lifestyles? What does the archaeological evidence tell us about early agriculture in each area?

12. Compare and contrast early agricultural practices in Mesoamerica and South America. What were the principal similarities? What were the principal differences? How did early agricultural practices in North America differ from each?

13. Did the adoption of an agricultural way of life result in an improvement of the human condition? Why, or why not?

14. If you were an archaeologist seeking evidence for the transition from hunting and gathering to a way of life dependent upon food production, where would you go and what kind of evidence would you look for? What are some of the techniques you would use to recover useful information?

15. What are the ways that food production and the adoption of a sedentary lifestyle affect human population? What are the specific ways that these cultural changes had an impact on human health and reproduction?

CHECKING YOUR UNDERSTANDING - A PRACTICE EXAMINATION

We suggest that you take this practice exam and then check your answers against the key provided at the end of this section. Use the questions that you got wrong as a guide to further study. Try to learn why specific answers are right and wrong. You may even want to take the practice exam a second time to review what you have learned.

True - False Questions

1. Between the late Pleistocene and the early Holocene epochs, the world's climate became markedly colder.

2. The term "broad-spectrum collecting" refers to a technique for recovering ancient plant remains.

3. Ground stone tools were made by modifying microlithic tools.

4. The first animals to be domesticated were dogs.

5. Pottery can be used indirectly as evidence for domestication, because it always appears after the shift to a food-producing way of life.

6. Finding early plant or animal remains at a particular site means that the species were domesticated there.

7. Modern farmers in Ghana, West Africa, harvest over 200 species of wild plants on a seasonal basis.

8. Farming practices such as those found at archaeological sites dating to 3,500 years ago are still in use today.

9. In contrast to hunting and gathering, agriculture takes much more time and energy.

128

10. Although there is no consensus on the exact reasons for domestication, most archaeologists agree that the "Neolithic revolution" occurred within a short period of time.

11. The term "pastoralism" refers to a way of life characterized by the central importance of planting, harvesting, and storing a particular grain

12. The adoption of agriculture in Europe was due in part to the introduction of barley from Southwestern Asia.

13. Archaeological research has revealed that the megalithic monument of Stonehenge was built over a span of two thousand years.

14. The earliest domesticated plants in Southeast Asia were probably root crops.

15. Early American civilizations were dependent upon the plow.

16. In South America, the evidence for the use of crops such as cotton precedes the appearance of pottery.

17. The earliest evidence for plant cultivation in Peru dates to 2,000 years ago.

18. In a number of areas, the advent of domesticated crops actually contributed to a decline in human health.

19. Wheeled carts and wagons were not used by ancient American civilizations of Mesoamerica because there were no appropriate materials for making wheels.

20. Agricultural production, and the ability to store surplus food, led to the appearance of the first economies based on hunting and fishing.

Multiple Choice Questions

21. The most significant cultural adaptation in the past 15,000 years has been the ability of humans to:
    A. make and use stone tools
    B. survive cold climatic conditions
    C. live in mobile band societies
    D. produce their own food

22. The most common chipped-stone tools of the Mesolithic period are known as:
    A. megaliths
    B. microliths
    C. handaxes
    D. manos and metates

23. The site of Starr Carr provided evidence for large-scale utilization of:
    A. stands of wild wheat and barley
    B. shellfish beds
    C. obsidian quarries
    D. elk and red deer

24. The practice of growing plants is known as:
    A. domestication
    B. artificial selection
    C. cultivation
    D. pastoralism

25. One of the differences between wild wheat and barley and domesticated varieties of the same plants is that the domesticated plants have a rachis that is:
    A. brittle
    B. edible
    C. tough or firm
    D. elongated

26. The principal technique used for obtaining plant remains from archaeological deposits is known as:
    A. flotation
    B. broad-spectrum collecting
    C. ethnobotany
    D. coprolite analysis

27. The hypothesis that Upper Paleolithic hunters may have been intentionally maximizing the yield of wild sheep herds is supported by evidence for:
    A. increases in the size of sheep jaws and teeth over time
    B. wool production and new types of clothing
    C. replacement of wild goat herds by wild sheep herds
    D. selective killing of male sheep

28. Domestication is most likely to have occurred:
    A. in areas where wild ancestors of domesticates are found
    B. where human populations were small and highly dispersed
    C. prior to the end of the Ice Age
    D. as a result of chance discovery of domesticated varieties

29. The study of the interrelationship between ancient plants and human populations is called:
   A. agroecology
   B. archaeoagronomy
   C. paleohorticology
   D. paleoethnobotany

30. According to the "Oasis Theory," domestication occurred as a result of a major climate change that resulted in _____ at the end of the Pleistocene or "Ice Age."
   A. warmer temperatures and increased rainfall
   B. severe droughts that reduced the ranges of wild species
   C. colder and wetter climates in the Middle East
   D. dramatic decreases in human populations

31. Robert Braidwood, of the University of Chicago, hypothesized that domestication occurred throughout the world in:
   A. "nuclear" zones, where humans became familiar with the habitats and productive potentials of wild species
   B. "oases," where humans, plants, and animals lived together as a result of reliable sources of water
   C. environmental zones outside the areas where plants and animals normally flourished
   D. areas of excessive population pressure

32. Archaeologists agree that world populations increased at the end of the Pleistocene, but it is still unclear whether:
   A. there were significant changes in world climate
   B. humans were living near wild ancestors of domesticates
   C. population growth came before or after food production
   D. hunting and gathering peoples were mobile or sedentary

33. According to archaeologist David Rindos, the initial domestication of plants and their coevolution with human populations was:
   A. the result of careful and intelligent experimentation
   B. mostly unconscious, accidental, and unintentional
   C. an idea that originated in one place and spread by diffusion
   D. the only possible solution to world population pressure

34. Silica gloss is a distinctive feature found in/on:
   A. coprolites from Natufian sites
   B. microlithic flint blades used for cutting grasses
   C. storage bins and granaries that once held grass seeds
   D. horns of domesticated goats from Neolithic deposits

35. Which of the following would you NOT expect to find at a site of the Natufian culture?
    A. carbonized seeds of domesticated wheat and barley
    B. houses with stone foundations and storage chambers
    C. differential social status indicated by grave goods
    D. imported items such as seashells and obsidian

36. According to archaeological evidence, the earliest settlement at the site of Jericho was probably a:
    A. campsite occupied by hunter-gatherers on a seasonal basis
    B. walled village with towers, a defensive ditch, and mud-brick houses
    C. homestead of early wheat farmers
    D. cave that was shelter to a family of Neanderthals

37. In Europe, Mesolithic patterns of hunting and gathering without agriculture persisted for the longest period of time in:
    A. Great Britain
    B. southeastern Europe
    C. France and Spain
    D. Scandinavia

38. The earliest megalithic constructions were:
    A. chambered tombs
    B. circles of upright stones
    C. paved roads
    D. fortification walls

39. The earliest evidence for grinding stones and artifacts with sickle gloss in Africa dates to approximately:
    A. 180,000 B.C.
    B. 80,000 B.C.
    C. 18,000 B.C.
    D. 8,000 B.C.

40. In the western Sahara Desert region, archaeological sites have yielded pottery sherds with impressions of:
    A. maize and beans
    B. wild and domesticated rice
    C. sorghum and millet
    D. bananas and coconuts

41. The use of side-looking imaging radar has confirmed the hypothesis that the ancient Maya:
    A. did not use intensive forms of agriculture
    B. had sophisticated methods of turning swamplands into farms
    C. built extensive networks of canals for irrigating tropical rainforests
    D. once maintained large tracts of grazing lands for domesticated animals

42. *Manos* and *metates* were used for:
    A. taming wild horses
    B. transporting food products over long distances
    C. recording calendric information
    D. processing maize kernels into meal

43. Modern foods that are made from plants domesticated by ancient South Americans include:
    A. french fries and peanut butter
    B. pretzels and beer
    C. coffee and sugar
    D. onion rings and watermelons

44. Among the most important domesticates in highland South America were:
    A. donkeys and sheep
    B. horses and cattle
    C. pigs and goats
    D. guinea pigs and llamas

45. The Hohokam of the southwestern U.S. utilized _____ to assist with specialized dry-land farming.
    A. drought-resistant species of citrus fruits
    B. a domesticated form of prickly-pear cactus
    C. irrigation systems and carefully scheduled planting
    D. terracing of high mountain slopes

46. The principal benefit of plant cultivation for human populations is that it:
    A. improves the quality of human nutrition by the introduction of proteins and carbohydrates
    B. allows more food to be be obtained from a given piece of land, thus supporting a larger human population
    C. creates more leisure time for non-subsistence activities, such as child-rearing
    D. permits the domestication of herd animals, such as sheep, goats, and cattle

47. During the Neolithic period, worldwide populations:
    A. increased dramatically
    B. declined rapidly as a result of the spread of infectious diseases through farming populations
    C. were about the same as during the Upper Paleolithic
    D. are known to have been highly mobile

48. Harris lines are:
    A. traces of ancient irrigation systems in highland Peru
    B. late Neolithic plow marks at sites in Great Britain
    C. geographic boundaries of ancient cultivated plants
    D. indications of physiological stress caused by famines

49. It is likely that _____ was much higher in early agricultural communities that in our own society.
    A. life expectancy
    B. infant mortality
    C. social mobility
    D. gender equality

50. In the transition from the Mesolithic to the Neolithic, there was a clear trend of increased _____ in societies all over the world.
    A. social stratification
    B. geographic mobility
    C. nutritional health
    D. egalitarian behavior

Suggested Readings

CHILDE, V. GORDON. 1936. *Man Makes Himself*. London: Watts.

CLARK, J. DESMOND, AND STEVEN A. BRANDT, EDS. 1986. *From Hunters to Farmers: The Causes and Consequences of Food Production in Africa*. Berkeley: University of California Press.

CLARK, J.G.D. 1979. *Mesolithic Prelude*. Edinburgh: Edinburgh University Press.

COHEN, MARK N. 1977. *The Food Crisis in Prehistory*. New Haven, CT: Yale University Press.

COHEN, MARK, AND GEORGE J. ARMELAGOS, EDS. 1984. *Paleopathology at the Origins of Agriculture*. New York: Academic Press.

COWAN, C. WESLEY, AND PATTY JO WATSON. 1992. *The Origins of Agriculture: An International Perspective*. Washington, D.C.: Smithsonian Institution Press.

FAGAN, BRIAN M. 1989. *Peoples of the Earth: An Introduction to World Prehistory*, 6th ed. Glenview, IL: Scott, Foresman.

GREGG, SUSAN, ED. 1991. *Between Bands and States*. Center for Archaeological Investigations, Occasional Paper No. 9. Carbondale, IL: Southern Illinois University.

HARRIS, D.R., AND G.C. HILLMAN, EDS. 1989. *Foraging and Farming: The Evolution of Plant Exploitation*. London: Unwin Hyman.

HAYDEN, BRIAN. 1990. Nimrods, Piscators, Pluckers, and Planters: The Origin of Food Production. *Journal of Anthropological Archaeology* 9:31-69.

KEEGAN, WILLIAM F., ed. 1987. *Emergent Horticultural Economies of the Eastern Woodlands*. Center for Arcaeological Investigations, Occasional Paper No. 6. Carbondale, IL: Southern Illinois University.

REDMAN, CHARLES L. 1978. *The Rise of Civilization: From Early Farmers to Urban Society in the Ancient Near East*. San Francisco: W.H. Freeman and Company.

REED, CHARLES, ED. 1977. *Origins of Agriculture*. Mouton: The Hague.

RINDOS, DAVID. 1984. *The Origins of Agriculture: An Evolutionary Perspective*. New York: Academic Press.

UCKO, PETER J., AND G.W. DIMBLEBY. 1969. *The Domestication and Exploitation of Plants and Animals*. Chicago: Aldine.

Answer Key with Page Numbers

1. F 146	18. T 163	35. A 154
2. F 147	19. F 164	36. A 155
3. F 147	20. F 164	37. D 157
4. T 148	21. D 146	38. A 158
5. F 150	22. B 147	39. C 159
6. F 150	23. D 147	40. C 160
7. T 151	24. C 148	41. B 160
8. T 151	25. C 148	42. D 161
9. T 151	26. A 149	43. A 162
10. F 154	27. D 149	44. D 162
11. F 155	28. A 150	45. C 162
12. T 157	29. D 151	46. B 163
13. T 158	30. B 151	47. A 163
14. T 158	31. A 152	48. D 163
15. F 160	32. C 153	49. B 164
16. T 162	33. B 153	50. A 164
17. F 162	34. B 154	

CHAPTER 9

THE RISE OF THE STATE AND COMPLEX SOCIETY

Chapter Outline

Chapter Highlights

Because we ourselves live in a **state** society, theories for the origins of the state have been a central focus of anthropological investigation since its inception. The state, a more precise term for **civilization**, is both qualitatively and quantitatively different from a non-state society. That is, both the organization and structure of a state society and the size and complexity of its settlements, economy, and ideological systems set it apart from bands, tribes, and chiefdoms.

V. Gordon Childe offered a classic definition of civilization that included ten criteria: 1) urban centers; 2) a division of labor that included non-agricultural specialization; 3) distinct social classes; 4) surplus food production and storage; 5) monumental architecture; 6) numbers and writing systems; 7) exact sciences; 8) sophisticated art styles; 9) long-distance trade; and 10) a full-time military. While most archaeologists view this definition as too rigid (the Inca, for example, did not have a writing system), these characteristics are still valuable for studying ancient states.

The most important characteristic of a state is the existence of institutionalized **social stratification**--a formal **hierarchy** of **social classes** with different rights and privileges. This stratification is also evident in the presence of **administrative bureaucracies**. States have highly **centralized** governments, headed by highly privileged leaders. The term **agricultural state** refers to states with economies based on the production of agricultural **surplus**. (Most modern states are based on industrial production.) The earliest states to emerge from agricultural villages in their respective areas were in: 1) Mesopotamia (3500 B.C.); 2) Egypt (3500 B.C.); 3) China (2500 B.C.); 4) the Indus Valley, Pakistan (2500 B.C.); 5) Peru (300 B.C.); and 6) Mexico (300 B.C.). Each influenced the rise of complex society in neighboring regions.

Most states, because of their complex governments and economies, had systems of **writing** or recording. Control of information is a source of power, and the evolution of notation accompanied the centralization of decision making and wealth. Early writing systems used a variety of types of **symbols** to communicate information. **Pictographs** were actual representations of the objects they stood for (a picture of a bull to indicate that animal). **Ideographs** were pictures used to represent ideas (a picture of a flower to represent springtime). **Hieroglyphs** were symbols used to represent actual sounds (either a picture of a sheep or an abstract symbol could be used to represent either the word "sheep" or "baa"). In **syllabic writing**, symbols are used to represent consonant-vowel combinations (triangle = "tee"). In **alphabetic writing**, each symbol represents either a consonant or a vowel. Writing systems were developed by the ancient civilizations of Mesopotamia, Egypt, China, Indus Valley, and Mesoamerica. The Incas used a *quipu*, or system of knotted cords of different textures and colors, for accounting records.

Because states are characterized by institutionalized social hierarchy and bureaucracy, archaeologists expect to find artifacts and features that reflect this organization. Objects such as clay seals bearing symbols of authority or finely-crafted items of gold, pottery, or obsidian for the personal use of royalty would be examples of these. Features of a kind that could only be constructed with a highly controlled labor force, such as full-time artisans, manual laborers, or slaves, are also indicative of ancient states. These would include road systems, **ziggurats**, and pyramids. Examples of ziggurats, temple platforms built of mud brick around 5000 years ago, are found at the **Sumerian** city of **Warka** in Mesopotamia. Egyptian pyramids at **Giza** were built of stone blocks and served as massive tombs for Old Kingdom pharaohs at around the same time. **Maya** pyramids at **Tikal** (Guatemala), built of rubble faced with cut stone and stucco around 1500 years ago, served as both platforms for ceremonies and tombs for dead rulers.

The objects associated with ancient agricultural states are good indicators of social complexity. **Grave goods** can be used to interpret the status of individuals buried in cemeteries or tombs. These will often include evidence for **long-distance trade** in exotic materials. State-sponsored trade, underwritten by capital from agricultural surpluses, can also include importation of raw materials for processing by skilled craftspeople. Archaeologists can study patterns of trade and exchange by looking at the sources of different materials. One valuable technique is **trace element analysis**, which uses minute quantities of different elements in pottery or stone to identify their geological sources.

Explanations for state formation can be divided into **integrationist theories**, which concentrate on how state organization benefited society as a whole, and **conflict theories**, which emphasize the need to protect the rights of a dominant ruling class. Integrationist theories include the **hydraulic hypothesis** proposed by **Karl Wittfogel**, in which state formation occurs in response to the need for centralized administration of water rights for irrigation agriculture. Other theories emphasize the need for state administration of trade, markets, and specialized craft production. **Systems models**, which avoid attributing state formation to a single factor, point out that state authority is required to organize the economy, the military, and manage the huge amounts of information associated with social complexity.

Although the authors of the textbook label **Robert Carneiro's circumscription theory** an "integrationist" interpretation, it is based on the notion that political power and class structure were achieved through conflict. **Circumscription** refers to the existence of geographical boundaries (such as mountains) or social boundaries (other populations) that placed pressure on growing agricultural populations. Competition for resources within a circumscribed region resulted in warfare, the result of which was a society comprised of the victors (who become the upper stratum) and the vanquished (who become the subordinate class). Conflict models, also proposed by **Morton Fried**, interpret the formation of the state as an aid to the forceful dominance of a population by a ruling elite. **Jonathan Haas** emphasizes that monumental construction required coercion of peasants through taxation, tribute, and forced labor. **Elizabeth Brumfiel** uses the example of the **Aztecs** to show that coercion was political in nature, and functioned through the consolidation of power by an elite.

Critics of conflict theories, such as **Elman Service**, point out that there is no clear evidence for state formation as a result of class conflict in the archaeological record. They prefer the integrationist view that state systems exist to provide benefits, and that coercion is only required when state authority is weakened. They also criticize the underlying assumption that exploitation of the weak by the powerful is universal.

Needless to say, it is impossible to provide a simple explanation for the emergence of state society. The reasons for the emergence of ancient states were probably widely varied, and the process was influenced by a range of demographic, economic, ideological, environmental, and historical factors. There are merits to both integrationist and conflict theories. Archaeologists are currently investigating the many implications of the different hypotheses presented here—as well as several others—through active research on complex societies.

Terms and Concepts You Should Know

civilization (167)

state (167)

agricultural state (170)

complex society (170)

pictograph (171)

ideographic writing system (171)

hieroglyphic writing (171)

syllabic writing (171)

alphabetic writing (171)

central place theory (172)

settlement hierarchy (172)

clay sealing (173)

ziggurat (173)

stucco (174)

nagual (174)

fresco (174)

obsidian (174)

grave good (175)

trace element analysis (175)

integrationist theory (176)

conflict theory (176)

hydraulic hypothesis (178)

circumscription theory (178)

systems model (178)

People to Know About

V. Gordon Childe (167)

Elman Service (170)

Bruce Trigger (170)

Jack Goody (170)

Walter Christaller (172)

Karl Wittfogel (178)

Robert Carneiro (178)

Morton Fried (179)

Jonathan Haas (179)

Elizabeth Brumfiel (179)

Places to Know About

Warka (Uruk) (173)

Teotihuacan (174)

Cultures to Know About

Sumerians (173)

Maya (174)

Moche (176)

Thinking About What You Have Read

The following questions or problems may be of help to you in studying the material presented in both the text and in your class. You may want to write out the answers to these questions (writing something down always seems to help solidify it in one's mind) or just think about them.

1. How do archaeologists and anthropologists define the word "civilization"?

2. What were the principal changes that occurred during the Neolithic period to lay the foundations for the emergence of state-level society?

3. List the ten characteristics of urban civilization defined by V. Gordon Childe. Do you agree or disagree with the use of these criteria? Why?

4. What are the structural differences between the state and other types of political organization? How might these differences be recognized from archaeological evidence?

5. What were the principal factors that led to the emergence of writing systems in ancient states?

6. Define the differences between pictographic, ideographic, hieroglyphic, syllabic, and alphabetic writing systems. What are the advantages and disadvantages of each?

7. What is meant by "central place theory"? Why are the concepts of central place theory relevant to the study of ancient states? What types of archaeological evidence of administration can be found outside of primary centers?

8. In the emergence of state societies from non-stratified ones, what are the specific processes that would result in the erection of monumental architecture such as that found at Warka, Giza, Tikal and other sites?

9. Define "specialization" as it applies to the evolution of ancient states. When does specialization first appear, and how can it be recognized archaeologically? What is the difference between specialization as seen in state societies and specialization in Neolithic societies?

10. How can anthropologists recognize status and social ranking in the archaeological record? What are the principal lines of evidence that reveal class differences?

11. Why are trade and exchange important for the emergence of state societies? How does an archaeologist know that a society has been engaging in both inter- and intraregional trade?

12. Describe the "integrationist" theories of state formation that have been presented by various scholars. How do these differ from "conflict" theories?

13. What is the scenario that has been offered by anthropologist Robert Carneiro for the origins of the state? Do you agree with this model or not? Why?

14. How do the interpretations of state society presented by Morton Fried differ from those of Elman Service? How do these different perspectives affect the way one interprets the formation of states in antiquity?

15. What are some of the methods archaeologists can use to test whether integrationist theories are better than conflict theories for the emergence of the state? (A "better" theory is one that is consistent with the evidence, explains more information, and can predict new discoveries.)

CHECKING YOUR UNDERSTANDING: A PRACTICE EXAMINATION

We suggest that you take this practice exam and then check your answers against the key provided at the end of this section. Use the questions that you got wrong as a guide to further study. Try to learn why specific answers are right and wrong. You may even want to take the practice exam a second time to review what you have learned.

True - False Questions

1. Most archaeologists do not consider a society to be a civilization unless it has all of the features specified in V. Gordon Childe's classic definition.

2. In early states, political authority was primarily based on the control of agricultural surpluses.

3. The division between the world of the supernatural and that of social institutions was more distinct in ancient states than it is in modern ones.

4. There are no obvious differences in social, political, and economic organization between societies that had writing and those that did not.

5. Hieroglyphic writing systems use symbols that have direct relationships to the sounds of words.

6. The Egyptians and the Mayas developed hieroglyphic writing systems independently of one another.

7. The world's first cities began as Neolithic villages.

8. Monumental architecture was not erected by pre-state societies.

9. Pyramids and ziggurats have very similar types of monumental construction.

10. All of the ancient agricultural states produced brilliantly painted pottery, sculpture, and other artwork.

11. At Teotihuacan, an ancient city in central Mexico, the houses were strikingly uniform in terms of size and furnishings.

12. The quantity of a material acquired through trade that is found at archaeological sites usually descreases as distance from its source increases.

13. Integrationist theories of state formation assume that the state was a positive, integrative response to conditions faced by a society.

14. The archaeological evidence from Egypt and India suggests that, instead of large-scale irrigation contributing to the rise of the state, it was actually a consequence of state development.

15. According to Robert Carneiro, the state has its origin as a result of warfare when the winners dominated the losers.

16. In the conflict model presented by Morton Fried, the state exists to protect its citizens against domination by a ruling elite.

17. According to Jonathan Haas, chiefdoms could extract sufficient labor and tribute from their populations to construct large-scale monumental architecture.

18. The Aztec rulers centralized their authority through organizational reforms that reduced the power of subordinate rulers and nobles.

19. According to Elman Service, the archaeological record is filled with evidence for class-based conflicts that resulted in state formation.

20. Most archaeologists agree that there is only one acceptable model for the emergence of the state.

Multiple Choice Questions

21. The use of techniques such as irrigation, terracing, plow cultivation, and the use of fertilizers were adopted by human populations of the Old World around the:
   A. end of the Upper Paleolithic period
   B. beginning of the Mesolithic period
   C. beginning of the Neolithic period
   D. end of the Neolithic period

22. Which of the following features was NOT part of V. Gordon Childe's definition of ancient urban civilizations?
   A. settlements of between 7,000 and 20,000 inhabitants
   B. a ruling class of religious, civil, and military leaders
   C. use of numbers and writing systems for record keeping
   D. specialized production of bronze and iron implements

23. States are structurally distinct from bands, tribes, and chiefdoms because they have:
    A. systems of centralized leadership
    B. institutionalized social stratification
    C. individuals who participate in long-distance trade
    D. economies based on agriculture

24. Jack Goody has concluded that literacy in ancient states gave great power to:
    A. bureaucrats and priests
    B. common citizens
    C. military leaders
    D. merchants and traders

25. Archaeological research directed towards the location of early libraries or archives of written material has been particularly important in:
    A. Peru
    B. Guatemala
    C. Iraq
    D. the Indus Valley

26. Syllabic writing systems _____ than ideographic or hieroglyphic writing systems:
    A. use more symbols
    B. use fewer symbols
    C. use about the same number of symbols
    D. are more ancient

27. The most efficient form of writing, because it uses the fewest number of distinct symbols, is the _____ system.
    A. alphabetic
    B. syllabic
    C. hieroglyphic
    D. pictographic

28. According to central place theory, if the topography, resources, and opportunities within a given region were uniform:
    A. there would only be one "central place"
    B. political and economic centers would be evenly spaced
    C. all archaeological sites would be the same size
    D. only large, administrative centers would be necessary

29. The term "settlement hierarchy" refers to:
    A. an idealized pattern of central places arranged on a uniform landscape
    B. the centralized organization of towns, villages, and homesteads based on size and importance
    C. a stratified social system with a clearly bureaucratic structure
    D. rulership from a settlement with hieroglyphic writing

30. Even if a site is smaller in size than other settlements, its role as a primary center can be indicated archaeologically by the existence of:
    A. exotic trade and craft materials in burials
    B. irrigation canals, terracing, or other signs of agricultural intensification
    C. walls, ditches, or other fortifications
    D. monumental architecture, administrative buildings, and large storage facilities

31. The purpose of most monumental architecture in agricultural states was primarily _____ in nature:
    A. commercial
    B. military
    C. religious
    D. governmental

32. The Great Pyramid at Giza, measuring 481 feet tall and covering an area of 13 acres, was constructed approximately _____ years ago.
    A. 14,000
    B. 6,400
    C. 4,600
    D. 2,300

33. One of the most significant differences between Neolithic villages and urban centers of state civilization was the existence of:
    A. gender equality
    B. full-time craft workshops
    C. irrigation agriculture
    D. political authority

34. In Mesoamerican states, evidence has been found for workshops that specialized in the manufacture of finely crafted artifacts made of:
    A. obsidian and chert
    B. copper and bronze
    C. ebony and ivory
    D. leather

35. Teotihuacan, a planned city with perhaps as many as 120,000 inhabitants at its peak occupation, flourished in Mexico between:
    A. 4500 and 3000 B.C.
    B. 2500 and 1800 B.C.
    C. A.D. 150 and 750
    D. A.D. 1000 and 1500

36. Archaeologists study grave goods found in burials in order to understand the _____ of the individual with whom they were buried.
    A. age
    B. health
    C. status
    D. cause of death

37. The centralized control of mercantile exchange is indicated by the existence of:
    A. goods that were brought long distances
    B. large numbers of finely crafted artifacts
    C. precious stones, metals, and amber
    D. standardized weights and measures

38. Of the following sources of data, which would yield the best information about the place a particular pottery vessel was manufactured?
    A. fragments of rocks and minerals mixed into the clay
    B. the size and shape of the finished vessel
    C. food residues found inside the pot
    D. decoration on the outside of the pot

39. Trace element analysis is typically used to determine the _____ of an obsidian artifact.
    A. chronological age
    B. raw material source
    C. patterns of use
    D. quality of preservation

40. Archaeologists have been able to use _____ to reconstruct ancient religious rituals of the Moche culture in coastal Peru.
    A. detailed depictions on pottery and murals
    B. sacrificial knives discarded in temples
    C. poems and stories written on clay tablets
    D. trace element analysis of obsidian tools

41. Conflict theories of state formation:
    A. emphasize domination and exploitation
    B. assume state formation was beneficial
    C. see state authority as advantageous to the peasantry
    D. emphasize revolts against monopoly control

42. The "hydraulic hypothesis" offered by Karl Wittfogel linked the development of the state with:
    A. trade and exchange
    B. warfare among villages
    C. irrigation agriculture
    D. population circumscription

43. One of the principal criticisms of the hydraulic hypothesis is that:
    A. irrigation projects can be organized without administration by centralized governments
    B. population centers can be circumscribed by factors other than geography
    C. inter- and intraregional trade probably predates state formation
    D. expansion of intensive agriculture created problems and disputes among landowners

44. Anthropologist Robert Carneiro's circumscription theory suggests that states originated because:
    A. labor had to be recruited, mobilized, fed, and organized to resolve problems of large-scale agriculture
    B. economies became dependent upon the exchange of items produced by full-time craft specialization
    C. dominant ethnic groups used surgical modifications of male genitalia as a sign of divinely-sanctioned authority
    D. intergroup competition in regions with clearly defined boundaries resulted in warfare and political dominance

45. The term "social circumscription" refers to:
    A. a public gathering to conduct a rite of passage
    B. population expansion restricted by neighboring groups
    C. cautious behavior in the presence of a dominant elite
    D. population growth in a valley bounded by mountains

46. Systems models emphasize the requirements of agricultural states to do all of the following EXCEPT:
    A. organize large populations
    B. control and manage information
    C. insure equal opportunities for all
    D. maintain military organizations

149

47. In the view of anthropologist Morton Fried, the state:
   A. is just, and prohibits the emergence or maintenance of social inequalities
   B. is coercive, and utilizes force to perpetuate economic and political inequalities
   C. is ineffective, and yields to the will of a multiplicity of special interest groups
   D. is liberating, and seeks to eliminate the repression of subordinate groups and private citizens

48. For Jonathan Haas, large-scale monument construction required:
   A. a ruling elite that could force peasants to pay tribute and provide labor
   B. the organizational capacity of a chiefdom-level society
   C. written, scientific calculations that were understood by specialized architects
   D. large herds of state-owned beasts of burden, such as oxen, horses, or llamas

49. Elizabeth Brumfiel, citing the example of the rise of the Aztec state, hypothesizes that coercion and repression evolved from _____ determinants.
   A. economic
   B. political
   C. religious
   D. agricultural

50. According to critics of the different conflict theory models for state formation, state systems:
   A. are fundamentally different from chiefdom societies
   B. derive political authority from the provision of benefits to a wide range of social groups
   C. are usually ineffective at reducing conflicts within their own societies
   D. depend upon repression and coercion to maintain order

Suggested Readings

BRUMFIEL, ELIZABETH. 1983. Aztec State Making: Ecology, Structure, and the Origin of the State. *American Anthropologist*, 85(2), 261-284.

CARNEIRO, ROBERT. 1970. A Theory of the Origin of the State. *Science*, 169, 733-738.

CHILDE, V. GORDON. 1950. The Urban Revolution. *The Town Planning Review* 21:3-17.

COE, MICHAEL D. 1993. *Breaking the Maya Code.* New York: Thames and Hudson.

COHEN, RONALD AND ELMAN SERVICE, EDS. 1978. *Origins of the State: The Anthropology of Political Evolution.* Philadelphia: ISHI.

CONNAH, GRAHAM. 1987. *African Civilizations: Precolonial Cities and States in Tropical Africa: An Archaeological Perspective.* Cambridge: Cambridge University Press.

FLANNERY, KENT V. 1972. The Cultural Evolution of Civilizations. *Annual Review of Ecology and Systematics*, 4, 399-426.

FRIED, MORTON. 1967. *The Evolution of Political Society: An Essay in Political Anthropology.* New York: Random House.

HAAS, JONATHAN. 1982. *The Evolution of the Prehistoric State.* New York: Columbia University Press.

JOHNSON, ALLEN, AND EARLE, TIMOTHY. 1987. *The Evolution of Human Societies: From Foraging Group to Agrarian State.* Stanford, CA: Stanford University Press.

REDMAN, CHARLES L. 1978. *The Rise of Civilization: From Early Farmers to Urban Society in the Ancient Near East.* San Francisco: W.H. Freeman.

SERVICE, ELMAN. 1962. *Primitive Social Organization: An Evolutionary Perspective.* New York: Random House.

_____. 1975. *Origins of the State and Civilization: The Process of Cultural Evolution.* New York: W.W. Norton & Co., Inc.

TRIGGER, BRUCE. 1993. *Early Civilizations: Ancient Egypt in Context.* Cairo: American University in Cairo Press.

WRIGHT, HENRY T. 1977. Recent Research on the Origin of the State. *Annual Review of Anthropology*, 6, 355-370.

Answer Key with Page Numbers

1.	F 167	18.	T 180	35.	C 174
2.	T 170	19.	F 180	36.	C 175
3.	F 170	20.	F 180	37.	D 175
4.	T 170	21.	D 167	38.	A 175
5.	T 171	22.	D 167	39.	B 176
6.	T 171	23.	B 170	40.	A 176
7.	T 172	24.	A 170	41.	A 176
8.	F 173	25.	C 171	42.	C 178
9.	F 173	26.	B 171	43.	A 178
10.	T 174	27.	A 171	44.	D 178
11.	F 174	28.	B 172	45.	B 178
12.	T 175	29.	B 172	46.	C 178
13.	T 176	30.	D 173	47.	B 179
14.	T 178	31.	C 173	48.	A 179
15.	T 178	32.	C 174	49.	B 180
16.	F 179	33.	B 174	50.	B 180
17.	F 179	34.	A 174		

CHAPTER 10

CULTURE

Chapter Outline

Culture Is Learned
Symbols and Symbolic Learning
The Components of Culture
Ideal versus Real Culture
Culture Is Shared
Values
Beliefs
Norms
> FOLKWAYS
> MORES

Cultural Diversity
Food and Adaptation
Dress Codes and Symbolism
Cultural Universals

Chapter Highlights

The **concept of culture** is at the core of all anthropology. Culture is a shared way of life. Culture is not inherited, not instinctual. It is learned. Culture is shared within a group and passed on from generation to generation within **society**. A society is different from a culture. A society is a group of animals that occupy a specific region or area. Hence, a culture could be defined as a set of learned beliefs, behaviors, values, and ideals that are characteristic of a particular society. There are probably as many definitions of culture as there are anthropologists. Anthropologists do not have to agree upon a definition, but anthropologists do agree on what makes up culture. The hybrid term **sociocultural** has been used recently to refer to what were formerly called either cultural or social phenomena. It acknowledges the close interrelationship between shared thoughts and actions in human groups.

A couple of questions that you might keep in the back of your mind as you progress through this course in anthropology are the following: "How much of human behavior is learned (*nurture*), and how much is biologically based (*nature*)?" "How does culture influence biology, and how, in turn, does biology influence culture?"

Culture is shared and is passed on from one generation to the next within a society through **learning**.   Humans learn their culture through direct experience (**situational learning**), observation (**social learning**), and the ability to use and interpret symbols (**symbolic learning**). **Symbols** are arbitrary units of meaning that stand for different abstract or concert phenomena that are distinctive from society to society.   Many anthropologists think that symboling is a uniquely human trait that is the basis of culture. Humankind's most important symbolic vehicle is language.

Culture consists of material and nonmaterial items and entities.   **Material culture** has a physical reality, and consists of such things as cars, clothing, houses, and pots.   In archaeology these items would be called **artifacts**. The material components of a culture reflect the ideas, categories, and meanings found within that specific culture.

The ethereal aspects of a culture, the values, beliefs, ideologies, norms, morals, meanings, mores, categories, and rules, are known as **nonmaterial culture**.   **Beliefs** are culturally shared agreements or views of nature, the universe, and humankind's place within these contexts.   **Values**, usually more limited in scope, are notions of what is good or bad. Anthropologists often refer to the **worldview** of a people or society.   This concept refers to a collection of beliefs about the character of natural and supernatural realities.   Worldviews aid individuals in ordering the universe so it is understandable.   It also helps them order their lives and comprehend their role within the cosmos.   Beliefs that are articulated and manipulated to express and support the interests of a specific group within a society (often through the use of symbols) are called an **ideology**.

When discussing nonmaterial culture, many anthropologists refer to **ideal culture** and **real culture**.   Ideal culture is what an individual says he or she does or should do.   On the other hand, real culture is what actually happens.   As a student of anthropology, many of the things that you will be exposed to in this class are considered ideal cultural rules. You need to realize that sometimes the ideal solution does not work, or it is impossible to accomplish.   When this occurs, people simply do other things to accomplish their goals. For example, if your culture had a marriage rule that specified that you marry your cross-cousin (*the ideal cultural rule*), and if you did not have any cross-cousins, this does not mean that you will remain single the rest of your life—you will probably marry someone else (*real culture*).

Cultural diversity has always been a topic of interest to anthropologists.   Different languages, values, mores, and ideologies have intrigued anthropologists.   In fact, the comparative method (contrasting two or more cultures or behaviors) has been used effectively by ethnologists for years as a means of better understanding human cultural variation and behavior.   As anthropologists, we are now critically aware of the fact that written descriptions of other cultures are often **ethnocentric** in nature.   That is, the person writing the description often judges the other society on the basis of his or her own cultural values or standards. Ethnocentrism appears to be a universal feature of humans.   We learn our culture as we grow up (**enculturation**), and we tend to think that our culture has all the answers and is the correct way of doing things.   We then view other cultural traditions as strange, weird, inferior, or stupid.   Toward the close of the nineteenth century anthropologists began to realize that ethnocentrism was getting in the way of objective scientific inquiry.   To deal with this problem, anthropologists developed the notion of **cultural relativity**, the view that a society's customs and behaviors should be viewed

154

within the context of that society's values, ideals, and standards. This perspective allows anthropologists to examine other cultures without imposing ethnocentric interpretations. Obviously, it is very difficult to maintain a completely cultural relativist view and not invoke any ethnocentric feelings while dealing with another culture. However, by being aware of these two perspectives, you may be able to handle multicultural encounters in a much more humane and understanding manner.

One of the goals of anthropology is to understand the relationship between culture and biology. How does biology affect culture and how, in turn, does culture affect biology? How do humans **adapt** to different environments? How does culture influence our behavior. These types of questions will be explored throughout this text. Also, certain aspects of cultural diversity may be the result of **adaptations** (a beneficial adjustment of an organism or society with the environment) to different environments. Still other differences are due to symbolic creations, such as dress, hairstyles, and music. These symbolic codes enhance the beliefs and values of the individuals within the specific culture, while at the same time, creating a source of cultural diversity.

There are many **universal** patterns of human behavior. This universal distribution of certain cultural traits suggests that we all have similar biological requirements and tendencies that influence behavior. It probably also reflects the fact that we all live in a society or societies that have certain dynamics and problems that are universal, such as reproduction, nurture, and the creation of functioning adults. Anthropologists strive to understand the basis for both human universality and diversity.

Terms and Concepts You Should Know

culture (183):

society (183):

sociocultural (183):

situational learning (184):

social learning (184):

symbolic learning (184):

symbol (184):

sign (184):

material culture (186):

nonmaterial culture (186):

values (186):

beliefs (186):

worldview (186):

ideology (186):

cultural hegemony (187):

norms (187):

ethos (187):

folkways (187):

mores (187):

multiculturalism (188-189):

ideal culture (190):

real culture (190):

ethnocentrism (191):

cultural relativity (191):

adaptation (191-192):

Rastafarians (193):

cultural universals (194):

People to Know About

E.B. Tylor (183):

Leslie A. White (185):

Marvin Harris (192):

George Murdock (194):

Thinking About What You Have Read

The following questions or problems may be of help to you in studying the material presented in both the text and in your class. You may want to write out the answers to these questions (writing something down always seems to help solidify it in one's mind) or just think about them.

1. What are the defining characteristics of culture? How do you define culture? What do anthropologists mean when they say that cultures are generally adaptive and integrating?

2. Suppose that you had to organize a ethnographic tour of your college or town for a group of extraterrestrials. Your goal is to provide these visitors with a thorough knowledge of your culture. How would you organize this tour? Where would the visitors stay? What aspects of your culture would you emphasize, de-emphasize, or hide? What would you send back with him, her, or it as representative artifacts? Why?

3. Compare and contrast situational learning, social learning, and symbolic learning. How do signs differ from symbols?

4. Define and describe norms, ethos, folkways, mores, and beliefs. Provide examples from your own culture.

5. Define worldview and ideology. Can you describe your worldview and ideology? Why do you hold these views? Why are these beliefs true? How do you evaluate competing truth claims?

6. What is multiculturalism? How can anthropologists aid in such endeavors as multicultural education for businesses, communities, public service groups, and schools?

7. Define ethnocentrism. Using examples from your own experience, explain how ethnocentrism can serve both as a positive and negative force within human groups. Be specific.

8. The goal of cultural relativism is to understand other peoples. Understanding does not mean condone. Use an anthropological cultural relativist view and explain the Nazi's attempt to exterminate the Jews and others groups labeled as *untermensch* or subhuman.

9. Examine your clothing and hairstyle. Why do you dress in a certain manner? Did someone tell you what to wear? How does your dress style vary from situation to situation (e.g., at work, at school, at home, on a date, at a fancy restaurant). What do these varying styles symbolize for you?

10. "We totally depend upon culture. Our survival as a biological entity depends upon culture." Do you agree or disagree with this statement? Why or why not?

CHECKING YOUR UNDERSTANDING: A PRACTICE EXAMINATION

We suggest that you take this practice exam and then check your answers against the key provided at the end of this section. Use the questions that you got wrong as a guide to further study. Try to learn why specific answers are right and wrong. You might even consider taking this practice test more than once, several days apart.

True-False Questions

1. Culture is unique to human beings, while other types of animals may live in groups or societies.

2. Culture can be defined as a particular group of people who occupy a specific territory.

3. Society is a shared way of life that includes technology, values, beliefs, and norms passed on from one generation to the next.

4. Symbols are arbitrary meaningful units or models we use to represent reality.

5. A sign is an arbitrary, meaningful unit or model used to represent reality.

6. Many anthropologist view symbolic learning as the major distinction between humans and nonhuman primates.

7. Culture is transmitted from generation to generation through symbolic learning and language.

8. Values, beliefs, norms, and mores are all aspects of what anthropologists call material culture.

9. Beliefs are the standards by which members of a society define what is good or bad, right or wrong, holy or unholy, and beautiful or ugly.

10. The idea that eating insect larvae is disgusting is one that is culturally determined.

11. A worldview consists of various beliefs and cosmologies about the nature of reality.

12. An ideology consists of cultural symbols and beliefs that reflect and support the interests of specific groups within a society.

13. Norms are the ideological control over beliefs and values by one dominant ethnic group in a society.

14. Cultural understandings are shared equally by all members of a particular society.

15. Ethnocentrism is the view that no cultural traditions are inherently superior or inferior.

16. Cultural relativism is the practice of judging another society or culture by the values and standards of your own society.

159

17. Cultural universals are essential behavioral characteristics of societies, and they are found all over the world.

18. Since there are many cultural universals (remember George Murdock's list in the book), parts of culture must be inherited as part of our biological makeup.

19. Although there is an enormous diversity in the expression of human culture, practices like marriage and food taboos are universal.

20. Donald E. Brown (*HumanUniversals*) argues that, in their quest for finding and describing cultural diversity anthropologists have overlooked many basic similarities in human culture and behavior.

Multiple Choice Questions

21. What types of learning take place when an organism adjusts its behavior on the basis of direct experience?
    A. instinctual learning
    B. symbolic learning
    C. situational learning
    D. social learning

22. Arbitrary units of meaning that we use to represent reality are known as
    A. signs
    B. vexations
    C. ideograms
    D. symbols
    E. mores

23. What type of learning takes place when an organism adjusts its behavior on the basis of arbitrary meaningful units or models used to represent reality?
    A. instinctual learning
    B. situational learning
    C. symbolic learning
    D. casual learning
    E. environmental learning

24. A dog learning to drink or eat when it hears a whistle blown or a chimpanzee learning to run from danger when another chimpanzee emits a specific sound are examples of
    A. symbols
    B. mores
    C. cultural items
    D. signs
    E. values

25. What type of learning takes place when an organism adjusts its behavior on the basis of observing other organisms responding to a stimulus or interacting with other organisms?
    A. situational learning
    B. social learning
    C. latent learning
    D. symbolic learning

26. Humans learn most of their behaviors and concepts through:
    A. situational learning
    B. trial-and-error learning
    C. social learning
    D. symbolic learning

27. The cultural conventions concerning true or false assumptions, specific descriptions about the nature of the universe and humanity's place in it are called:
    A. inspirations
    B. values
    C. beliefs
    D. norms
    E. mores

28. "Education is good" is a basic _____ in American society, whereas "Grading on the curve is the best way to evaluate students" is a _____ that reflects assumptions about the best way to determine educational achievement.
    A. norm / mores
    B. mores / norm
    C. value / belief
    D. ideal / truism

29. The standards by which members of a society define what is good or bad, desirable or undesirable, holy or unholy, and beautiful or ugly are called:
    A. values
    B. norms
    C. mores
    D. folkways
    E. set by instinct

30. Norms guiding ordinary, everyday activities of humans are often so ingrained or taken for granted that an individual is hardly aware that these norms even exist. What do anthropologists call these norms?
    A. folkways
    B. values
    C. ideologies
    D. ideal cultural elements

31. The norms of a society whose violation is met by severe punishments are known as
    A. mores
    B. folkways
    C. lifeways
    D. norms
    E. paradigms

32. The control of a population by a specific, dominant group that maintains its power by asserting particular values and beliefs is referred to as:
    A. Communism
    B. cultural hegemony
    C. ethnic cleansing
    D. apartheid

33. Since the nineteenth century the U.S. has become more ethnically and culturally diverse. This mixture of peoples is called
    A. assimilation
    B. cultural molding
    C. multiculturalism
    D. ethnic fusion
    E. enculturation

34. The practice of judging another society by the values and standards of one's own culture is called:
    A. ethnocentrism
    B. cultural relativism
    C. multiculturalism
    D. cultural ideology

35. The view that no cultural traditions are inherently superior or inferior is called
    A. ethnocentrism
    B. cultural universals
    C. cultural relativism
    D. social conformity
    E. wishful thinking

36. "Man, those people sure do some stupid, immoral things. I'm glad our culture has devised superior methods of dealing with that problem." This is an example of
    A. ethnocentrism
    B. clear, logical reasoning
    C. cultural relativism
    D. normative prejudice
    E. multicultural mores

37. _____ culture consists of what people *say* they do or should do, whereas _____ culture refers to their *actual behaviors*.
    A. Learned / assumed
    B. Personal / shared
    C. Ideal / real
    D. Genuine / artificial
    E. Impeccable / flawed

38. Cultural relativism is the view that:
    A. all human cultures are related to one another
    B. some cultures are more highly developed than others
    C. social norms are highly situational
    D. cultural traditions cannot be judged out of context

39. Marvin Harris suggests that cultural dietary preferences frequently have adaptive significance. This idea is exemplified by the Judaic and Islamic pork taboo. According to Harris, pigs are taboo because
    A. they are considered valued members of the family, and one does not eat ones relatives.
    B. they carry diseases such as trichinosis.
    C. they are direct competitors with humans for food, they are not adapted to hot, dry regions, and they need artificial shade and moisture to keep cool.
    D. they are abominable, dirty, smelly animals just like chickens and goats.

40. In the Rastafarian movement of Jamaica, individuals express a feeling of kinship with the spirit of the lion by:
    A. shaving their heads
    B. tattooing their faces
    C. growing long hair
    D. dyeing their hair blond

41. By using _____, George Murdock was able to compile a lengthy list of cultural universals from hundreds of societies.
    A. inductive reasoning
    B. deductive modeling
    C. cross-cultural analysis
    D. normative values
    E. valued-controlled research methods

Suggested Readings

ANGELINO, E., Ed. 1994. *Annual Editions: Anthropology 94/95*. Guilford, CT: Dushkin.

BARASH, DAVID. 1981. *The Whispering Within: Evolution and the Origin of Human Nature*. New York, NY: Penguin Books.

_____. 1986. *The Hare and the Tortoise: Culture, Biology, and Human Nature*. New York, NY: Penguin Books.

BARRETT, RICHARD A. 1984. *Culture and Conduct*. Belmont, CA: Wadsworth.

BELLAH, ROBERT N. et al. 1986. *Habits of the Heart: Individualism and Commitment in American Life*. New York, NY: Harper & Row.

GEERTZ, CLIFFORD. 1973. *The Interpretation of Cultures*. New York, NY: Basic Books.

HALL, EDWARD AND MILDRED HALL. 1987. *Hidden Difference: Doing Business with the Japanese*. New York, NY: Anchor Books.

_____. 1989. *Understanding Cultural Differences: Germans, French, and Americans*. Yarmouth, ME: Intercultural Press.

HARRIS, MARVIN. 1974. *Cows, Pigs, Wars, and Witches: The Riddle of Culture*. New York, NY: Vintage.

_____. 1977. *Cannibals and Kings: The Origins of Culture*. New York, NY: Vintage.

_____. 1985. *The Sacred Cow and the Abominable Pig: Riddles of Food and Culture*. New York, NY: Touchstone.

HARRIS, PHILIP R. AND ROBERT T. MORAN. 1985. *Managing Cultural Differences*. Houston, TX: Gulf Publishing Company.

Answer Key with Page Numbers

1. T 183	15. F 191	29. A 186
2. F 183	16. F 191	30. A 187
3. F 183	17. T 194	31. A 187
4. T 184	18. F 194	32. B 187
5. F 184	19. T 194	33. C 188-189
6. T 184	20. T 194	34. A 191
7. T 184	21. C 184	35. C. 191
8. F 186-187	22. D 184	36. A 191
9. F 186	23. C 184	37. C 190
10. T 186	24. D 184	38. D 191
11. T 186	25. B 184	39. C 191-192
12. T 186	26. D 184	40. C 193
13. F 187	27. C 186	41. C 194
14. F 190	28. C 186	

CHAPTER 11

PSYCHOLOGICAL ANTHROPOLOGY

Chapter Outline

Enculturation and Emotions
Culture and Mental Illness
What is Abnormal?
Culture-Specific Disorders
The Limits of Enculturation
Unique Biological Tendencies
Individual Variation

Chapter Highlights

One of the principal concerns of anthropology is the relationship between culture and **individual behavior**. **Enculturation** is the process by which a person learns the process of **social interaction** within a specific culture. Human beings are animals, and there are certain innate reflexes and **drives** that affect our behavior. However, the way that we act is determined by interactions between individual psychology and **learned culture**.

Humans require interaction with other humans from the instant they are born. Studies of **feral children**, raised in situations where they were deprived of contact with other humans, have shown that social interaction early in one's life is critical for normal psychological development.

Ethnographic studies have sought to demonstrate relationships between psychology and culture. Anthropologist **Ruth Benedict**, for example, suggested that certain personality types were typical of individual cultures. **Margaret Mead**, who studied adolescent girls on the island of Samoa, concluded that the process of psychological maturation varied cross-culturally. Her findings have been disputed by **Derek Freemen**, who pointed out contradictory data and flaws in Mead's research methodology, but her work on the effects of childhood training, culture, and personality laid the foundations for a productive area of anthropological research.

Culturally determined styles of childhood training are believed to affect individual personality. **Cora Du Bois** introduced the notion of **modal personality** - a psychological profile that is the most common in a given society as a result of childhood enculturation. Cross-cultural studies, such as the **Six Cultures Project**, have demonstrated that there is great diversity in the ways children are raised in different societies.

Sigmund Freud, through his theories of **psychoanalysis**, has had an important influence on psychological anthropologists. Freud believed that all humans are born with innate, **unconscious** drives for sex and aggression. The **repression** of these drives and the redirection of energy caused by unconscious desires influenced individual psychology and behavior. An example of Freud's influence is the work of **Melford Spiro**, who used the concept of the **Oedipus complex** to explain patterns of kinship relationships in the Trobriand Islands.

167

Incest is one topic studied by psychological anthropologists. **Incest avoidance** is universal in human societies, with a few specific exceptions. There are several theories for why this is so. One hypothesis is that the incest **taboo** originated as a means of encouraging alliances based on marriage. Another is that it helps to sustain the family as an institution. The **childhood familiarity hypothesis** holds that children raised together develop a mutual aversion to sexual relationships with one another, while the notion of kinship amity suggests that sexual-aggressive tendencies are reduced among related individuals who depend on one another for mutual support. Psychological anthropology is also concerned with cross-cultural differences in attitudes about sexuality and homosexuality.

How humans think, or the process of **cognition**, is also of interest to psychological anthropologists. Theoretical frameworks include the **structuralism** of **Claude Levi-Strauss**, which emphasizes the role of **binary opposition** in human thought, and **Jean Piaget**'s four-stage model of human cognitive development.

There are significant cross-cultural differences in the way humans define emotions. Some emotions, such as sadness, anger, happiness, and surprise, are shared by all cultures. Others, such as love, fear, and disgust, vary widely. Anthropologists use an **interactionist** approach that acknowledges the existence of both universal and culture-specific emotions to study the relationship between enculturation and emotional development.

Just as emotions can vary from culture to culture, **mental illness** can be defined differently from one society to another. The definition of what is "abnormal" depends on one's culture, and there are a number of mental disorders that are culture-specific. These include *amok* rages in Southeast Asia, the cannibalistic *windigo* psychosis of certain Canadian Indian groups, and *piblotok* or "**Arctic hysteria**" among Eskimos.

Enculturation is a different process for every individual. Because a person's personality is affected by factors such as heredity, health, and life experience, the role of culture in conditioning human behavior is a very complex issue.

Terms and Concepts You Should Know

psychological anthropologist (198):

enculturation (198):

instinct (199):

drive (201):

closed biogram (201):

open biogram (201):

personality's three components (202):

feral child (202):

Apollonian society (203):

Dionysian society (203):

collectivistic society (208):

uchi and *soto* (209):

two-way enculturation (209):

ade (209):

id (212):

ego (212):

superego (212):

repression (212):

Oedipus complex (212):

incest avoidance (213):

incest taboo (213):

royal incest (213):

childhood familiarity hypothesis (214):

169

kibbutzim (214):

kinship amity (215):

xanith (216):

berdache (216):

hijira (216):

structuralism (217):

cognitive development (218):

sensorimotor stage (218):

preoperational stage (218):

concrete-operational stage (218):

formal-operational stage (218):

basic cross-cultural emotions (220):

culture-specific disorders (221):

latah (221):

amok (221):

windigo (221):

piblotoq (221):

People to Know About

Victor, the Wild Child of Aveyron (202):

Anna (202):

Ruth Benedict (203):

Margaret Mead (204):

Derek Freeman (205):

Cora Du Bois (207):

Six Cultures Project (208):

Joy Hendry (208):

Francis Hsu (211):

Sigmund Freud (212):

Melford Spiro (212):

E.B. Tylor (214):

Bronislaw Malinowski (214):

Arthur Wolf (214):

Paul Roskow (215):

John Messenger (216):

Unni Wikan (216):

Serena Nanda (216):

Claude Levi-Strauss (217):

Jean Piaget (218):

Karl Heider (220):

Richard Schweder (220):

Cultures to Know About

Plains Indians (203):

Pueblo Indians (203):

Kwakiutl (203):

Dobu (203):

Samoans (203):

Alorese (207):

Mixtecans (208):

Tarong (208):

Orchard Town (208):

Japanese (208):

Kaluli (209):

Lepcha (216):

Inis Beag Islanders (216):

Thinking About What You Have Read

The following questions or problems may be of help to you in studying the material presented in both the text and in your class. You may want to write out the answers to these questions (writing something down always seems to help solidify it in one's mind) or just think about them.

1. What are some of the ways that children become enculturated in the United States? How might these differ from the way children are enculturated in Mexico? France? Japan?

2. Does enculturation differ among ethnic groups? Does it differ among social classes? Does it differ between boys and girls? What are the principal variables an ethnologist must consider when trying to define the enculturation process?

3. How would you go about testing hypotheses that propose a relationship between heredity and human behavior? Who would you study, and why? What would be an experiment you could use to test a specific hypothesis?

4. Do you think that there is a relationship between culture and personality? Give some examples of personalities that you think might be common to particular ethnic groups. How could you go about testing this relationship?

5. Doing experiments to test the effects of social deprivation on small children can be highly unethical and even dangerous. What are some of the problems faced by anthropologists and psychologists who want to understand the experience of "feral" children?

6. Margaret Mead conducted research in the 1920s to study whether or not adolescent behavior was similar cross-culturally. How would you do research on this problem today? What would you do to avoid criticisms like Derek Freeman's criticism of Mead?

7. How might the concept of cultural relativism affect research on child development in different societies? Can you think of any ethical dilemmas that might arise in such research?

8. What were the principal aims of studies like Cora Du Bois' investigation of the Alorese and the Six Cultures Project? What were some of the conclusions produced by this research?

9. What have ethnographers like Joy Hendry been able to learn about Japanese childrearing practices? What do you think she might have concluded if she studied your own upbringing?

10. How have the theories of Sigmund Freud influenced modern psychological anthropology? What was the specific influence of Freud on Melford Spiro's research?

11. What are some of the explanations for why humans avoid incest? Which one do you favor, and why?

12. Has your own sex drive been influenced by your specific enculturation experience? Do you think it would be different if you had been raised in another culture? Why or why not?

13. Is homosexual behavior wrong? Is it possible to answer this question without representing the views of a specific culture or belief system?

14. Can you think of any mental disorders that are specific to your own culture? Do you think that disorders such as PMS (pre-menstrual syndrome), post-traumatic stress syndrome, or attention deficit disorder are culture-specific?

CHECKING YOUR UNDERSTANDING: A PRACTICE EXAMINATION

We suggest that you take this practice exam and then check your answers against the key provided at the end of this section. Use the questions that you got wrong as a guide to further study. Try to learn why specific answers are right and wrong. You may even want to take the practice exam a second time to review what you have learned.

True-False Questions

1. Most animals, including mammals, have instinctual behavior.

2. Genes encode for narrowly defined types of human behavior.

3. A child that was raised with no human contact from birth until the age of six would probably grow up with an abnormal adult personality.

4. Ruth Benedict attributed differences in typical personality type between Pueblo and Plains Indians to the fact that they came from genetically distinct populations.

5. Government records indicate that, during the time of Margaret Mead's research, the incidence of rape in Samoa was twice as common as it was in the U.S.

6. Cora Du Bois noted that Alorese infants did not receive intimate maternal care and regular breast feeding.

7. Japanese children are raised in such a way that they completely lose their sense of individuality.

8. The notion of "self" exists in all human societies.

9. Sigmund Freud believed that individuals had little or no control over their own behavior.

10. Freud's theory that the unconscious played an important role in the development of personality has been disproven by psychological anthropology.

11. Incest has been strictly prohibited in all human societies by the enforcement of incest taboos.

12. Malinowski maintained that the incest taboo served to reduce family friction and conflict.

13. Unrelated children who are raised in close association with one another usually develop a strong sexual attraction as adults.

14. The concept that individuals should not engage in sexual activity before the onset of puberty is a cultural universal.

15. Children of the same age raised together in Israeli *kibbutzim* almost never marry one another.

16. All human societies recognize only two genders: male and female.

17. According to Claude Levi-Strauss, the natural way of classifying the natural and social world is in combinations of opposites.

18. Jean Piaget demonstrated that human use of symbols begins at birth.

19. Researchers studying African infants have discovered that the sensorimotor stage is identical in both African and European babies.

20. The concept of mental illness is highly subjective and conditioned by cultural norms.

Multiple Choice Questions

21. The process by which an individual learns how to behave within a particular society is known as:
     A. cognition
     B. cultural relativism
     C. cultural adaptation
     D. enculturation

22. Most anthropologists have come to agree that human behavior _____.
     A. is mostly determined by genetic inheritance
     B. is usually automatic and instinctual
     C. results from learning only
     D. results from a combination of biology and culture

23. Humans are considered to have an "open biogram" because they:
     A. react automatically to loud noises
     B. cannot avoid instinctual behavior
     C. learn new behaviors easily
     D. are always looking for new experiences

24. The human capacity for culture is:
     A. learned after birth
     B. genetically programmed
     C. weaker than for instinctual behavior
     D. severely limited

25. "Feral" children are children who:
     A. have "wild" behavior
     B. were adopted by animals as infants
     C. were raised in isolation from other humans
     D. display symptoms of autism or psychosis

26. Studies of children who have been deprived of interaction with other humans for several years reveal that:
    A. they are rapidly enculturated once they are put into a normal environment
    B. language skills can be acquired in a matter of weeks
    C. periods of isolation are actually beneficial and stimulate attention spans
    D. long periods of social isolation can result in permanent emotional damage

27. In her classic work *Patterns of Culture* (1934), Ruth Benedict used the terms Apollonian and Dionysian to describe:
    A. cultural "personalities" of Pueblo and Plains Indians
    B. religious cults of northern and southern Greece
    C. rituals of warfare and celebration in the South Pacific
    D. contrasting models of cultural diffusion

28. According to Margaret Mead, which of the following was NOT true of Samoan adolescents?
    A. They were not exposed to conflicting values and religious beliefs.
    B. They grew up in a society that emphasized group harmony.
    C. They placed a high value on preserving virginity prior to marriage.
    D. They did not develop strong emotional ties to any one adult.

29. Anthropologist Derek Freeman challenged Margaret Mead's assertions about Samoan adolescents, claiming that:
    A. the Samoan people lacked strong passions, aggression, or a sense of sin or guilt
    B. Samoan girls were excessively promiscuous
    C. adolescents in Samoa were rarely punished for defiant behavior
    D. hormonal changes affect adolescent behavior in all societies

30. One of the principal criticisms of the culture-and-personality school is that:
    A. there is no evidence for a biological link between culture and personality
    B. it tends to assume greater uniformity in personality than actually exists in society
    C. the investigation of personality should be done by psychologists, not anthropologists
    D. individual behavior is more important than the behavior of a whole society

31. The "modal personality" is defined as the _____ psychological profile for a given culture.
    A. average
    B. most common
    C. composite
    D. majority

32. Cora Du Bois concluded that the modal personality of the Alorese was:
    A. open and trusting, with a tendency for close personal relationships
    B. hot-tempered and aggressive, with a tendency to violent behavior
    C. jealous and suspicious, with an inability to engage in sustained interpersonal relationships
    D. innocent and naïve, with exceptional gullibility

33. The Six Cultures Project sought to investigate:
    A. language acquisition
    B. the effects of diet and nutrition
    C. poverty and family life
    D. child rearing and personality

34. Among the conclusions of the Six Cultures Project was the observation that children:
    A. who were poorly nourished tended to be aggressive
    B. in male-dominated families were dependent, submissive, and less responsible
    C. raised in relative affluence were self-centered and vain
    D. learned to speak at different rates in different societies

35. Studies in psychological anthropology have revealed that, for children, the process of enculturation:
    A. is mostly passive and unconscious
    B. does not occur until around the time of puberty
    C. is one in which they are actively engaged from a very young age
    D. is identical in all human cultures

36. Joy Hendry, who conducted a study of child-raising practices in Japan, concluded that Japanese children:
    A. develop a sense of self based on their individual talents and abilities
    B. are taught to believe that individualism is a negative characteristic
    C. receive much less attention as infants than children in the U.S.
    D. are taught to feel more comfortable with the outside world than in their own home

178

37. Among Kaluli children on Papua New Guinea, the *ade* relationship is characterized by:
    A. husbands negotiating with their wives for sex by providing food
    B. younger brothers appealing to older sisters for goods, services, and attention
    C. grandparents teaming up with grandchildren to influence the generation in between
    D. uncles providing their nieces with money and shelter

38. The *ade* relationship in Papua New Guinea is an example of:
    A. unconscious enculturation
    B. 2 conscious enculturation of others
    C. two-way enculturation
    D. conspiratorial enculturation

39. According to Marcel Mauss, the concept of an individual "self":
    A. came into Western consciousness through Eastern philosophy
    B. arose in relationship to the emergence of modern capitalism
    C. is a fundamental aspect of the "situation-centeredness" of Chinese society
    D. developed as a Christian notion during the Medieval period in Europe

40. One of the basic theories of Sigmund Freud was that:
    A. all human behavior is learned behavior
    B. the intellect is more important than emotions in influencing behavior
    C. people are often unaware of the real reasons for their feeling and actions
    D. all emotional behavior is rational behavior

41. Freud believed that the repression of natural sexual and aggressive drives:
    A. redirected energy into socially approved forms of expression
    B. resulted in mental and emotional exhaustion
    C. was essential for the emotional development of a responsible adult
    D. could be controlled through mediation and physical therapy

42. According to Freud, the conscience of an individual was based on an internalization of social and cultural norms and values. He termed this level of consciousness the:
    A. id
    B. ego
    C. superego
    D. Oedipus complex

43. According to Melford Spiro, the belief in evil ghosts among Ifaluk people in Micronesia serves to:
    A. encourage the expression of innate aggressive desires
    B. hinder cooperation between individuals
    C. stimulate fantasies and overt sexual behavior
    D. reduce interpersonal aggression and stimulate cooperation

44. According to Spiro's neo-Freudian psychoanalytic interpretation of Trobriand Islanders, the Oedipus complex:
    A. appears in Trobriand children
    B. is particular to European culture
    C. does not exist
    D. cannot be documented in ethnographic studies

45. Research on the "childhood familiarity hypothesis" supports the notion that:
    A. unrelated children raised together make good marriage partners
    B. children who have grown up in the same household share sexual attractions
    C. children living in close association with one another develop an aversion to incest
    D. unrelated adolescents who live together are likely to become erotically involved

46. Among certain highland cultures of Papua New Guinea, prepubescent boys are initiated into secret societies where they perform regular oral sex on older males and are forbidden to engage in heterosexual relations for ten years. After this, they marry women, father children, and maintain heterosexual relationships. These individuals are considered to be _____ by other members of their society.
    A. homosexuals
    B. heterosexuals
    C. bisexuals
    D. normal

47. Gender is defined according to:
    A. genetics
    B. behavior
    C. anatomy
    D. culture

48. The term *berdache* is used to refer to men in Native American societies who:
    A. asserted their personal power through public displays of heterosexual prowess
    B. chose to abstain from sex so that they could focus on spiritual growth
    C. wore female clothing and offered sexual services to male warriors
    D. participated in homosexual activity only when they were preparing for war

49. The classification of foods into categories of "kosher" (edible) and "*traif*" (not edible) is an example of:
    A. preoperational reasoning
    B. cognitive dissonnance
    C. binary opposition
    D. ethnocentric enculturation

50. The "windigo psychosis" is characterized by:
    A. an insatiable craving for human flesh
    B. uncontrollable, random violence
    C. wild screaming of obscenities
    D. obsessive eating and regurgitation

Suggested Readings

BARNOUW, VICTOR. 1985. *Culture and Personality*. Homewood, IL: Dorsey Press.

BENEDICT, RUTH. 1928. "Psychological Types in the Cultures of the Southwest." (Reprinted in Mead, Margaret, *An Anthropologist at Work: Writings of Ruth Benedict*. Boston: Houghton Mifflin, 1959.)

_____. 1934. *Patterns of Culture*. Boston: Houghton Mifflin.

BLOCH, MAURICE. 1985. "From Cognition to Ideology." In R. Fardon, ed. *Power and Knowledge: Anthropological and Sociological Approaches*. Edinburgh: Scottish Academic Press.

BOURGUIGNON, ERIKA. 1979. *Psychological Anthropology: An Introduction to Human Nature and Cultural Differences*. New York: Holt, Rinehart & Winston.

FREEMAN, DEREK. 1983. *Margaret Mead and Samoa: The Making and Unmaking of an Anthropological Myth*. Cambridge, MA: Harvard University Press.

HENDRY, JOY. 1987. *Understanding Japanese Society*. London: Croon Helm.

HSU, FRANCIS. 1981. *Americans and Chinese: Passage to Differences* (3rd ed.). Honolulu: University of Hawaii Press.

MEAD, MARGARET. 1928. *Coming of Age in Samoa*. New York: Morrow.

_____. 1950. *Sex and Temperament in Three Primitive Societies*. New York: Mentor.

SHWEDER, RICHARD. 1991. *Thinking Through Cultures: Expeditions in Cultural Psychology*. Cambridge, MA: Harvard University Press.

SPIRO, MELFORD. 1982. *Oedipus in the Trobriands*. Chicago: University of Chicago Press.

WHITE, GEOFFREY M., & JOHN KIRKPATRICK, eds. 1985. *Person, Self, and Experience: Exploring Pacific Ethnopsychologies*. Berkeley: University of California Press.

WOLF, ARTHUR. 1970. "Childhood Association and Sexual Attraction: A Further Test of the Westermark Hypothesis." *American Anthropologist* 72:503-515.

VAN DEN BERGHE, PIERRE. 1980. "Incest and Exogamy: A Sociobiological Reconsideration." *Ethnology and Sociobiology* 1:151-162.

Answer Key with Page Numbers

1. T 200	18. F 218	35. C 208
2. F 201	19. T 219	36. A 209
3. T 203	20. T 221	37. B 209
4. F 203	21. D 198	38. C 209
5. T 205	22. D 198	39. B 210
6. T 207	23. C 201	40. C 211
7. F 209	24. B 201	41. A 212
8. F 211	25. C 202	42. C 212
9. F 212	26. D 203	43. D 212
10. F 212	27. A 203	44. A 213
11. F 213	28. C 204	45. C 214
12. T 214	29. D 206	46. D 216
13. F 214	30. B 205	47. C 216
14. F 215	31. B 207	48. C 216
15. T 215	32. C 207	49. C 217
16. F 217	33. D 208	50. A 71
17. T 218	34. B 208	

CHAPTER 12

LANGUAGE

Chapter Highlights

Imagine your life without language. That is hard to do, isn't it? **Language** (a symbolic system with standardized meanings) is one of the most vital components of culture. Language is the most important vehicle for transmitting and expressing wisdom, feelings, knowledge, and values. Through language, culture is transmitted from one individual to another and from generation to generation (what we call **enculturation**). Our major mode of **communication** (the transfer of information) is language.

One intriguing question that has been asked by anthropologists is how does animal, especially nonhuman primate, communication differ from human language? **Anthropological linguists** and **ethologists** have spent much time developing criteria that distinguish human languages from nonhuman communication. **Productivity**, **displacement**, and **arbitrariness** are three features that set human languages apart from animal communication systems. Productivity means that languages are open systems that allow humans to create sentences and messages that are unique and that have never been uttered before. Primate communication is a much more rigid and closed system, not allowing for this type of flexibility. Displacement means being able to refer to something that is not physically present. It allows humans to discuss the present, past, and future. A language is an arbitrary system in the sense that there does not have to be any physical connection between the symbol and the object. For example, we say "father" to refer to a male person who was partially responsible for our existence. The Portuguese refer to the same person as "*pai*", the Finns to "*isä*", and the Spanish to "*padre*".

When did language start? Were neandertals capable of making the same sounds (**phones**) as modern humans? Questions such as these have been asked by anthropologists for years. There is a great deal of research and debate. Obviously, it is difficult to determine exactly when language started, but it has been suggested that this was one of the last critical evolutionary steps of the hominids.

The structure of different languages is studied by anthropological linguists by examining sound patterns (**phonology**), the meaning of words (**morphology**), and how these meaningful units are put together in well formed utterances, phrases, and sentences (**syntax**). They are also interested in the meaning or **semantics** of the different terms that are used to classify reality. Peoples in various societies use a variety of terms to describe kinship relations, classify animals and plants, and describe other physical phenomena. Linguistic anthropologists have found some universals. Two such universals appear to be basic color terms and bird classifications. These studies challenge **linguistic relativism**, the idea that a specific language molds the cognition and perception of individuals so that they have a view of reality that is wholly different from speakers of other languages. These studies have opened up the interesting possibility that we have a common biological structure that determines how we perceive certain aspects of reality.

How did you learn your native language? Behaviorists such as B.F. Skinner would say that language is learned through positive and negative social conditioning. In opposition to this view, the linguist Noam Chomsky has suggested that all humans use an innate or genetically encoded capability for learning grammar and syntax. Chomsky's model, referred to as the **transformational-generative theory**, posits the existence of two major components: **deep structure** and **surface structure**. According to Chomsky, everyone has language competence (the capability to comprehend the basic principles underlying language) that they are not consciously aware exists. That is, they speak correctly without knowing how or why. This theoretical view has prompted some interesting research on **Creole** and **pidgin** languages.

The relationship among language, thought, and culture is another topic that has been explored by linguistic anthropologists. The **Sapir-Whorf hypothesis** contends that language predisposes individuals to perceive the world in a certain manner, guiding their thinking and behavior. Language acts as a filter for classification and perception of reality. Research has found that this hypothesis exaggerates the extent to which language determines the perception of time, space, and other aspects of reality. Anthropological linguistics do not speak of the *influence* that language has on the speaker's worldview and thinking.

The study of how languages are related to each other, and how they have separated from each other is included in the study of **historical linguistics**. One technique that has been developed to date on the divergence of languages is called **glottochronology**, which relies upon phonological and morphological changes. Using this method, linguistics have reconstructed languages and generated "family trees" for many languages in the world.

The relationship between language and society is studied by **sociolinguists** who are interested in the social context of language. They study social interactions and the ways in which people use particular linguistic expressions that reflect **dialect** patterns of their speech community. Sociolinguists have shown that many languages have subtle nuances in linguistic usage, such as greeting patterns, **honorific forms**, or in speech patterns that vary according to age, gender, and status.

Human beings not only communicate through language, but through smell, tone of voice, pace of speech, emphasis, facial expressions, body position, and gestures. These aspects of **nonverbal communication** are usually lumped into **kinesics** (body language), **proxemics** (study of the meaning and manipulation of space), and **paralanguage** (non-linguistic elements of communication that accompany speech, such as tone of voice, tempo, and crying). Nonverbal communication varies across the world, and yet, some forms of nonverbal communication appear to be universally understood.

Terms and Concepts You Should Know

language (226):

communication (226):

ethologist (228):

productivity (229):

displacement (229):

arbitrariness (229):

Broca's area (230):

Wernicke's area (230):

phoneme (229, 232):

semantics (230-233):

phonology (231-232):

morphology (231-232):

syntax (231-233):

phones (232):

minimal pairs (232):

morpheme (232):

free morpheme (232):

bounded morpheme (232):

cognitive anthropology or ethnosemantics (233):

linguistic relativism (236):

grammar (237-238):

deep structure (238):

surface structure (239):

transformational-generative grammar (238-239):

pidgin and Creole (239):

Sapir-Whorf hypothesis (240-242):

historical linguistics (242):

protolanguage (242):

glottochronology (243):

sociolinguistics (244):

dialects (245):

honorific forms (246):

kinesics (248-249):

proxemics (249):

People or "Primates" To Know About

"Washoe" (226-227):

Allen & Beatric Gardner (226):

"Koko" (226-227):

"Lana" ((226-227):

"Kanzi" (226-227):

"Nim" (226-227):

Jane Goodall (228):

Noam Chomsky (237-238):

Dell Hymes (245):

Cultures You Should Know

Hopi (241):

Thinking About What You Have Read

The following questions or problems may be of help to you in studying material presented in both the text and in your class. You may want to write out the answers to these questions (writing something down always seems to help solidify it in one's mind) or just think about them.

1. What is communication? What is language? What are signs and symbols, and how are they different?

2. Describe the work of Herbert Terrace and Sue Savage-Rumbaugh. Do you agree with their interpretations concerning language acquisition in nonhuman primates?

3. What are some of the differences between nonhuman primate communication and human language? Is language qualitatively different from animal communication systems or does it vary only in degree?

4. Could early hominids speak? When did language evolve? Do you think that language was critical in the adaptation and survival of the early hominids?

5. What is ethnosemantics or cognitive anthropology? Talk about them in terms of kinship terminology and classification of some aspect of reality (trees, cars, buildings, dogs, plants).

6. "Language is a guide to social reality." "The world in which different societies live are distinct worlds, not merely the same world with different labels attached." Explain how you either agree or disagree with these quotes by Edward Sapir.

7. In what ways is a language's vocabulary affected by culture? What are some of the ways people vary in their use of language according to situation?

8. Human communication is based largely on symbols. What are some of the common nonverbal symbols in your society? Were these symbols devised for a particular purpose (such as advertising), or did they develop spontaneously? What social functions are served by those that developed spontaneously?

9. The structure of language determines the structure of thought of its speakers. Explain how you either agree or disagree with this statement of the Sapir-Whorf hypothesis.

10. How do children learn a language?

11. Given the findings of Ekkehart Malotki, how would you evaluate the phenomenon known as "politically correct speech"?

12. What is sociolinguistics? What does it study? Can you think of examples of dialects, greeting behaviors, and language honorifics from your own experience that are similar or different from those given in the text?

13. Dell Hymes uses the acronym S-P-E-A-K-I-N-G as a formula for sociolinguists to study the speech act in different situations. Using this formula, evaluate and describe a linguistic exchange you have witnessed.

14. What is nonverbal communication? What types of nonverbal communication do you use in your daily communication? Do some of the things you do appear to be automatic?

CHECKING YOUR UNDERSTANDING: A PRACTICE EXAMINATION

We suggest that you take this practice exam and then check your answers against the key provided at the end of this section. Use the questions that you got wrong as a guide to further study. Try to learn why specific answers are right and wrong. You might even consider taking this practice test more than once, several days apart.

True-False Questions

1. A system of symbols with standard meanings through which members of a society communicate with each other is a syntax.

2. The act of transferring information to others is called communication.

3. Herbert Terrace's study of Nim Chimpsky showed that chimps learn and understand syntax.

4. The gorilla named "Koko" was able to write her own name and verbally communicate her needs to humans using English.

5. Scientists who study the behavior of animals in their natural setting are called ethologists.

6. Jane Goodall's work with Kanzi and Washoe demonstrated that these chimpanzees could communicate with each other through American Sign Language.

7. Human languages are inherently flexible and creative and not closed systems. This human language trait is called productivity.

8. Displacement is a dialect spoken by both the Zulu and Tusi so they can conduct intergroup trade.

9. The portion of the brain associated with understanding the meaning of words and sentences is called Wernicke's area.

10. The voice box containing the vocal cords is called the larynx.

11. Philip Lieberman and Jeffrey Laitman have conclusively demonstrated that *Homo habilis* and *Homo erectus* could produce speech just like modern *Homo sapiens*.

12. Scientific attempts to teach apes to speak human languages have been extremely successful, especially with chimpanzees.

13. Morphology is the study of the sounds in a language

14. The sounds of language are called phones

15. The English word "*dogs*" contains one free morpheme and one bound morpheme.

16. A phoneme is the unit of a language that conveys meaning.

17. Ethnosemantic research has shown that classification systems of natural phenomena (colors, animals) across the world are completely random and without any structural similarities.

18. Cecil Brown has found that all languages exhibit universal tendencies in the ways in which they name the days of the seven-day week, the four cardinal directions, plants, animals, parts of the human body, and time cycles.

19. According to Noam Chomsky, children are born with the ability to speak a language.

20. Linguist Noam Chomsky argues that each language provides the speaker with a built-in filter that heightens, dims, or eliminates certain perceptions, thus determining how we perceive reality.

21. The Sapir-Whorf hypothesis assumes that a close relationship exists between language and culture in that language defines experiences for us.

22. Modern anthropologists think that language determines thought.

23. Historical linguistics have determined that the original language spoken by the first humans was called Glottochronology.

24. Sociolinguistics study the evolution of languages using family tree methodology to determine branching locations of trunk languages.

25. Linguist Dell Hymes has developed a method of studying language usage in different social contexts using the acronym T-A-L-K which means: Timing, Allocation, Language, and Knowledge.

Multiple Choice Questions

26. The set of grammatical rules governing the way words combine to form sentences is
    A. proxemics
    B. syntax
    C. a lexigram
    D. semantics

27. Ethologists have found that many types of animals produce certain sounds or vocalizations that produce specific meanings. This is called a
    A. syntax
    B. call system
    C. language
    D. productivity system

28. Words in human languages seldom have any necessary connection with the concrete objects or abstract symbols they represent. This human language trait is called
    A. displacement
    B. productivity
    C. clarity
    D. arbitrariness

29. In human languages the meaning of sounds can refer to people, places, events, or things that are not present. This trait of human language is known as
    A. displacement
    B. productivity
    C. remoteness
    D. arbitrariness

30. A unit of sound that makes a difference in meaning is called a
    A. morph
    B. morpheme
    C. phoneme
    D. syntax

31. In the English words "cat" and "hat", the /c/ and the /h/ are considered
    A. syntaxes
    B. proxemics
    C. grammatical units
    D. phonemes

32. The portion of the brain that is associated with the production of sound or pronunciation and with grammatical abilities is called
    A. Broca's area
    B. Wernicke's area
    C. the pharynx
    D. Wendel's region

33. The part of the vocal tract between the back of the tongue and the vocal cords that extends into the nasal cavity is
    A. Broca's area
    B. the larynx
    C. the pharynx
    D. Wendel's region

34. The study of sounds made in language is called
    A. morphology
    B. syntax
    C. phonology
    D. ethology

35. The words "call" and "hall" are what are called
    A. maximal units
    B. semantic components
    C. minimal pairs
    D. phonal divergence

36. How many phones does the English word "house" have?
    A. 1
    B. 5
    C. 10
    D. zero, "house" does not have any phones

37. The study of words of human languages is called
    A. morphology
    B. phonology
    C. syntax
    D. semantics

38. The study of sentence structure of a language is known as
    A. phonology
    B. morphology
    C. syntax
    D. proxemics

39. This type of anthropology focuses on the meaning of language as it relates to different societal circumstances:
    A. ethnosemantics
    B. lingual anthropology
    C. syntactic anthropology
    D. application anthropology

40. The study of the meaning of language is
    A. phonology
    B. syntax
    C. morphology
    D. semantics

41. The view that the specific language spoken within a society organizes people's objective experiences and perceptions in ways unique to that language is called
    A. ethnosemantics
    B. cognitive anthropology
    C. linguistic absolutism
    D. linguistic relativism
    E. kinesics

42. Noam Chomsky calls the unconscious basic structure that enables us to learn any type of syntax or grammar in any language the
    A. deep structure
    B. generative component
    C. semantic component
    D. critical stage

43. In Noam Chomsky's transformational-generative model, the sentence as it is actually spoken in called the
    A. syntax
    B. surface structure
    C. coded component
    D. linguistic emergent unit

44. A _____ is a parent language for many ancient and modern languages.
    A. glottochronology
    B. protolanguage
    C. syntax
    D. paternal dialect

45. The study of language change and the historical relationships among different languages is
    A. kinesics
    B. glottochronology
    C. historical linguistics
    D. sociolinguistics

46. The study of the use of language in different social contexts is
    A. kinesics
    B. proxemics
    C. localemics
    D. socioemics

47. A social unit within which speakers share various ways of speaking is a
    A. dialectical community
    B. speech community
    C. speak-easy group
    D. normative unit

48. Linguistic differences in pronunciation, vocabulary, or syntax that may differ within a single language are known as
    A. honorifics
    B. dialects
    C. glottos
    D. subcultures

49. Many societies that maintain social inequality and hierarchy have language that is used to express differences in social level between speakers. These languages contain what are called:
    A. ethnic boundary units
    B. honorific forms
    C. social leveling components
    D. proxemic spacing units

50. The study of body motion and gestures used in nonverbal communication is
    A. proxemics
    B. kinesics
    C. motionoptics
    D. gesturology

51. The study of how people in different cultures perceive and use space is called:
    A. proxemics
    B. kinesics
    C. relativity
    D. structurology

Suggested Readings

ASANTE, MOLEFI K. AND WILLIAM B. GUDYKUNST. 1989. *Handbook of International and Intercultural Communication*. Beverley Hills, CA: Sage.

BARNLUND, DEAN C. 1989. *Communicative Styles of Japanese and Americans: Images and Realities*. Belmont, CA: Wadsworth.

BAUMAN, RICHARD. 1986. *Let Your Words Be Few: Symbolism of Speaking and Silence Among Seventeenth Century Quakers*. Prospect Heights, IL: Waveland Press.

BONVILLAIN, NANCY. 1993. *Language, Culture, and Communication: The Meaning of Messages*. Englewood Cliffs, NJ: Prentice Hall.

CAZDEN, COURTNEY B.; JOHN P. VERA; AND DELL HYMES. 1986. *Functions of Language in the Classroom*. Prospect Heights, IL: Waveland Press.

CHOMSKY, NOAM. 1968. *Language and Mind*. New York, NY: Harcourt, Brace & World.

CLARK, VIRGINIA P.; PAUL A. ESCHHOLZ, AND ALFRED F. ROSA, eds. 1981. *Language: Introductory Readings*. New York, NY: St. Martin's Press.

CONDON, JOHN C. 1985. *Good Neighbors: Communicating with the Mexicans*. Yarmouth, ME: Intercultural Press.

CRYSTAL, DAVID. 1988. *The Cambridge Encyclopedia of Language*. New York, NY: Cambridge University Press.

DOE, JOHN. 1988. *Speak Into the Mirror: A Story of Linguistic Anthropology*. Lanham, MD: Univeristy Press of America.

FARB, PETER. 1975. *Word Play: What Happens When People Talk*. New York, NY: Bantam Books.

GRACE, GEORGE W. 1987. *The Linguistic Construction of Reality*. New York, NY: Croom Helm.

HALL, EDWARD. 1964. *The Hidden Dimension*. New York, NY: Doubleday.

_____. 1973. *The Silent Language*. New York, NY: Doubleday.

_____. 1977. *Beyond Culture*. New York, NY: Doubleday.

197

HELLER, MONICA. 1988. *Codeswitching: Anthropological and Sociolinguistic Perspectives.* New York, NY: Mouton de Gruyter.

HYMES, DELL, ed. 1964. *Language in Culture and Society: A Reader in Lingustics and Anthropology.* New York, NY: Harper & Row.

MARSHALL, TERRY. 1990. *The Whole World Guide to Language Learnin*g. Yarmouth, ME: Intercultural Press.

MOERMON, MICHAEL. 1988. *Talking Culture: Ethnography and Conversation Analysis.* Philadelphia, PA: University of Pennsylvania Press.

PULLUM, GEOFFRY K. 1990. *The Great Eskimo Vocabulary Hoax.* Chicago, IL: University of Chicago Press.

RADFORD, ANDREW. 1988. *Transformational Grammar: A First Course.* New York, NY: Cambridge University Press.

SAMOVAR, LARRY A. AND RICHARD PORTER. 1991. *Intercultural Communication: A Reader.* Belmont, CA: Wadsworth.

SCHIEFFELIN, BAMBI B. AND ELINOR OCHS. 1986. *Language Socialization Across Cultures.* New York, NY: Cambridge University Press.

SPRADLEY, JAMES P. 1985. *Culture and Cognition: Rules, Maps, and Plans.* Prospect Heights, IL: Waveland Press.

TRUDGILL, PETER. 1983. *Sociolinguistics: An introduction to Language and Society.* New York, NY: Penguin Books.

WEST, FRED. 1975. *The Way of Language: An Introduction.* New York, NY: Harcourt Brace Jovanovich.

Answer Key with Page Numbers

1.	F 226	18.	T 238	35.	C 232
2.	T 226	19.	T 238-239	36.	B 232
3.	F 227	20.	F 240-241	37.	A 232
4.	F 227	21.	T 240-241	38.	C 232-233
5.	T 228	22.	F 240-242	39.	A 233
6.	F 227-228	23.	F 243	40.	D 233
7.	T 229	24.	F 243-244	41.	D 236
8.	F 229	25.	F 245	42.	A 238-239
9.	T 230	26.	B 227	43.	B 239
10.	T 230	27.	B 228	44.	B 242
11.	F 231	28.	D 229	45.	C 242
12.	F 231	29.	A 229	46.	A 244-245
13.	F 231-232	30.	C 229	47.	B 245
14.	T 232	31.	D 229	48.	B 245-246
15.	T 232	32.	A 230	49.	B 246-247
16.	F 232	33.	C 230	50.	A 248-249
17.	F 236-237	34.	C 231	51.	A 249

CHAPTER 13

ANTHROPOLOGICAL EXPLANATIONS

Chapter Outline

Nineteenth-Century Explanations
Unilineal Evolution: Tylor
Unilineal Evolution: Morgan
    MORGAN AND KINSHIP THEORIES
A Critique
Diffusionism
British Diffusionism
German Diffusionism
The Limitations and Strengths of Diffusionism
Historical Particularism
Boas versus the Unilineal Evolutionists
Functionalism: British Anthropology
Structural Functionalism: Radcliffe-Brown
Psychological Functionalism: Malinowski
The Limitations of Functionalism
Twentieth-Century Evolutionism
Steward and Cultural Ecology
    A CASE STUDY: THE SHOSHONE
The Strengths of Neo-evolutionism
Criticisms of Cultural Ecology
Cultural Materialism
Marxist Anthropology
Evaluation of Marxist Anthropology
Sociobiology
A Case Study: Sexual Behavior
Inclusive Fitness and Kin Selection
Sociobiology: A Critique
Symbolic Anthropology
Criticisms of Symbolic Anthropology
Materialism versus Culturalism

Chapter Highlights

Chapter thirteen provides an overview of anthropological **theory**, beginning with nineteenth century notions of **cultural evolution** and concluding with modern **sociobiology** and **symbolic anthropology**. As a science, anthropology seeks to provide explanations for human society and behavior. These are presented in the form of **models** or theories - conceptual frameworks that seek to explain observations in a complete, logically consistent, and predictive manner. A basic division in anthropological theory is between **materialist explanations** that focus on technological, environmental, biological, and economic factors that influence culture, and **culturalist explanations**, that focus on the way culture is used to give meaning to life.

Modern anthropology began in the nineteenth century as Western scholars sought to explain physical and cultural variation among humans as imperialistic expansion and colonialism brought about increased contact with non-Western societies. Inspired by Darwin's model for biological evolution, **Edward B. Tylor** and **Lewis Henry Morgan** formulated theories for the **unilineal evolution** of human culture. They described stages of "savagery" and "barbarism" through which societies passed on their way to **"civilization."** Morgan emphasized the importance of both social structure and technology for cultural development. Although they presented many valuable ideas, these theories were flawed by **ethnocentrism** and the belief that all societies could be ranked in terms of their success or failure at becoming like modern Western society.

In the early twentieth century, theories of **diffusionism** suggested that civilization spread from specific core areas. The **British school** held that Egypt was the center, while the **German school** emphasized that culture spread in circles (*Kulturkreise*) from several centers. Diffusionist theories tended to be ethnocentric in attributing the lack of civilization to degeneration. However, although anthropologists have rejected specific diffusionist models for cultural evolution, they agree that diffusion is an important process in culture change.

Anthropologist **Franz Boas** led a movement to reject unilineal models of cultural evolution in favor of **historical particularism**, maintaining that each society must be understood as a product of its own history. Boas emphasized the importance of fieldwork over **"armchair anthropology"** and argued that no society could be considered superior or inferior to any other. He pioneered research in all areas of anthropology and helped repudiate racism through studies of physical type and intelligence.

Functionalism is a school of thought based on the idea that societies are comprised of **institutions** that serve vital purposes (functions) for the people in them. **Structural functionalism**, practiced by **Radcliffe-Brown**, stressed the role of economic, social, political, and religious institutions for a society's survival. **Psychological functionalism**, like that of **Malinowski**, concentrated on how society functioned to serve the needs of individuals. Functionalism presented new ways of interpreting culture but has been criticized for ignoring historical factors in cultural diversity.

After World War II, cultural evolution was revived by scholars like **Leslie White** and **Julian Steward**. White sought to quantify **general evolution** in terms of **energy** use. Steward, who introduced the notion of **cultural ecology**, emphasized the role of environmental factors in the **specific evolution** of individual societies. He demonstrated how desert habitats limited the evolution of groups like the **Shoshone** while fertile river valleys supported the emergence of agricultural civilizations.

Cultural materialism stresses the role of material factors such as technology, environment, and economic production for culture change and evolution. **Marxist anthropology** is a form of materialism that is based on **Karl Marx's** argument that systems for the production of material goods determine a culture's social, political, and spiritual character.

During the 1980s, **sociobiology** emerged from the work of entomologists and animal behaviorists. It emphasizes the role of **natural selection** and the influence of the biological need to reproduce on human **social behavior**. An example of a sociobiological theory is the idea that humans develop cultural strategies to ensure that their own children mature and reproduce in order to maximize their own **reproductive success**.

Symbolic anthropology, drawing upon **culturalist** rather than **materialist** theory, interprets material and biological aspects of culture as secondary to symbols, values, and beliefs. Symbolic anthropologists focus on the interpretation of **symbols** within the worldviews of specific societies. They seek to make the values, beliefs, and cosmologies of other cultures meaningful and intelligible.

Terms and Concepts You Should Know

unilineal evolution (254):

progress (254):

civilization (254):

diffusionism (255):

British diffusionism (255):

German diffusionism (255):

Kulturkreise (255):

armchair anthropology (256):

202

historical particularism (256):

cultural relativism (256):

culture-and-personality theory (257):

functionalism (257):

structural functionalism (257):

psychological functionalism (257):

neo-evolutionism (258):

sociocultural systems (257):

cultural evolution (258):

general [cultural] evolution (259):

cultural ecology (259):

ecological anthropology (259):

specific [cultural] evolution (259):

cultural materialism (260):

infrastructure (260):

structure (260):

superstructure (260):

Marxist anthropology (260):

class struggle (261):

capitalist (261):

proletariat (261):

sociobiology (262):

general strategies [of behavior] (262):

inclusive fitness (263):

kin selection (263):

nepotism (263):

symbolic anthropology (263):

thick description (263):

materialists (264):

culturalists (264):

People to Know About

Edward B. Tylor (253):

Lewis Henry Morgan (254):

G. Elliot Smith (255):

William J. Perry (255):

Father Wilhelm Schmidt (255):

Franz Boas (256):

A.R. Radcliffe-Brown (257):

Bronislaw Malinowski (257):

Leslie White (258):

James Steward (259):

Karl Marx (260):

Marshall Sahlins (263):

Richard Barrett (264):

Cultures to Know About

Trobriand Islanders (257):

Shoshone (259):

Thinking About What You Have Read

The following questions or problems may be of help to you in studying the material presented in both the text and in your class. You may want to write out the answers to these questions (writing something down always seems to help solidify it in one's mind) or just think about them.

1. What aspects of the way anthropology was conducted in the nineteenth century would have influenced the formulation of theories of unilineal anthropology? How did these change in the early twentieth century?

2. Give an example of a diffusionist explanation for culture change? Is the diffusionistic approach a meaningful one? What are its strengths and weaknesses?

3. Who was Franz Boas? What were his principal contributions to anthropology? How did he influence the directions taken by anthropological theory in the early twentieth century?

4. What are some of the differences between structural functionalism and psychological functionalism? What are some examples of functionalist explanations? Do you think that functionalism can explain features of our own culture?

5. How is the concept of "sociocultural systems" relevant to neo-evolutionism? What are some of the advantages of viewing cultures as systems?

6. Do you find any value in Leslie White's hypothesis that cultural complexity evolves with changes in the use of energy? What are the implications of this theory for advances in energy technology such as the capture of unlimited solar power?

7. Compare and contrast the concepts of "general evolution" and "specific evolution." What are the fundamental differences between the two? Is it more important to understand one than the other?

8. Do you think that Julian Steward would have supported models of unilineal evolution that proposed all human cultures would evolve into civilizations? Why or why not?

9. What would be the differences between the way a cultural materialist and a sociobiologist might explain the custom of the father giving away the bride at a wedding?

10. What is meant by "sociobiology"? Describe the principal theoretical perspective of sociobiology. What have been some of its main criticisms? Do you think that the theories of sociobiology are reasonable ones?

11. What might be included in a "thick description" of a major league baseball game? Why would this kind of analysis be worthwhile?

12. Do you think it would be possible to study cultural evolution by combining the views of the sociobiologists, Marxists, and symbolic anthropologists in one grand theoretical perspective? Or, are these views so different that they simply cannot be combined in any manner?

CHECKING YOUR UNDERSTANDING: A PRACTICE EXAMINATION

We suggest that you take this practice exam and then check your answers against the key provided at the end of this section. Use the questions that you got wrong as a guide to further study. Try to learn why specific answers are right and wrong. You may even want to take the practice exam a second time to review what you have learned.

True-False Questions

1. Anthropological research has resulted in the formulation of laws that can be used to predict human action.

2. Edward B. Tylor's theory of social evolution was influenced by the work of Charles Darwin.

3. Unilineal evolution is the view that all societies evolve (or have evolved) in a single direction, from "primitive" to "civilized."

4. For Lewis Henry Morgan, the crucial distinction between civilized and "savage" societies was the existence of institutions based on private property.

5. Diffusionism is the term used for the idea that culture could not be transmitted from one race of people to another.

6. Diffusionism has been shown to be an invalid concept, and is no longer relevant to the analysis of human culture.

7. Franz Boas was one of the principal contributors to the model of unilineal evolution.

8. Historical particularism maintains that each society must be understood as a product of its own history.

9. Ruth Benedict and Margaret Mead were both students of Franz Boas.

10. A "structural functionalist" might explain the need for males to marry outside of their group as biological drive.

11. Malinowski suggested that fishing magic functioned to reduce the anxieties of fishermen.

12. Functionalists were concerned with the historical development of specific cultural institutions.

13. Leslie White hypothesized that society evolved in response to the ability to use new forms of energy.

14. A cultural ecologist would probably to attribute the small group organization of the Shoshone to the environment in which they lived.

15. Cultural ecology has helped to explain sociocultural similarities and differences between cultures.

16. Marxist anthropology is a form of cultural materialism.

17. A criticism of Marxist anthropology is that its practitioners tend to accept Marx's unilineal model of cultural evolution.

18. Sociobiologists believe that all human behavior is genetically programmed.

19. According to sociobiologists, women are more discerning than men in their choice of sexual partners because they can produce fewer direct offspring.

20. A "thick description" of a cultural event would attempt to interpret the meanings of its symbolic elements.

Multiple Choice Questions

21. The principal theoretical objective of modern anthropology is:
    A. to document differences between ethnic groups
    B. to study the close relationship between genetics and culture
    C. to provide useful explanations of human society and behavior
    D. to formulate laws for predicting human behavior and thought

22. As anthropology emerged from the intellectual atmosphere of the Enlightenment, early anthropologists were interested in explaining the similarities and differences among the diverse cultures of the world. E.B. Tylor attempted to answer the question of why societies were at different or similar levels of evolution and development by the explanation of
    A. spontaneous generation
    B. unilineal evolution
    C. diffusionism
    D. historical particularism
    E. functionalism

23. E.B. Tylor and other eighteenth century thinkers asserted that "primitives" around the world would eventually evolve through the stages of barbarism to become civilized like Europeans, but that these "primitives" would need some help from the civilized world to reach this ultimate, ideal stage. This perception that Western society is the center of the civilized world and that non-Western societies are inherently inferior is called
   A. logical negativism
   B. logical positivism
   C. ethnocentrism
   D. functionalism
   E. devolution

24. According to Lewis Henry Morgan, a crucial distinction between civilized society and earlier societies was the importance of:
   A. private property
   B. domesticated animals
   C. metallurgy
   D. the bow and arrow

25. The principal criticism of nineteenth century theories of "unilineal evolution" is that:
   A. they were ethnocentric, holding that Western society was superior to all others
   B. they relied too heavily upon Biblical teachings
   C. they were based on inadequate knowledge of the fossil record
   D. they neglected the civilizations of ancient China and India

26. The German school of diffusionism differed somewhat from that of the British in that it:
   A. argued for multiple centers from which civilization had spread instead of just one
   B. concentrated on psychological aspects of culture instead of general behaviors linked to kinship patterns
   C. embraced some of the assertions of unilineal evolution
   D. traced its intellectual history to the work of Franz Boas

27. One of Boas' principal criticisms of nineteenth-century anthropologists was that:
   A. they failed to make use of archaeological evidence for pre-literate societies
   B. their theories were based on "armchair anthropology" and not their own fieldwork
   C. there was too much cultural relativism in their interpretations
   D. they failed to assign adequate importance to biological effects on culture

28. The belief that each society must be understood as a product of its own particular history rather than as part of a general evolutionary trajectory is called:
    A. cultural relativism
    B. historical particularism
    C. structural functionalism
    D. neo-evolutionism

29. The term "functionalism" in anthropology refers to the notion that:
    A. ethnographers are competent observers of human culture
    B. some societies are "functional" while others are "dysfunctional"
    C. cultural practices function to fulfill specific needs in a given society
    D. culture is transmitted through functions like rituals and ceremonies

30. The existence of a "joking relationship" - one in which interactions are typified by friendly teasing - between a man and his brothers-in-law would be explained by anthropologist Radcliffe-Brown as:
    A. a structured relationship whose function is to reduce potential hostility
    B. evidence for cultural influences on individual personality
    C. an example of the importance of cultural relativism in kinship roles
    D. the basis for materialistic behavior

31. According to Malinowski, the principal function of fishing magic in the Trobriand Islands was to:
    A. make the fish come into the fishermen's nets
    B. reduce fishermen's internal anxieties and tensions
    C. provide a metaphysical explanation for bad weather and other hazards of offshore fishing
    D. increase the wealth of magicians and medicine men

32. The reformulation of models for cultural evolution by anthropological theorists in the twentieth century is referred to as "neo-evolutionism" because:
    A. cultural evolution suffered serious setbacks during World War I and World War II
    B. it represented a third stage, preceded by "paleo-" and "meso-evolution-ism"
    C. nineteenth-century evolutionary theory had been rejected by Boas and his students
    D. evolutionary biologists recognized the effects of increased radioactivity

33. The quote, "Culture evolves as the amount of energy harnessed per capita per year is increased, or as the efficiency of the instrumental means of putting the energy to work is increased.", captures the essence of
    A. the functional perspective of cultural evolution
    B. neo-evolutionism (general evolution) of Leslie A. White
    C. Steward's cultural ecology
    D. the Marxist view of societal evolution
    E. the cultural materialist viewpoint

34. Julian Steward, who helped to establish the field of cultural ecology, believed that:
    A. all hunting and gathering societies existed in marginal environments
    B. parallels in cultural evolution could be explained by similar environmental conditions
    C. the rise of civilization could be explained through a theory of general evolution
    D. social organization developed independently of environmental conditions

35. The case study of the Shoshone Indians of the Great Basin is important to the theory of cultural ecology because:
    A. it demonstrates the effects of intensive horticulture on primitive social organization
    B. the Shoshone are an example of foragers subsisting in a rich environment
    C. environment and natural resource availability had a definite influence on the form of social organization
    D. the ecology of the Great Basin allowed for the emergence of a complex system of tribal government

36. According to Steward, the social organization of the Shoshone:
    A. remained simple due to the restrictions of their desert habitat
    B. evolved free of the constrictions of limited natural resources
    C. was similar to that of ancient Mesopotamian states
    D. reflected the effects of high population density

37. One of the principal criticisms of cultural ecology is the charge that it:
    A. reduces human behavior to simple adaptations to the external environment
    B. places humans within ecosystems as if they were just another type of organism
    C. ignores the fundamental role of subsistence needs in the organization of human culture
    D. is overly dependent upon historical or political factors

211

38. In the theory of cultural materialism, the term "superstructure" would refer to:
    A. philosophy, art, music, religion, ideas, and values
    B. technology and practices for producing food, shelter, and clothing
    C. family structure, political organization, and gender roles
    D. classes, castes, and division of labor

39. According to cultural materialists, the term "infrastructure" would refer to:
    A. philosophy, art, music, religion, ideas, and values
    B. technology and practices for producing food, shelter, and clothing
    C. family structure, political organization, and gender roles
    D. classes, castes, and division of labor

40. According to cultural-materialist theory, the structure and superstructure of sociocultural systems is determined primarily by:
    A. the domestic economy (family, domestic division of labor, age and gender roles)
    B. philosophy, art, music, religion, ideas, science, and values
    C. the political economy (political organization, class, castes, police, military)
    D. the technology and the practices used for expanding or limiting the production of food, clothing, and shelter.

41. The theory that systems for the production of material goods affect the organization of society and the general character of the social, political, and spiritual processes is central to the writings of:
    A. Lewis Henry Morgan
    B. Julian Steward
    C. Karl Marx
    D. A.R. Radcliffe-Brown

42. Marx believed that human existence was characterized by:
    A. long-term stability
    B. constant struggle and conflict
    C. mindless submission to authority
    D. a preoccupation with food and sex

43. Marxist anthropology:
    A. was practiced only in the former Soviet Union
    B. has been demonstrated to be a flawed theory
    C. continues to provide fruitful hypotheses for investigation
    D. predicts that all capitalist societies will someday become communist

44. The systematic study of the biological basis of social behavior, including aspects of human culture, is known as:
    A. genetic anthropology
    B. bioculturalism
    C. population dynamics
    D. sociobiology

45. Sociobiologists attribute the "double standard" that tolerates male promiscuity while condemning females with multiple sexual partners to:
    A. ideological rationalization
    B. reproductive strategy
    C. instinctual behavior
    D. twentieth century morality

46. Sociobiologists tend to view the particular sexual behaviors of males and females as the result of:
    A. fixed, unchanging instincts that have evolved over millennia of human evolution
    B. enculturation processes that are the same in every human culture
    C. conscious or unconscious strategies to insure the reproduction and survival of their own genes
    D. an interaction of biology and sociology

47. "Inclusive fitness" is the assumption that living organisms, including humans:
    A. can only survive if they are physically fit
    B. maximize reproductive fitness through their offspring
    C. avoid reproducing with individuals who are not kin
    D. include fitness as one of the requirements for survival

48. The politician who hires his relatives for key positions in his administration or the father who dies saving his son and his brother are examples of what sociobiologists call
    A. kin selection
    B. fatalism
    C. simplistic acts
    D. evolutionary reductionism
    E. symbolic gestures

49. Marshall Sahlins has criticized sociobiology by pointing out that:
    A. kin selection and kinship systems are organized by cultural rather than biological categories
    B. human behavior cannot be compared to animal behavior
    C. sociology and biology are separate disciplines with completely different aims and methodologies
    D. only the behavior of individuals in band societies is instinctual, and this model cannot be applied to more highly developed societies

50. Symbolic anthropologists suggest that cultural symbols:
    A. derive primarily from the material conditions and adaptive mechanisms of a given society
    B. represent unconscious, universal archetypes that are common to all human societies
    C. may be completely independent of the material aspects of human existence
    D. can be understood only through cross-cultural analysis

Suggested Readings

BARRETT, RICHARD A. 1984. *Culture and Conduct: An Excursion in Anthropology.* Belmont, CA: Wadsworth.

BOAS, FRANZ. [1940] 1966. *Race, Language, and Culture.* New York: The Free Press.

CHAGNON, N.A., & W. IRONS, eds. 1979. *Evolutionary Biology and Human Social Behavior.* North Scituate, MA: Duxbury Press.

GEERTZ, CLIFFORD. 1973. *The Interpretation of Cultures: Selected Essays by Clifford Geertz.* New York: Basic Books.

HARRIS, MARVIN. 1968. *The Rise of Anthropological Theory.* New York: Thomas Y. Crowell.

_____. 1977. *Cannibals and Kings: The Origins of Cultures.* New York: Random House.

_____. 1979. *Cultural Materialism: The Struggle for a Science of Culture.* New York: Random House.

HATCH, ELVIN. 1973. *Theories of Man and Culture*. New York: Columbia University Press.

MALINOWSKI, BRONISLAW. 1922. *Argonauts of the Western Pacific*. New York: Dutton.

MANNERS, R.A., & D. KAPLAN, eds. 1968. *Theory in Anthropology: A Sourcebook*. Chicago: Aldine.

MORGAN, LEWIS HENRY. [1877] 1964. *Ancient Society*. Cambridge, MA: Harvard University Press.

SAHLINS, MARSHALL. 1976. *The Use and Abuse of Biology: An Anthropological Critique of Sociobiology*. Ann Arbor: University of Michigan Press.

STEWARD, JULIAN. 1955. *Theory of Culture Change: The Methodology of Multilinear Evolution*. Urbana: University of Illinois Press.

SYMONS, DONALD. 1979. *The Evolution of Human Sexuality*. Oxford: Oxford University Press.

TERRAY, EMMANUEL. 1972. *Marxism and "Primitive" Societies: Two Studies*. New York: Monthly Review Press.

WHITE, LESLIE. 1959. *The Evolution of Culture*. New York: McGraw-Hill.

WILSON, E.O. 1978. *On Human Nature*. Cambridge, MA: Harvard University Press.

Answer Key with Page Numbers

1. F 253	18. F 262	35. C 259
2. T 253	19. T 262	36. A 259
3. T 254	20. T 264	37. A 260
4. T 254	21. C 253	38. A 260
5. F 255	22. B 254	39. B 260
6. F 255	23. C 254	40. D 260
7. F 256	24. A 254	41. C 261
8. T 256	25. A 255	42. B 261
9. T 257	26. A 255	43. C 261
10. F 257	27. B 256	44. D 262
11. T 258	28. B 256	45. B 262
12. F 258	29. C 257	46. C 262
13. T 258	30. A 257	47. B 263
14. T 259	31. B 258	48. A 263
15. T 260	32. C 258	49. A 263
16. T 261	33. B 258	50. C 263
17. F 261	34. B 259	

CHAPTER 14

ANALYZING SOCIOCULTURAL SYSTEMS

Chapter Outline

217

Political Structure
  Types of Political Systems
  Decision Making in a Political System
  Warfare and Feuds
  Law and Social Control
    LAW AS FORMALIZED NORMS AND SANCTIONS
Religion
  Myths
  Rituals
  Religious Specialists
  Religious Movements
Cross-Cultural Research

CHAPTER HIGHLIGHTS

Anthropological knowledge is generated through careful study and scientific inquiry. Much of this sociocultural information is obtained by **ethnological fieldwork** that is conducted in contemporary societies across the globe. However, before going into the field, the anthropologist prepares by becoming familiar with the different theoretical perspectives and insights provided by earlier scholars. This background information is often vitally important in developing a **research design** or strategy for examining a particular culture or topic of interest. One of the most productive methods of obtaining ethnological information is **participant observation**. The anthropologist learns the language and culture of the people by immersing himself or herself in their daily lives. Through **naturalistic observation**, participant observation, **unstructured** and **structured interviews**, **random sample questionnaires**, and **key informants**, anthropologists gain an increasingly complete picture of a people and their way of life. Cultural anthropologists will work with both **qualitative** and **quantitative data**. Both are necessary to create a full and complete **ethnography**—one that is both objective and subjective. An ethnographer usually asks and answers three basic questions: What do these people do? How do they do it? Why do they do it in that way? Only in this manner do we obtain a whole and comprehensive picture of a people and their culture.

A cultural anthropologist must not only use good methodology, but must also be cognizant of his or her feelings, biases, and beliefs. These affect the ability to follow the methodology and to draw conclusions from the field data. If you have ever felt "out of place" while experiencing something new, you have an inkling of what **culture shock** is like. Culture shock is when the gestures, spacing, language, facial expressions, and many other aspects of culture are different from what you expect. All the subtle, and not so subtle, cues you and we depend upon are missing in their familiarity. They are new and different. It becomes very easy to "misread" situations and interactions with other people. We have to use much energy to correctly "read" the situation around us. This type of response can become very stressing, often resulting in psychological shock. It is something that each individual must work out on his or her own terms. It cannot be done for us. If you travel, you may have seen some Americans trying to avoid culture shock by staying in American hotels, only associating with fellow Americans, and eating American food while abroad—the "McDonald Syndrome".

Ethnologists must not only be trained in scientific methodology and theory, but they must also be acutely aware of potential **ethical problems** while working in a field setting. Often anthropologists are privy to information that may cause embarrassment or even harm to the peoples they study. Ethnologists attempt to keep such information confidential. Many times the real identities of key informants are kept secret, and pseudonyms may be used in place of real individual, village, culture, or area names. **Ethical guidelines** have been published by the American Anthropological Association for individuals contemplating or engaged in fieldwork.

Sociocultural systems are composed of numerous **variables** that interact in a functioning whole. Anthropologists are interested in delineating and studying these variables. The major variables that are of interest include (1) subsistence and physical environment, (2) demography, (3) technology, (4) economy, (5) social structure, (6) political organization, and (7) religion. Cause and effect relationships among different variables are very important in anthropological analysis of sociocultural systems. Anthropologists use a multidimensional approach when they examine the interaction among a variety of variables. This perspective and methodology provide explanations for the similarities and differences observed among societies.

The interaction between the environment and **subsistence patterns** is of particular interest to many anthropologists. They examine different **biomes** (major environmental areas characterized by a particular climate and certain types of plants and animals, e.g., tropical rainforest, Arctic tundra) in order to determine the influence of the environment on societal development. How humans adapt, both culturally and biologically, to varying environments is often a key to understanding similarities or differences among cultures.

The size, composition, and distribution of human populations are studied by **demographic anthropologists** interested in the dynamics of the population. Three key variables are examined: **fertility**, **mortality**, and **migration**. These variables are responsible for the growth, decline, or stability of populations. An understanding of the major demographic variables may provide insight into interpreting other features and cultural practices of a people.

In an analysis of society and culture, **technological** and **economic** variables must be considered. A society's technology and economy produce distinctive differences in the **division of labor**. Cultural values and norms influence the technology and economic conditions. There are two ways of examining economic systems. The **formalist** approach assumes that all economic systems are similar and can be compared. Formalists think that all peoples attempt to maximize their returns. They argue that all cultures can be studied using modern, Western economic theory. **Substantivists**, on the other hand, argue that each economic system is unique because it is part of a particular sociocultural system, including its values, beliefs, mores, and norms. This is essentially a cultural relativist view of economics. Today, both approaches are usually combined in a single study.

Social structure provides the building blocks for a society. An important feature of social structure is **status** or the position a person occupies within a society. This status is usually composed of **ascribed** and **achieved** components. Inequity in status usually leads to **social stratification**.

When analyzing any society, anthropologists study major social components such as the family, marriage, kinship, residence patterns, divorce, gender, and age. One of the most basic units in almost all societies is the **family**, a social group composed of two or more people related by blood, marriage, or adoption who reside together, sharing economic resources and caring for their children. Two common types of families are found across the world. **Nuclear families** are composed of two parents and their children (their own or adopted), while **extended families** are basically nuclear families plus other kin.

Marriages are important not only for producing families but are often integral parts of larger social networks involving subsistence patterns, economics, politics, and other social features. Many societies have **marriage rules** that prescribe who one can marry and who one should not marry. **Endogamous** marriages are those between two individuals who belong to the same social group or category, while **exogamous** marriages are unions between people from different groups. Even though **monogamy** is the most frequent form of marriage (primarily because of economics), many societies allow individuals to have multiple spouses (**polygamy**). One can either have multiple wives (**polygyny**) or multiple husbands (**polyandry**).

Gender relations comprise an important part of the social matrix of any society. Gender, specific traits attached to each sex by the society, is based on cultural criteria. On the other hand, **sex** refers to the biological and morphological differences between males and females. Anthropologists are interested in gender roles, the relationship between gender and the division of labor in societies, gender and status, and gender and enculturation.

Age is a universally recognized feature that is used to prescribe status. The human life cycle provides the basis for status and roles that have both a cultural and biological dimension. Societies divide the human life cycle into categories, often assigning specific roles and statuses to particular stages or **age grades**. One of the more interesting aspects of the life cycle are the **rites of passage** that are associated with changes in status. These rites have been the focus of many anthropological inquires.

Anthropologists explore different types of **political organizations** and **legal systems**. Based on detailed ethnographies and cross-cultural comparisons, anthropologists have concluded that specific types of political and legal systems have been influenced by a variety of social conditions. In order to analyze different forms of political systems, anthropologists classify societies into **bands, tribes, chiefdoms**, and **states**. These different types of societies will be discussed in the chapters that follow.

The anthropology of **religion** is devoted to the examination of the diverse religious beliefs and **worldviews** found throughout the world. Myths, rituals, religious specialists (**shamans** and **priests** or **priestesses**), and **religious movements** are examined in relationship to other aspects of the society of which they are a part.

The immense complexities involved in analyzing culture and society are recognized by anthropologists. Anthropologists cannot isolate a single variable as determining conditions within a society. They must use a multidimensional approach in exploring the interconnections among different variables. Part of this exploration involves comparing and contrasting cultural practices across the world (**cross-cultural research**). Cross-cultural studies provide us with information on the diversity and similarities of the human experience.

Much of the rest of the text is devoted to examining the features discussed in this chapter as they relate to bands, tribes, chiefdoms, and states. You might find it helpful to refer back to this chapter from time to time for basic definitions and a focus.

<u>Terms and Concepts You Should Know</u>

naturalistic observation (268):

time-allocation (268):

participant observation (268):

random sample (269):

quantitative data (269-270):

qualitative data (269-270):

culture shock (270):

independent variable (273-274):

dependent variable (273-274):

ecology (274):

niche (274):

biome (275):

demography (275):

fertility and mortality (275):

fecundity (277):

carrying capacity (277):

division of labor (279):

formalism or formalist (279):

substantivism or substantivist (279):

status (280):

ascribed status (280):

achieved status (280):

family (280):

family of orientation (280):

family of procreation (28):

nuclear family (281):

extended family (281):

marriage (281):

endogamy (281):

exogamy (281):

monogamy (281):

polygamy (281):

polygyny (281):

polyandry (281):

gender versus sex (281-282):

age grade (283):

rite of passage (284):

band (284-285):

tribe (285):

chiefdom (285):

state (285):

sanctions (286):

religion (288):

myth (289):

ritual (289):

shaman (289):

priest or priestess (289):

People to Know About

Arnold Van Gennep (284):

Thinking About What You Have Read

The following questions or problems may be of help to you in studying the material presented in both the text and in your class. You may want to write out the answers to these questions (writing something down always seems to help solidify it in one's mind) or just think about them.

1. How do anthropologists conduct ethnological fieldwork. Are there problems that one should be aware of while doing this type of research?

2. What is demography? Why is it important to anthropology? What variables do demographic anthropologists study? Explain what they are and their importance in studying the demographic patterns of a society.

3. Compare and contrast the formalist and substantivist views to studying the economy. If you had to use either of these approaches, which one would you use and why?

4. What is social structure? What are some of the important components of social structure?

5. What is a family? What are some of the functions a family fulfills? What forms does the family take?

6. How are sex, gender, enculturation, division of labor, and status related?

7. How does age relate to enculturation, division of labor, and status? Give examples from your own culture.

8. What is a rite of passage? Have you ever gone through a rite of passage? Why are rites of passage important? What is their purpose?

9. What is a political organization? What roles do political power and authority play in the political organization of a society?

10. What is religion and worldview? How are these studied by anthropologists?

11. How is ethnological research conducted? What research strategies are employed by anthropologists in the field?

12. What are some of the ethical concerns of anthropologists who conduct ethnological research?

13. What is a subsistence pattern? Why are subsistence patterns of interest to anthropologists?

14. Think about the members of your family; now diagram (using triangles for males and circles for females) your family of orientation and family of procreation. Who are members of your nuclear family, your extended family? Does your culture practice any type of exogamy or endogamy? Is polygamy (either polygyny or polyandry) allowed? If so, what are some of the features? If not, why not?

15. Discuss how the human life cycle is the basis of social statuses and roles that have both a biological and cultural dimension.

16. How do you define "old age"? Take a survey of your friends and family and see if there is any variation in the definition of "old age." Do you think that different cultures define "old age" differently, or are specific age categories universally set by the biological phenomenon of aging? Do the "aged" occupy the same roles and statuses in all societies? How are "old people" viewed in the United States?

17. How do anthropologists study religion? What are some of the goals of these studies? What types of questions about religion do anthropologists avoid?

CHECKING YOUR UNDERSTANDING: A PRACTICE EXAMINATION

We suggest that you take this practice exam and then check your answers against the key provided at the end of this section. Use the questions that you got wrong as a guide to further study. Try to learn why specific answers are right and wrong. You might even consider taking this practice test more than once, several days apart.

True-False Questions

1. Time-allocation studies have been used by anthropologists to assess how different societies use their time in various activities.

2. When anthropologists study a culture by asking anyone they happen to meet about the culture, they are employing the research strategy called random sampling.

3. A person who experienced profound depression after spending time living in a foreign country may have suffered from culture shock.

4. An ethnography is a written description of a culture.

5. An environmental niche refers to the locale that contains various plants, animals, and other ecological conditions to which a species must adapt.

6. A biome is a type of armed combat occurring *within* a political community and usually involves one kin group taking revenge against another kin group.

7. Fertility, or the potential number of children that women in a society are capable of bearing, exerts a major influence on the actual fecundity of the women.

8. A demographic study of a society is crucial for understanding population change, distribution, and composition.

9. The carrying capacity is the maximum population that can be supported in a specific region.

10. The carrying capacity for a given biome cannot be changed.

11. Social structure provides the framework for all human societies.

12. Exploring the causes of differing patterns of social stratification and how they relate to other facets of society is an important objective in ethnological research.

13. A nuclear family consists of two parents, their parents, and the children of the parents.

14. The family is a universal aspect of social organization.

15. Polygyny is the marriage between one husband and two or more wives.

16. Polygyny and polyandry are two different forms of polygamy.

17. For anthropologists, sex and gender are the same thing.

18. In the United States, the following designations convey a particular social status: "preschool", "kindergarten", "elementary school", and "high school". These designations are what anthropologists call age grades.

19. Since the individuals within bands, tribes, and chiefdoms are related, these are also known as kin-structured societies.

20. States are political systems with centralized bureaucratic institutions to establish power and authority over large populations in distinctive territories.

21. Since warfare, violence, and aggression are all genetic traits that are inherited, human beings must continually suppress these traits using various cultural means so that there is not warfare and aggression in every society at all times.

22. For an anthropologist the term "myth" applies to specific religious beliefs that have been found to be false or incorrect through scientific scrutiny.

23. Shamans are part-time religious practitioners who are believed to have contact with supernatural forces and beings.

24. Cross-cultural research is an important component of many anthropological studies.

25. The HRAF contains descriptive ethnographic data on more than 300 societies.

26. An ethnologist who collects most of her information by talking to two or three elderly women would be making use of:
    A. time-allocation analysis
    B. naturalistic observation
    C. key informants
    D. archival information

27. Asking for answers to the same series of questions from all adult males in a community would be an example of:
    A. structured interviews
    B. unstructured interviews
    C. random sampling
    D. qualitative evaluation

28. In a random sample of ethnographic information:
    A. only quantitative data can be collected
    B. each individual has an equal chance of being interviewed
    C. key informants play the most important role
    D. the ethnographer is unaware of her results

29. Qualitative data is:
    A. non-statistical information
    B. highly subjective
    C. rarely collected
    D. statistical information

30. An ethnographer who made extensive use of photographs and videos of her informants would be doing:
    A. forensic anthropology
    B. ethnohistory
    C. visual anthropology
    D. oral history

31. An ethnography is:
    A. a research question about a foreign culture
    B. the norms, values, and ideas of a given society
    C. a description of a society
    D. a map or other graphic representation of a given culture.

32. An ethnographer, in describing the culture she is studying, seeks to:
    A. present the views of her informants as if they were her own
    B. offer a critique based on her own cultural values
    C. reveal the identities of all informants and collaborators
    D. reduce or eliminate bias, distortion, and error

33. If a study revealed that low income and family violence regularly occurred together, these two cultural variables could be said to be:
    A. dependent
    B. independent
    C. correlated
    D. uncorrelated

34. If it could be demonstrated that the age of first sexual intercourse had a direct effect on the number of children per couple, the age of first intercourse would be:
    A. an independent variable
    B. a dependent variable
    C. a multidimensional variable
    D. a spurious correlation

35. One of the principal arguments of the postmodernist critique of ethnographic research is that:
    A. ethnographies are objective science
    B. ethnographic objectivity cannot be achieved
    C. ethnographers must hide their own values
    D. subjectivity is to be avoided at all costs

36. The crude birthrate is defined as the:
    A. total number of births during a 5-year period
    B. number of births per woman in a given population
    C. number of live births per thousand individuals in a year
    D. number of live births per household

37. A population's mortality is calculated on the basis of:
    A. crude death rate
    B. crude birthrate
    C. net migration
    D. total morbidity

38. Which of the following variables does NOT help define a biome?
    A. geographical location
    B. temperature range
    C. population size
    D. annual precipitation

39. The potential number of children to whom a hundred women in a given society can give birth in one year is known as the:
    A. mortality rate
    B. morbidity rate
    C. fertility rate
    D. fecundity

40. Life expectancy represents:
    A. the average age of the oldest individuals
    B. the age at which most adults can expect to die
    C. the number of years the average newborn baby can expect to live
    D. the average age of all living individuals

41. One of the most significant variables affecting life expectancy is:
    A. infant mortality
    B. fecundity
    C. migration
    D. fertility

42. The life expectancy of a population will increase when there is a decrease in:
    A. natural growth rate
    B. crude birth rate
    C. infant mortality
    D. net migration

43. Human technology and cultural innovation will almost always _____ the carrying capacity of a given biome.
    A. increase
    B. decrease
    C. change
    D. conserve

44. The perspective that maintains all economic systems are fundamentally similar and can be compared with one another is called the:
    A. formalist approach
    B. substantivist approach
    C. globalist theory
    D. positivist approach

45. This status is attached to one as a result of birth.
    A. ascribed status
    B. achieved status
    C. neonatal status
    D. formal status

46. The family of _____ is the one in which people are born and receive basic enculturation, and the family of _____ is the family within which people have or adopt children of their own.
    A. procreation / orientation
    B. socialization / reproduction
    C. orientation / procreation
    D. life / enculturation

47. The marriage of a woman to more than one man is known as
    A. polygyny
    B. polyandry
    C. monogamy
    D. manygamy
    E. husbandamy

48. Sex refers to the biological and anatomical differences between males and females, while _____ refers to the specific human traits attached to each sex by society.
    A. status
    B. role
    C. gender
    D. sodality
    E. rite of passage

49. Learning one's culture is known as
    A. acculturation
    B. enculturation
    C. osmosis
    D. symbolic transference

50. Rituals associated with the life cycle and the movement of people between different age status levels is known as
    A. status transfer
    B. role movement
    C. rites of passage
    D. ritual of transference

Suggested Readings

ANDERSON, BARBARA G. 1990. *First Fieldwork: The Misadventures of an Anthropologist*. Prospect Heights, IL: Waveland Press.

BERNARD, H. RUSSELL. 1989. *Research Methods in Cultural Anthropology*. New York, NY: Sage Publications.

BERNARD, H. RUSSELL AND JESUS SALINAS PEDRAZA. 1989. *Native Ethnography: A Mexican Indian Describes His Culture*. Newbury Park, CA: Sage Publications.

BOHANNON, PAUL, ed. 1977. *Law and Warfare: Studies in the Anthropology of Conflict*. Garden City, NY: Natural History Press.

BOHANNON, PAUL AND MARK GLAZER. 1989. *High Points in Anthropology*. New York, NY: McGraw-Hill.

BROWN, DONALD. 1990. *Human Universals*. New York, NY: McGraw Hill.

CAMPBELL, BERNARD. 1983. *Human Ecology: The Story of Our Place in Nature from Prehistory to the Present*. New York, NY: Aldine.

COHEN, RONALD AND JOHN MIDDLETON, eds. 1967. *Comparative Political Systems: Studies in the Politics of Pre-industrial Societies*. Garden City, NY: Natural History Press.

CRANE, JULIA G. AND MICHAEL V. ANGROSINO. 1984. *Field Projects in Anthropology: A Student Handbook*. Prospect Heights, IL: Waveland Press.

DALTON, GEORGE, ed. 1976. *Tribal and Peasant Economies: Readings in Economic Anthropology*. Austin, TX: University of Texas Press.

DEVITA, PHILIP R. 1990. *The Humbled Anthropologist: Tales From the Pacific*. Belmont, CA: Wadsworth Publishing Company.

FETTERMAN, DAVID M. 1989. *Ethnography: Step by Step*. Newbury Park, CA: Sage.

FOX, ROBIN. 1967. *Kinship and Marriage*. Baltimore, MD: Penguin Books.

GARBURN, NELSON, ed. 1971. *Readings in Kinship and Social Structure*. New York, NY: Harper & Row.

HEIDER, KARL G. 1976. *Ethnographic Film.* Austin, TX: University of Texas Press.

JACKSON, BRUCE. 1987. *Fieldwork.* Urbana, IL: University of Illinois Press.

KEESING, ROGER M. 1975. *Kin Groups and Social Structure.* New York, NY: Holt, Rinehart & Winston.

LESSA, WILLIAM A. AND EVON Z. VOGT, eds. 1979. *Reader in Comparative Religion: An Anthropological Approach.* New York, NY: Harper/Row.

MCCURDY, DAVID W. AND JAMES P. SPRADLEY. 1988. *Issues in Cultural Anthropology: Selected Readings.* Prospect Heights, IL: Waveland Press.

OSWALT, WENDELL. 1976. *An Anthropological Analysis of Food-Getting Technology.* New York, NY: Wiley.

SCHUSKY, EARNEST L. 1965. *Manual for Kinship Analysis.* New York, NY: Holt, Rinehart & Winston.

SPRADLEY, JAMES P. 1979. *The Ethnographic Interview.* New York, NY: Holt, Rinehart & Winston.

_____. 1980. *Participant Observation.* New York, NY: Holt, Rinehart & Winston.

SPRADLEY, JAMES P. AND DAVID W. MCCURDY. 1988. *The Cultural Experience: Ethnography in Complex Society.* Prospect Heights, IL: Waveland Press.

STORTI, CRAIG. 1989. *The Art of Crossing Cultures.* Yarmouth, ME: Intercultural Press.

WALLACE, ANTHONY F.C. 1966. *Religion: An Anthropological View.* New York, NY: Random House.

Answer Key with Page Numbers

1. T 268	18. T 283	35. A 271-272
2. F 269	19. T 285	36. C 275
3. T 270	20. T 285	27. A 275
4. T 271	21. F 287	38. C 275
5. T 274	22. F 289	39. D 277
6. F 275	23. T 289	40. C 277
7. F 276-277	24. T 290	41. A 277
8. T 275	25. T 290	42. C 277
9. T 277	26. C 268	43. A 277
10. F 277	27. A 269	44 A 279
11. T 280	28. B 269	45. A 280
12. T 280	29. A 270	46. C 281
28. F 281	30. C 270	47. B 281
14. T 281	31. C 271	48. C 281-282
15. T 281	32. A 271	49. B 283
16. F 281	33. C 271	50. C 284
17. F 282-3	34. A 271	

CHAPTER 15

BAND SOCIETIES

Chapter Highlights

Human societies that are small in size, **seasonally mobile**, and rely primarily on hunting and gathering (also known as **foraging**) for their subsistence are referred to by anthropologists as **band societies**. From the first appearance of humans at around two million years ago until the domestication of plants and animals and the appearance of sedentary, agricultural ways of life around 12,000 years ago, all human societies lived in bands. The band is the form of human society that persisted for the longest period of time. It is also the form that is ancestral to all subsequent societies. Because they were dependent upon wild resources, band societies lived in intimate relationships with the natural world. Although once universal, occupying the richest natural habitats, band societies are now virtually extinct.

Given that all human societies have evolved from band societies, this way of life disappeared in most places as a result of population growth and technological change. Many band societies can be understood only through their archaeological remains. Modern band societies have existed only in remote areas such as deserts, tropical rainforests, and arctic regions - environments that have had little or no value to agricultural peoples. They are not representative of all prehistoric band societies, many of which existed in very rich environments.

The **!Kung San** are a band society of the Kalahari Desert in southwestern Africa. Until recently, they lived by collecting nuts, roots, fruit, and berries. Hunting provided only 20 to 30 percent of the diet. Other desert foragers include the **Shoshone** of the Great Basin in the U.S. and **Australian Aborigines**.

Among tropical rainforest **hunter-gatherers** are the **Mbuti Pygmies** of Zaire. The Mbuti, who have occupied the Ituri Forest for at least 5000 years, live by gathering plants and hunting wild game. Another group is the **Semang** of Malaysia and Thailand, who live by fishing, hunting small game, and gathering wild fruits and vegetables.

Eskimos of the Arctic regions also had a band society based on seasonal hunting and fishing. Vegetable foods were only a small part of their diet. The principal sources of food were whales, seals, and walruses on the coast, while groups farther inland hunted caribou, musk oxen, and occasional polar bears.

Mobility, made necessary by a reliance upon wild resources whose availability varies with season and location, is the most important characteristic of band societies. In order to survive, foragers must know which plants and animals will be abundant in specific locations at specific times of the year. They must also be skilled at obtaining food, especially when resources are scarce.

Another characteristic of band societies is small group size, which becomes essential to survival when food is limited. The specific size of a band is dependent upon the carrying capacity of the environment given a specific subsistence technology. Band societies have a variety of means by which they limit population size. Methods of population control include **fissioning**, **infanticide**, abortion, delayed **menarche** (menstruation) due to low body fat or physiological stress, and increased **birth spacing** due to prolonged breast-feeding or sexual abstinence.

The technologies used by foraging societies are ingenious and highly effective, making use of stone, wood, bone, horn, ivory, fibers, sinews, leather, and other natural materials. Hunting implements include **throwing sticks**, bows and arrows, blowguns, spears, harpoons, traps, and snares. The most common all-purpose tool was the **digging stick**. Foragers also used a variety of nets, bags, bowls, and **grinding stones**. Travel was assisted by the use of canoes and dogsleds.

Foraging societies utilized a reciprocal economic system that enabled them to remain egalitarian. Differences in social status were determined by age, sex, skill, and knowledge rather than personal wealth. **Reciprocity**, or sharing, helped to maintain close ties between individuals. Property was owned collectively, rather than individually. **Marshall Sahlins** called the band **"the original affluent society"** based on the data indicating foragers spent only a few hours a day collecting food and therefore had a great deal of leisure time. **Richard Lee** and **Irven DeVore**, who conducted research on the !Kung San, came to the conclusion that foragers were usually healthy and well nourished. These interpretations have been challenged by ethnographers who dispute Sahlins' time allocation data and by medical research that shows that the !Kung San suffered from inadequate caloric intake and periodic starvation. However, it is important to remember that conditions of modern hunter-gatherers living in **marginal environments** may not be typical of past societies.

Bands are usually composed of clusters of nuclear families, and may contain up to five or more **extended families**. **Monogamy** is the most common marriage practice, and marital arrangements are typically used to strengthen alliance within or between bands. **Brideservice** is a custom in which a man lives with his wife's parents' band (**matrilocal residence**) for a certain amount of time before the couple returns to his father's band (**patrilocal residence**). **Wife exchange** and divorce are also practiced by foraging societies.

The division of labor in band societies is usually based on gender. The most typical arrangement is that men are responsible for hunting and fishing, while women collect plant foods and care for infants. However, the relative importance of these activities varies widely. Gender relations are more **egalitarian** in foraging societies than in other societies. Another important basis for status is age. Roles for children and the elderly are closely linked to specific subsistence strategies. Although the elderly make fewer direct contributions to hunting or gathering, they serve as important sources of knowledge about long-term cycles, human relationships, and spiritual matters.

Leadership in foraging societies is informal and situational. Political leaders, chosen to resolve specific problems on a temporary basis, are not allowed to control economic resources and do not have a substantially higher social status than other members of the band. A pattern of **reverse dominance** ensures that the group will control anyone who tries to exert undue authority, and serves as a leveling mechanism to maintain an egalitarian structure.

In general, foraging societies are peaceful. Warfare is occasional and sporadic, as is any type of violence or homicide. The flexible structure of band societies, which can fission if tensions become too great, serves to reduce conflict. Individual behavior is moderated by group approval or disapproval, often based in certain age groups. Among the Mbuti, for example, children play a key role by ridiculing individuals who are selfish or lazy. More serious conflicts are resolved by respected elders.

The religions of modern foragers are usually based on the natural environment. **Animism**, the belief that both animate and inanimate objects have spirits, is common to many band societies. The Australian notion of **"dreamtime"** is part of a **cosmology** in which ancestral beings interact with the living. The order it conveys provides a moral structure for Aborigine behavior relative to one another and to the environment. Eskimo religion involves the actions of a **shaman**, a curer or healer who can assist with physical, emotional, and spiritual growth for individuals or the community.

Terms and Concepts You Should Know

hunter-gatherer (294):

forager (294):

marginal environment (294):

fissioning (298):

infanticide (299):

fertility (299):

menarche (299):

digging stick (300):

reciprocal exchange system (300):

reciprocity (300):

generalized reciprocity (300):

egalitarian society (301):

balanced reciprocity (301):

negative reciprocity (301):

altruism (301):

communistic society (301):

"original affluent society" (302):

band (303):

extended family (303):

cross-cousin marriage (304):

restricted marital exchange (304):

brideservice (304):

matrilocal residence (304):

wife exchange (305):

division of labor (306):

patriarchal societies (307):

rites of passage (307):

hopi (307):

Elima (307, 312):

restrained warfare (310):

song duel (311):

animism (311):

dreamtime (311):

soul loss (312):

shamanism (312):

People to Know About

Richard Lee (295):

Colin Turnbull (296):

Marshall Sahlins (302):

Cultures to Know About

!Kung San (295):

Shoshone (296):

Arunta (296):

Mbuti (296):

Semang (297):

Eskimo (297):

Batak (306):

Thinking About What You Have Read

The following questions or problems may be of help to you in studying the material presented in both the text and in your class. You may want to write out the answers to these questions (writing something down always seems to help solidify it in one's mind) or just think about them.

1. What are some of the reasons that 99% of human existence has been characterized by the predominance of band societies?

2. How can a band limit population growth so that it is not exhausting the availability of natural resources? Which methods would be considered short-term solutions and which would be long-term?

3. Describe the characteristics of fertility, mortality, and life expectancy in band societies. What are the principal factors that influence each?

4. If you were a hunter-gatherer in the savannah regions of South Africa, what tools would you make and use on a regular basis? (Respond in a way appropriate to your gender.)

5. If you were a hunter-gatherer living in a wet, tropical rain forest, what would be the principal activities of the opposite sex? (Respond in a way appropriate to your gender.)

6. What are the three principal kinds of reciprocity (as described by Sahlins)? In what social contexts among gatherers does each of these kinds of exchange take place?

7. What is the nature of political leadership in a band society? What are its principal characteristics, and why is this so?

8. Give an example of a religious practice characteristic of a hunting and gathering society. What are the principal differences between religion in band societies and the religious activities practiced in our society?

241

9. Foraging societies usually engage in very limited warfare. What are some of the reasons that have been given for this pattern of conflict? How does this type of warfare contrast with modern warfare conducted by industrial nations?

10. Pick any leader with whom you are familiar and examine his or her leadership skills. Is the leader you chose exemplifying any of the characteristics discussed on pages 309-311 that typify leaders in band societies? If so, what are those characteristics? Is the leader you have chosen to examine doing anything that is different from that done by leaders of bands?

11. Outline the marital patterns found in forager groups. Are these patterns random, or are they related to other aspects of the culture? For example, what is the purpose of specific types of cousin marriages and post-marital residence rules?

12. Describe the concept of "dreamtime". Why is this belief and the associated behavior important to Australian Aborigines? Can you think of any parallels from your own experiences?

CHECKING YOUR UNDERSTANDING: A PRACTICE EXAMINATION

We suggest that you take this practice exam and then check your answers against the key provided at the end of this section. Use the questions that you got wrong as a guide to further study. Try to learn why specific answers are right and wrong. You may even want to take the practice exam a second time to review what you have learned.

True-False Questions

1. Modern hunting and gathering societies exist in isolation from modern industrial societies.

2. Today, most foraging societies are found in marginal environments.

3. Anthropological research has recently shown that because of the complexity of tropical regions, foragers have never been able to adapt to tropical forest environments.

4. Foraging societies have existed in all natural environments except the cold Arctic regions.

242

5. Most hunter-gatherer societies are sedentary, occupying a single settlement throughout the year.

6. Hunter-gatherers have a limited technology, consisting of elementary stone tools, because of the simplicity of their minds and the lack of skill inherent in a forager way of life.

7. All hunter-gatherers are distinguished by infrequent use of clothing.

8. Much of the technology involved in hunter-gatherer societies consists of sophisticated cultural knowledge concerning such things as where to find plants and animals, which ones are poisonous and edible, what plants and animals are scarce or abundant, and how resources fluctuate over the seasons.

9. The major form of economic system identified with band societies is known as a reciprocal economic system.

10. A type of reciprocal exchange that carries with it an explicit expectation of immediate return is know as instantaneous reciprocity.

11. Another word for negative reciprocity is theft.

12. Morgan's view that band societies were "communistic" because everyone shared the productive technology and economic resources is considered to be too simplistic.

13. The !Kung San never complain about having to share what they have with other members of their community.

14. The !Kung population has always been on the edge of starvation, and no individuals have ever lived beyond the age of 60.

15. Recent research has challenged the idea that all foragers represent the "original affluent society" because time-allocation studies of the Ache foragers of eastern Paraguay have shown that males spend about 40 to 50 hours per week in the quest for special kinds of food.

16. The specific number of people within a band depends on the carrying capacity of the natural environment.

17. Brideservice refers to the work that a woman must do for her husband's family after they are married.

18. Most marriages in forager societies are based on the universal concept of love.

19. Ethnological research has shown that gender roles in forager societies are often associated with the basic division of labor.

20. Ethnologists have found that warfare among foragers is widespread, very violent, and seemingly unending because band leaders are continually looking for new territories to conquer and occupy.

Multiple Choice Questions

21. The term "Paleolithic lifestyle" evokes for anthropologists a society that:
    A. is small in size and highly mobile
    B. exists as a large, sedentary community
    C. is organized as a tribe with a powerful chief
    D. subsists on domesticated plants and animals

22. For 99% of human existence, foraging societies were most numerous in:
    A. marginal environments
    B. rich environments
    C. tropical forests
    D. deserts and savannahs

23. Hunting and gathering lifeways have persisted in marginal environments because:
    A. those are the only types of environments in which they can exist
    B. hunting and gathering lifeways are very ancient
    C. foragers always live a marginal existence
    D. there is little competition for these environments from other groups

24. The study of foraging societies (hunter-gatherers) is important because
    A. foragers can survive for long periods of time without eating or drinking, thus giving us a basis to examine starvation
    B. foraging was the mode of subsistence for almost 99% of humanity's existence on earth
    C. foragers have a very sophisticated, complex technology that allows them to adapt readily to any environment
    D. foragers are able to make plants grow and produce food in almost any climate
    E. these groups lack leadership, cohesion, and family units; yet, they have survived for years

25. The !Kung San are a hunting and gathering society that has been the object of study in:
    A. Central Australia
    B. the Great Basin of the western U.S.
    C. the Kalahari Desert
    D. the Amazon rainforest

26. As shown by the study of the !Kung San, foragers
    A. must rise with first light of day and work until sundown in order to find enough to eat
    B. are almost always on the brink of starvation
    C. lead short, nasty, brutish lives
    D. only have to work at actual food procurement for about two to three days each week to get enough food to survive
    E. are unhealthy, as a rule

27. Anthropologist Richard Lee has estimated that the traditional !Kung San spent between _____ days each week finding food.
    A. 2 to 3
    B. 4 to 5
    C. 5 to 6
    D. 6 to 7

28. The time required to find food by foragers in the Kalahari Desert:
    A. keeps them constantly occupied with subsistence activities
    B. places significant restrictions on their ability to move around the land-scape
    C. leaves them with plenty of leisure time to play games or tell stories
    D. forces men, in particular, to devote most waking hours to hunting

29. Among the foods eaten by the Shoshone are:
   A. seeds and insects ground into a flour
   B. kangaroos, wallabees, and emus
   C. elephants, buffalo, and wild pigs
   D. raw whale meat and boiled blubber

30. Archaeological research in the Ituri rainforest suggests that the hunting and gathering lifestyle of the Mbuti is:
   A. relatively recent, dating to about 500 years ago
   B. unlikely to leave any datable traces
   C. very ancient, having lasted for over 5000 years
   D. all that is left of a once powerful and complex civilization

31. In the traditional society of the Mbuti pygmies of the Ituri rainforest, hunting is undertaken by:
   A. the older men of the village
   B. men, youths, women, and children
   C. boys who have undergone sacred puberty rites
   D. adult women of the hunting clans

32. The Semang of Malaysia, who hunt with blowguns, get most of their meat from:
   A. elephants and buffalo
   B. kangaroos and the ostrich-like emu
   C. fish, birds, and other small game
   D. monkeys and crocodiles

33. Hunting and gathering groups are characterized by:
   A. fission in the face of scarce resources
   B. year-round permanence of occupation
   C. rapid demographic expansion
   D. maintenance of stored food resources

34. For foraging groups, having too few people can result in:
   A. increased population pressure
   B. an increase in infanticides
   C. inefficient foraging strategies
   D. increased competition for abundant resources

35. There are a number of ways that foragers control their populations; among these are
   A. fissioning and infanticide
   B. warfare and raiding
   C. artificial birth control and warfare
   D. preferential male infanticide and mandatory gerontocide and senilicide

36. In the Great Basin, spring and fall are the times of the year when resources are most abundant, while summer and winter are seasons of scarcity. A woman is probably most likely to consider killing her baby if it is born in:
    A. March
    B. December
    C. August
    D. April

37. Birth spacing is a strategy for:
    A. increasing mobility
    B. decreasing mobility
    C. increasing family size
    D. taking advantage of abundant resources

38. Among the !Kung San, who subsist on a low caloric diet and expend a high level of energy, the onset of menstruation usually occurs:
    A. a few years earlier than the average in the U.S.
    B. a few years later than the average in the U.S.
    C. at the same age as the average in the U.S.
    D. between the ages of 19 and 22

39. The most likely reason why hunter-gatherer technology is limited to simple tools made of stone, wood, and bone is because foraging peoples:
    A. lack the basic intelligence necessary to make anything more complex
    B. are too busy looking for food to spend time on more advanced tools
    C. have not acquired knowledge of more sophisticated technologies
    D. have little use for objects that are expensive to make and to carry

40. An important mechanism for reducing envy and social tensions, distributing resources, and increasing cooperation among individuals in small-scale societies is:
    A. generosity in gift-giving
    B. designation of property rights
    C. barter
    D. wife-swapping

41. A common form of generalized reciprocity in our society is:
    A. common acceptance of the value of the dollar
    B. communal use of public restrooms
    C. a salary increase accompanying a job promotion
    D. getting and giving birthday presents

42. Despite the vast differences with respect to the physical environments, subsistence patterns, and technologies, most foraging societies have similar economic systems. The major form of economic exchange found in these societies is based on the premise of
   A. supply and demand
   B. what's mine is mine
   C. reciprocity
   D. false promises
   E. scarce commodities

43. Reciprocity means:
   A. trade or barter
   B. uneven exchange of goods and services
   C. a balanced economy
   D. sharing

44. "Negative reciprocity" is a term that refers to:
   A. a trade deficit
   B. theft of property
   C. currency devaluation
   D. common forms of gift giving

45. The !Kung San term *hxaro* refers to:
   A. a system for circulating material possessions among individuals
   B. a complex ritual performed by young boys before their first hunt
   C. trade with their agricultural neighbors
   D. a type of root obtained in the spring with pointed digging sticks

46. Examples of foraging groups include all of the following except
   A. !Kung
   B. Ache
   C. Mbuti
   D. Yanomamö
   E. Semang

47. It has been suggested that in forager societies that the more concentrated and the greater the predictability of resources,
   A. the less likely that the group will be egalitarian in nature.
   B. the least amount of reciprocity will occur.
   C. the more pronounced the conceptions of private ownership and exclusive rights to territories.
   D. the more likely it will be that negative reciprocity will occur when individuals meet.

48. A principal criticism of the theory that hunter-gatherers work fewer hours than do agriculturalists is that:
    A. it was based on the idea of work as only meaning working for food
    B. it took into account labor expended in toolmaking, cooking, and healing
    C. it was based mostly on archaeological evidence
    D. it neglected to take relations of reciprocity into account

49. Marital arrangements in foraging societies
    A. are usually made by the couple involved after they fall in love with each other.
    B. are intended to enhance economic, social, and political interdependence among bands and to promote band alliances.
    C. are random in nature because the bands are always on the move from one place to another and individuals cannot predict who they will meet in the future.
    D. must be approved by the chief before the couple can be married.

50. Warfare in forager societies is limited in nature because (which reason below is INCORRECT?):
    A. interpersonal competition is discouraged and these societies do not have a competitive male-status hierarchy.
    B. public displays of interpersonal violence and aggression are not culturally valued.
    C. property rights are not restricted in the sense that there is an emphasis on resource sharing.
    D. hunter-gatherers simply do not have the technological capabilities of making weapons of war.

Suggested Readings

BALIKCI, ANSEN. 1970. *The Netsilik Eskimo*. Garden City, NY: Natural History Press.

BICCHIERI, M.G., ed. 1972. *Hunters and Gatherers Today*. New York: Holt, Rinehart & Winston.

DAHLBERG, FRANCES, ed. 1978. *Woman the Gatherer*. New Haven, CT: Yale University Press.

DYSON-HUDSON, RADA, & ERIC ALDEN SMITH. 1978. "Human territoriality: An ecological reassessment." *American Anthropologist* 80(1):21-41.

EMBER, CAROL. 1978. "Myths about hunter-gatherers." *Ethnology* 17:439-448.

FRIED, MORTON. 1967. *The Evolution of Political Society: An Essay in Political Anthropology*. New York: Random House.

GLASCOCK, ANTHONY P. 1981. "Social assets or social burden: Treatment of the aged in non-industrial societies." In C.L. Fry, ed. *Dimensions: Aging, Culture and Health*. New York: Praeger.

HILL, K., H. KAPLAN, K. HAWKES, & A.M. HURTADO. 1985. "Men's time allocation to subsistence work among the Ache of eastern Paraguay." *Human Ecology* 13:29-47.

HOWELL, NANCY. 1979. *Demography of the Dobe !Kung*. New York: Academic Press.

LEE, RICHARD B. 1979. *The !Kung San: Men, Women, and Work in a Foraging Society*. Cambridge: Cambridge University Press.

_____. 1984. *The Dobe !Kung*. New York: Holt, Rinehart & Winston.

LEE, RICHARD B., & IRVEN DeVORE, eds. 1968. *Man the Hunter*. Chicago: Aldine.

MARTIN, KAY, & BARBARA VOORHIES. 1975. *Female of the Species*. New York: Columbia University Press.

SAHLINS, MARSHALL. 1972. *Stone Age Economics*. Chicago: Aldine.

SERVICE, ELMAN. 1979. *The Hunters*, 2nd ed. Englewood Cliffs, NJ: Prentice Hall.

SERVICE, ELMAN, & MARSHALL SAHLINS. 1960. *Evolution and Culture*. Ann Arbor: University of Michigan Press.

SHOSTAK, MARJORIE. 1981. *Nisa: The Life and Worlds of a !Kung Woman*. New York: Vintage Books.

STANNER, W.E.H. 1958. "The dreaming." In W.A. Lessa & E.Z. Vogt,eds. *Reader in Comparative Religion*. New York: Harper & Row.

TURNBULL, COLIN. 1961. *The Forest People: A Study of the Pygmies of the Congo*. New York: Simon & Schuster.

_____. 1972. *The Mountain People*. New York: Simon & Schuster.

YELLEN, JOHN. 1985. "Bushmen." *Science* 85:40-48.

Answer Key with Page Numbers

1. F 294
2. T 294-295
3. F 296
4. F 297
5. F 297
6. F 299
7. F 300
8. T 300
9. T 300
10. F 301
11. T 301
12. T 301
13. F 301
14. F 302
15. T 303
16. T 303
17. F 304

18. F 304-305
19. T 306
20. F 310
21. A 294
22. B 294
23. D 294
24. B 294
25. C 295
26. D 296
27. A 296
28. C 296
29. A 296
30. C 296
31. B 297
32. C 297
33. A 298
34. C 298

35. A 298-299
36. B 299
37. A 299
38. B 299
39. D 300
40. A 300
41. D 300
42. C 300
43. D 300
44. B 301
45. A 301
46. D 301-303
47. C 302
48. A 303
49. B 304
50. D 310

CHAPTER 16

TRIBES

Chapter Outline

Environment and Subsistence for Horticulturalists
Amazon Horticulturalists: The Yanomamö
New Guinea Horticulturalists: The Tsembaga
Horticulturalists in Woodland Forest Areas: The Iroquois
Environment and Subsistence for Pastoralists
East African Cattle Complex
THE NUER
Demographics and Settlement
Technology
Horticulturalist Technology
Pastoralist Technology
Economics
Money
Property Ownership
Social Organization
Family
Descent Groups
UNILINEAL DESCENT GROUPS
AMBILINEAL DESCENT GROUPS
BILATERAL DESCENT GROUPS
CLANS
PHRATRIES AND MOIETIES
Functions of Descent Groups
DESCENT GROUPS AND ECONOMIC RELATIONSHIPS
Marriage
POLYGYNY
BRIDEWEALTH EXCHANGE
POLYANDRY
THE LEVIRATE AND SORORATE
POSTMARITAL RESIDENCE RULES IN TRIBAL SOCIETIES
CAUSES OF POSTMARITAL RESIDENCE RULES
GENERALIZATIONS ON MARRIAGE IN TRIBAL SOCIETIES
DIVORCE

Chapter Highlights

In anthropology the term **tribe**, although vague and often criticized, usually means people who depend primarily upon **horticulture** (non-intensive and non-mechanized cultivation of plants) or **pastoralism** (maintenance of domesticated animals) for their **subsistence**. Most horticulturalists and pastoralists supplement their diets by collecting, hunting, fishing, and/or trading with other societies. The term tribe also refers to a form of political complexity and development that lies somewhere between **bands** and **centralized societies**.

Many tropical rainforest horticulturalists rely on **slash-and-burn** (or **swidden**) cultivation. This type of horticulture involves cutting the brush in an area, letting it dry, burning it, and then planting in the burned clearing. The ashes provide nutrients for the crops; however, the soil quickly leaches and a new area must be cleared. The old area is left fallow for a number of years (3 to 15, depending on the region). Two cultures that practice this type of subsistence are the **Yanomamö** (South America) and the **Tsembaga Maring** (Papua New Guinea). Even though most horticulturalists live in tropical rainforest areas, horticulture is not restricted to this biome. Many Native Americas, such as the **Iroquois** of the eastern woodlands, relied on horticulture.

Pastoralist subsistence revolves around the care of domesticated animals. Herds vary in size, type, and composition from region to region. In most cases pastoralists are mobile, often moving with the changing seasons. These movements are not aimless, but are well planned to take advantage of available food and water. Moves are usually coordinated to avoid political conflicts, and they often interface with the activities of other peoples (e.g., horticulturalists in the area with whom they trade). Examples of pastoral populations include the **Nuer** of the southern Sudan, the **Bedouins** of Arabia, the **Basseri** of Iran, and the **Tungus** of Siberia.

Food production raises the **carrying capacity** of the environment allowing tribal societies have greater population densities than foragers. Growth of the population is, however, slow because resources are usually limited. The technology of tribal groups is varied and broad. Horticulturalists usually have more material possessions than pastoralists because pastoralists are limited in what they can carry with them from camp to camp.

As in foraging societies, **reciprocity** is the predominant form of economic exchange found in tribal societies. However, unlike foragers, some tribal groups are involved in **monetary exchanges**. **Money**, a medium of exchange based on a standardized value, may take the form of shells, beads, feathers, or animal teeth. Often this money is used for specific purposes and limited exchanges only. The concept of property ownership becomes much more clearly defined in tribal societies than we saw for forager groups. **Corporate** kinship groups (e.g., **lineages** and **clans**) are usually the basis for property ownership.

The social organization of tribal societies is more complex and varied than among forager populations. The most common social unit is the **extended family** which is more stable and effective than the **nuclear family**. Larger social groups are based on **descent rules** (methods of tracing actual or supposed kinship relations).

If descent is traced through only one sex (**matrilineal**, through females or **patrilineal**, through males), it is called **unilineal descent**. If descent is traced through either the male or female line, it is known as **ambilineal descent**. On occasion, groups have what is called **bilateral descent** where relatives are traced through both male and female lines. **Lineages** are unilineal descent groups, the members of which can trace their descent to a common, known ancestor. These lineages can either be **matrilineages** or **patrilineages**. Larger social units, called **clans** (both **matriclans** and **patriclans**) are composed of individuals who purport to be able to trace their descent back to a common ancestor in the distant past (in fact, the ancestor may be a sacred plant or animal). Other, more loosely structured groups such as **phratries** and **moieties** are found in some tribal groups. One can think of these groups as the building blocks of a society: families are composed of individuals, lineages are groupings of families, clans are composed of two or more lineages, phratries consist of two or more clans, moieties are groupings of phratries, and two moieties, when combined make up the whole society. Obviously this is a simplification, but it helps in understanding the structure. These units are multi-functional, and many are **corporate** in nature.

Corporate descent groups play a major role in regulating marital relations within tribal societies. Most marriages are **exogamous** in relation to the descent groups discussed above. Often tribal groups have marriage rules (preferential **cross-cousin marriage**) that insure exogamy by specifying whom one should marry (e.g., mother's brother's daughter). In some patrilineal tribal societies **parallel-cousin marriage** (e.g., father's brother's daughter) ensures that marriages remain within the group (i.e., they are **endogamous** in nature).

In tribal societies marriage tends to be **polygynous**, and it usually involves **bridewealth** exchanges. Some groups practice **monogamy**, while others are **polyandrous**. The corporate nature of descent groups is reflected in two other marriage rules: the **levirate** (widow marries her deceased husband's brother) and **sororate** (widower marries a sister of his deceased wife). These rules ensure that kin ties are maintained, obligations met, and children and spouses cared for after the death of either the husband or wife. **Post-marital residence** and **divorce** are often intimately related to these social units.

Early research on tribes concluded that women had a fairly high **status**. Nonetheless, modern anthropologists tend to find that **patriarchy** dominates these societies. In fact, most anthropologists now argue that no **matriarchal** societies (a pattern where females dominate males economically and politically) have been identified in any archaeological, historical, or ethnological sources. Sometimes patriarchy is associated with **sexism** (prejudice and discrimination against the opposite sex) and the maltreatment of women in tribal groups. Why is patriarchy the **norm**? Researchers are investigating the relationships among subsistence, descent (matrilineal versus patrilineal), warfare, and biology in order to explain the prevalence of patriarchy.

Another important feature of tribal social organization is **age**. In some tribal situations, **age-sets** (corporate groups of individuals of about the same age who share rights and obligations) are the basis of economic, political, and religious organization. Transition from one age set to the next is usually accompanied by a **rite of passage**. In tribal societies an increase in age is often accompanied by an increase in power and prestige. In some situations, actual **gerontocratic** societies have arisen.

Decentralization and the absence of permanent political offices are characteristic of tribal political organization. Anthropologists suggest that these characteristics are the result of the non-permanence and mobility of settlements in both horticultural and pastoral groups. In tribes which depend upon horticultural subsistence strategies, village headmen and big men often organize and arrange intervillage political activities. Leadership is based on personal abilities and qualities. Among pastoralists, the lack of centralized leadership has often led to hierarchical, descent-based political organizations called segmentary lineages.

Warfare is more frequent in tribal societies than in forager groups. Most anthropologists reject the idea that warfare, aggression, and violence are biologically determined. Instead they often use a holistic perspective and focus on environmental, demographic, and sociocultural factors. Many tribal groups have developed more formalized legal mechanisms to deal with conflict resolution. Prominent among these techniques is the use of mediators, ordeals, oaths, or oracles.

Animism, shamanism, witchcraft, and sorcery are typical aspects of tribal religions or worldviews. These beliefs and practices help tribal peoples understand, explain and deal with illness, bad luck, death, and other crises. Tribal religion is often centered around the family. Ancestor worship and spirits communing with the living members of descent groups are common beliefs.

Terms and Concepts You Should Know

tribe (316):

horticulture (317):

slash-and-burn (317):

pastoralists (320):

money (322):

general-purpose money (322):

limited-purpose money (322):

descent group (324):

lineage (324):

consanguineal (consanguines) (324):

affinal (affines) (324):

unilineal descent (324):

patrilineal descent (324,325):

patrilineage (324):

matrilineal descent (324-325):

matrilineage (324):

double descent (324):

ambilineal descent (324):

bilateral descent (324):

kindred (324):

clan (325):

patriclan/matriclan (325):

ego (325):

phratry (phratries) (326):

moiety [moieties] (326):

primogeniture (326):

ultimogeniture (326):

matrilateral cross-cousin marriage (327):

parallel-cousin marriage (328):

polygamy (327):

polygyny (327):

polyandry (328):

fraternal polyandry (328):

levirate (328):

sororate (328):

postmarital residence rules (329):

matrilocal residence (329):

patrilocal (329):

avunculocal (329):

patriarchy (331):

sexism (332):

age sets (333):

gerontocracy (334):

headman (335):

big man (335):

segmentary lineage (336):

complementary opposition (336):

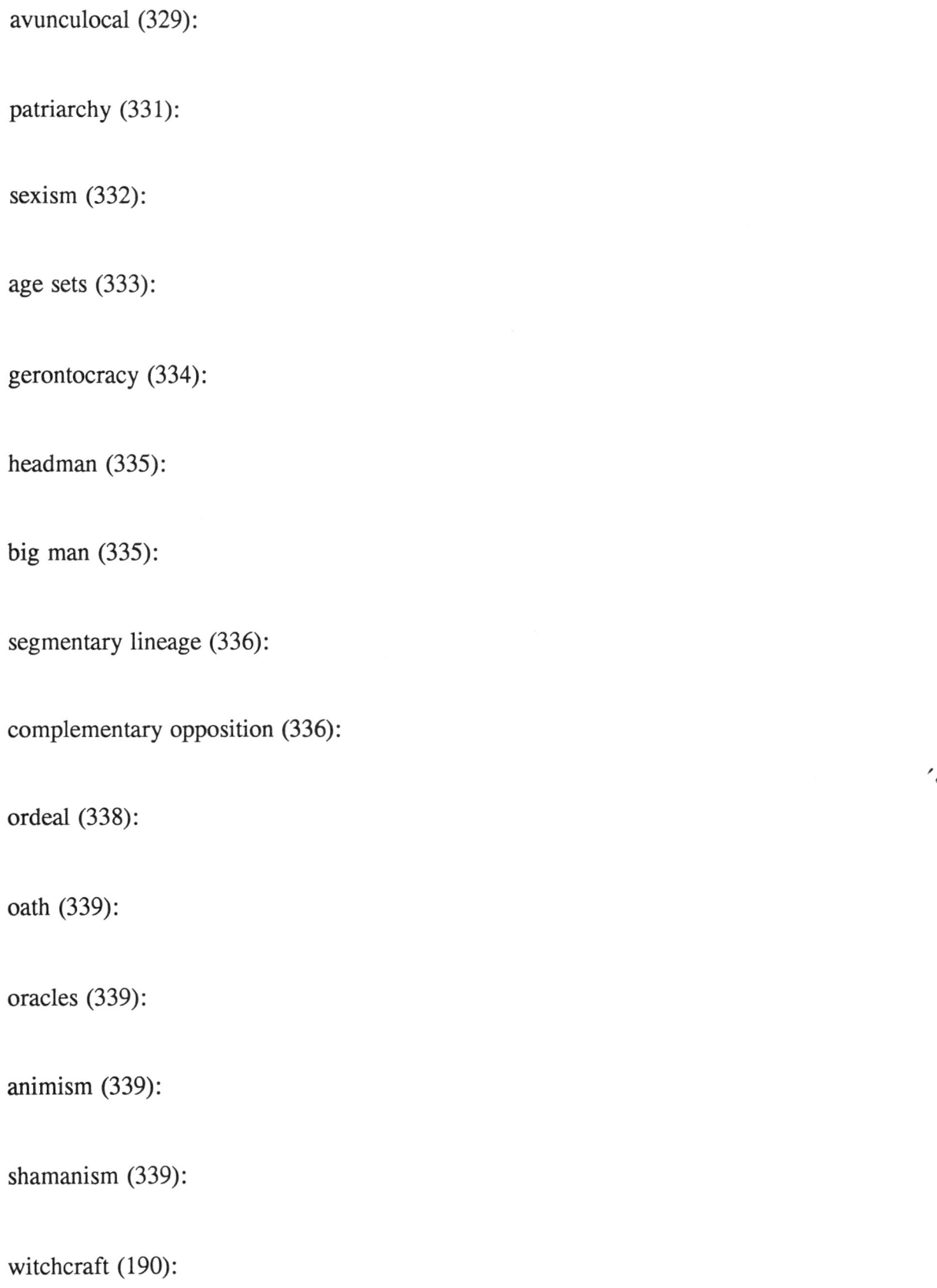

ordeal (338):

oath (339):

oracles (339):

animism (339):

shamanism (339):

witchcraft (190):

sorcery (190):

totem (190):

People to Know About

Napoleon Chagnon (318):

Roy Rappaport (318-319):

E.E. Evans-Pritchard (320):

Margaret Mead (330-331):

Cultures to Know About

Yanomamö (317-8,326-7,337):

Tsembaga Maring (318-9):

Iroquois (319,332-3):

Nuer (320-1,337):

Hopi (324,326):

Arapesh (330):

Mundugumor (330):

Tchambuli (Chambri) (330-1):

Nyakyusa (333):

Sebei (333):

Jivaro (339):

Azande (340):

Navajo (340):

Lugbara (341):

Thinking About What You Have Read

The following questions or problems may be of help to you in studying the material presented in both the text and in your class. You may want to write out the answers to these questions (writing something down always seems to help solidify it in one's mind) or just think about them.

1. What is a tribe? Why does Morton Fried object to the term? What do you think about Fried's arguments?

2. What is horticulture, and how does it differ from agriculture? What is *slash-and-burn horticulture*?

3. Describe, compare, and contrast the horticultural systems of the Yanomamö, the Tsembaga Maring, and the Iroquois.

4. What is pastoralism? Describe the Nuer pastoralist system.

5. Describe the demography and settlement patterns of tribal societies. Compare and contrast them with the demography and settlement patterns of foraging societies.

6. What is money? What are some of its functions? Define, explain, and give examples of general-purpose money and limited purpose money (special-purpose money). Can you identify both types in your society?

7. Describe property ownership in tribal societies. How does it compare to property ownership in foraging societies and in your society?

8. What types of descent groups are found in tribal societies? What types of descent groups do you have in your society?

9. What are some of the differences between a lineage and a kindred?

10. Draw a large kinship chart. Now, identify the following groups: kindred, matrilineage, and patrilineage. Also identify ego's cross-cousins and parallel cousins.

11. What are some of the functions of descent groups?

12. What are the differences between lineages and clans?

13. Describe the various forms of marriage in tribal societies. What are the advantages and disadvantages of monogamy, polyandry, polygyny, preferential cousin marriage (cross-cousin and parallel cousin marriage), bride price, levirate, and sororate?

14. Describe the various postmarital residence rules (patterns) that are found in tribal societies. Are these rules related to other any other aspect(s) of the sociocultural system?

15. How is divorce handled in tribal societies? Is the ease or difficulty of divorce related to any other cultural practice(s)?

16. Describe the role of gender in the social structure of tribal societies. What did Margaret Mead's study in Papua New Guinea show about gender and enculturation? How has her work been reappraised?

17. If Deborah Gewertz's study of the Chambri is accurate, it would seem to indicate that gender roles are more strongly influenced by biological factors and less strongly influenced by cultural factors than we had believed. How does this finding affect such concepts and "battles" as feminism, female rights and equality, male rights, child rights, and gender-role blurring?

18. Patriarchy, not matriarchy, is found throughout the archaeological, historical, and ethnological record. Why is this? How have sociobiologists, cultural materialists, and other anthropologists interpreted and explained this situation?

19. How do gender, subsistence, and female status interrelate? Are there any *causal variables* here? Does females status differ in matrilineal versus patrilineal societies? Describe the roles and status of Iroquois women.

20. How is age dealt with in tribal societies? How are the elderly treated? How does this compare to what happens in your society?

21. What are age sets? Do you belong to an age set? What are age grades? Are you a member of an age grade? Describe age sets among the Nyakyusa and the Sebei.

22. Describe the political organization of tribes. Compare the tribal political organiza-tion with that found in forager societies.

23. What is a gerontocracy? How does it work? Would it work in your society? Are there elements of a gerontocracy in the U.S.?

24. Why do political leaders in tribal societies lack much in the way of coercive power and formal authority? Describe, compare, and contrast the village headman and the big man (Melanesia). Are there any parallels to the village headman and big man in U.S. society?

25. What is a segmentary lineage system? What is complementary opposition, and how does it relate to segmentary lineages?

26. What types of warfare are found in tribal societies? Why do tribes conduct warfare? Describe and critically evaluate the theories that have been proposed to explain warfare, aggression, and violence.

27. Describe the legal systems of tribal societies. How do individuals in tribal societies resolve disputes? What are mediators, ordeals, oracles, and oaths?

28. What is animism and shamanism?

29. What are witchcraft and sorcery? Describe the role of witchcraft and sorcery in tribal societies. Do they work? Why? Do you have elements of witchcraft and sorcery in your society? Do you have magic?

30. What is familistic religion? Describe the ghost lineage among the Lugbara. Are their any elements of familistic religion in your culture?

31. Describe the art and music in tribal societies. Compare and contrast these elements to their counterparts found in forager societies.

CHECKING YOUR UNDERSTANDING: A PRACTICE EXAMINATION

We suggest that you take this practice exam and then check your answers against the key provided at the end of this section. Use the questions that you got wrong as a guide to further study. Try to learn why specific answers are right and wrong. You might even consider taking this practice test more than once, several days apart.

True-False Questions

1. According to many anthropologists, horticulturalists and pastoralists have what are called tribal political systems.

2. Under a slash-and-burn regime, after crops have been planted and harvested for a few year the garden plot is left to fallow for a period of time (3-15 years) in order to ensure continued productivity in the region.

3. Groups whose subsistence activities revolve around the care and maintenance of domesticated animals are called pastoral societies.

4. The care of herd animals requires random, aimless, and often haphazard movements from area to area in order to find water and grazing lands.

5. As humans developed the capacity of produce food, the carrying capacity of particular areas increased to support more people than would have been possible by foraging.

6. Slash-and-burn horticulturalists usually have a sophisticated hunting technology.

7. Unlike foragers, some tribal societies engage in transactions that involve money.

8. Most traditional tribal societies that practiced monetary exchange used limited-purpose money.

9. Tribal social organization is based on family, descent group, gender, and age.

10. The most common social grouping in tribal societies is what is termed the blert by anthropologists.

11. A patrilineage is a unilineal descent group, the members of which trace their descent through females back to a common, known male ancestor.

12. Primogeniture is the practice where land is transmitted from generation to generation to the eldest male.

13. Within tribal societies one function of corporate descent groups is to regulate marriages.

14. A polyandrous marriage is one in which a woman has more than one husband.

15. Postmarital residence is related to the form of descent groups found in the society.

16. Marriages in patrilineal societies tend to be less enduring than those in which matrilineal descent rules are followed.

17. Most tribal societies are matriarchal.

18. Iroquois society was matrilineal.

19. Women's status is generally higher in societies that recognize patrilineal descent.

20. Kinship is the primary basis for political organization, activities, and processes within tribal societies.

21. It has been suggested that since tribal societies often move from area to area because of slash-and-burn horticulture or because of pastoral activities that it is not possible to develop an effective, centralized form of political authority.

22. Since tribal societies are on the move most of the time looking for food, they never have any time to engage in warfare or feuding with other groups.

23. Warfare tends to be more common among foragers, who compete for scarce wild resources, than among horticultural tribes.

24. Many critics of single explanations for tribal warfare suggest that even though demographic and environmental factors are important, they must be combined with critical cultural factors such as prestige, honor, and the enhancement of status.

25. Sorcery is magic used for evil purposes only.

26. A form of food production in which people use a limited, nonmechanized technology to cultivate plants is known as
    A. pastoralism
    B. spot gardening
    C. horticulture
    D. agriculture
    E. foraging

27. Examples of horticultural societies include all of the following except:
    A. Yanomamö
    B. Tsembaga
    C. Iroquois
    D. Nuer

28. Early cultural ecologists assumed that periodic relocations of Yanomamö villages in South America were due to soil depletion caused by slash-and-burn cultivation. However, Chagnon has shown that Yanomamö population movements result mostly from:
    A. lack of adequate sources of fresh water
    B. desire to participate in a cash economy
    C. warfare and conflict with neighboring groups
    D. seasonal variation in fishing resources

29. Research has shown that a Yanomamö garden cleared from tropical forest can be used for approximately _____ before the soil is depleted and weeds take over.
    A. six months
    B. a year
    C. three years
    D. eight years

30. Approximately 80 to 90 percent of the Yanomamö diet comes from:
    A. garden products
    B. hunting wild game
    C. fishing in lakes and rivers
    D. cannibalism

31. The typical Iroquois dwelling was:
    A. a tipi
    B. an igloo
    C. a pithouse
    D. a longhouse

32. The term "fallow" refers to:
    A. any male member of a tribal society
    B. the concept that land must be cared for to be used by the next generation
    C. allowing a plot of land to regain its fertility through natural regeneration
    D. the practice of slashing and burning vegetation to clear land for gardening

33. It is fair to say that the Iroquois diet consisted:
    A. of cultivated plant foods like maize, beans, and squash
    B. of a mixture of hunted and gathered products
    C. of a combination of cultivated products, wild game, and wild plant foods
    D. almost exclusively of deer and fish

34. Most pastoralists are:
    A. seasonally mobile
    B. settled in villages throughout the year
    C. band-level societies
    D. found in coastal regions

35. Many different indigenous societies that are highly dependent on cattle for their principal means of subsistence can be found in:
    A. northwestern Brazil
    B. Papua New Guinea
    C. East Africa
    D. western Australia

36. Societies that base their subsistence activities on the care of domesticated animals are called
    A. animalologists
    B. pastoralists
    C. shepherds
    D. flock cultures
    E. domesticates

267

37. Pastoralists
    A. have population densities that are much less than foragers since pastoralists are nomadic
    B. have population densities that are greater than foragers even though pastoralist are mobile like foragers
    C. move about an undefined territory at random, hoping to find food for their herds
    D. are similar to foragers due to the fact that population growth is rapid and little or no population control is practiced

38. Like other cattle herders of the Sudan and Kenya, the Nuer subsist mainly on:
    A. fresh and salted meat from grain-fed bulls
    B. meat from calves and older animals that die natural deaths
    C. vegetables from household gardens
    D. foods made from blood and milk

39. "Limited-purpose money" differs from "general-purpose money" in that:
    A. it can be used as a medium of exchange for most economic transactions
    B. it serves as a uniform standard of value for goods and services
    C. its standard of value fluctuates radically from one time to another
    D. its use is restricted to the purchase of specific goods or services

40. Unlike foragers, some tribal societies engage in
    A. balanced reciprocity
    B. generalized reciprocity
    C. monetary exchange
    D. negative reciprocity

41. In tribal societies, property rights are usually held by:
    A. families and larger kinship groups
    B. wealthy and powerful warriors and chiefs
    C. individuals, through hereditary inheritance
    D. shamans and religious specialists

42. The most important factors affecting the social organization of tribal societies are:
    A. environmental resources and climate
    B. material culture and technology
    C. religion and ideology
    D. kinship structure and population size

43. Anthropologists define a "lineage" as:
    A. an extended family related by blood or marriage to a common ancestor
    B. a continuous line of male descendants related by blood to a common ancestor
    C. all of the children and grandchildren of a single couple
    D. all of the children born within a single generation

44. The predominant form of lineage in tribal societies traces descent from:
    A. a female ancestor
    B. an original couple
    C. a male ancestor
    D. an animal spirit

45. A form of descent group whose members trace their descent back to an unknown ancestor, a plant or an animal is called the
    A. nature-group
    B. lineage
    C. clan
    D. moiety

46. Descent groups perform a number of functions in tribal societies. Which is NOT one of the functions performed by these groups?
    A. play a role in determining marital relations
    B. regulate economic production
    C. regulate exchange of goods and services
    D. determine who will be the next chief of the tribe by running the campaigns and conducting the voting
    E. define family rights to land, livestock, or other resources

47. There is a practice that exits in some tribal societies that is also an adaptive strategy that makes it possible for males to have more land and livestock, control the allocation and exchange of more goods, and gain more prestige and wealth. This practice is called
    A. polygyny
    B. combative warfare
    C. competitive warfare
    D. phratry
    E. levirate

48. Marriage patterns are affected by descent groups to the extent that individuals are usually:
    A. allowed to marry only within their descent group
    B. allowed to marry only outside of their descent group
    C. forced to marry their nearest relatives
    D. free to choose a marriage partner from among all members of the society

49. The price paid by the family of the groom to the family of the woman he marries is known as:
    A. bridewealth
    B. matriline
    C. sororate
    D. levirate

50. A marriage rule in which a widow is expected to marry one of her deceased husband's brothers is called
    A. sororate
    B. fraternal right
    C. incest
    D. levirate

51. Marriage rules and postmarital residence rules are
    A. not found in tribal societies, only forager societies
    B. inviolate and cannot be changed for any reason
    C. are flexible and change as ecological, demographic, economic, and political circumstances change, hence exceptions to the rules are often made
    D. random rules that independently developed in order for tribal societies to remain distinct entities and avoid acculturation

52. In the vast majority of tribal societies, a married couple will go to live:
    A. in the house of the wife's mother
    B. in the house of the husband's father
    C. in the house of the wife's uncle
    D. in a new house occupied only by them

53. It has been suggested that a matrilocal residence pattern will develop in societies where:
    A. there is frequent warfare with neighboring societies close to home
    B. agricultural or pastoral activities have strong female participation
    C. warfare or labor require men's absence for long periods of time
    D. polygyny is a common practice

54. In comparing gender roles between the Arapesh, Mundugumor, and the Tchambuli societies of New Guinea, Mead noted that Tchambuli women were:
    A. always submissive to male members of society
    B. unaggressive, cooperative, passive, and sensitive to the needs of others
    C. sometimes dominant politically and economically while men cared for children
    D. universally concerned with what we regard as "feminine" values

55. Marriages in _____ descent groups tend to be less enduring that those in _____ groups because of corporate rights over children.
    A. bilateral / ambilineal
    B. matrilineal / patrilineal
    C. patrilineal / matrilineal
    D. ambilineal / bilateral
    E. loose / rigid

56. Who was the famous anthropologist who studied gender and enculturation in New Guinea?
    A. Melvin Ember
    B. Roger Keesing
    C. Louis Leakey
    D. Margaret Mead
    E. Leslie White

57. Female status tends to be relatively high in
    A. patriarchal societies
    B. matrilineal societies
    C. bilateral descent groups
    D. societies that practice avunculocal residence

58. In most _____ societies, mother's bother has the political authority and economic control within the family.
    A. patrilineal
    B. matrilineal
    C. tribal
    D. patriarchal
    E. acephalus

59. In tribal societies, political leadership is usually:
    A. passed from father to son within patrilineal descent groups
    B. limited and decentralized
    C. absolute and sanctioned by supernatural authority
    D. democratic and representational

60. There are two types or styles of tribal leadership, the
    A. chief and captain
    B. chief and shaman
    C. headman and big man
    D. cephalus and acephalus
    E. commander and skipper

61. Tribal political organizations in which numerous and distinct descent groups coexist and serve a variety of different political functions are known as:
    A. pastoralist societies
    B. conical clans
    C. segmentary lineage systems
    D. complimentary oppositions

62. Anthropologists have developed a number of hypotheses to explain tribal warfare. These theories focus on all of the following except
    A. demographic factors
    B. environmental reasons
    C. instinct or biological proclivity
    D. external political or cultural factors, including prestige and honor

63. Witchcraft refers to the innate, psychic ability of some individuals to harm others, while _____ is a magical strategy in which practitioners manipulate objects and supernatural forces in order to bring about harmful or beneficial effects.
    A. animism
    B. shamanism
    C. sorcery
    D. totemism
    E. oration

64. Clyde Kluckhohn suggested that an important function of the belief in witchcraft among Navajo peoples of the Southwestern U.S. was to:
    A. ensure success in raiding and warfare
    B. encourage redistribution of wealth within the community
    C. protect Indian communities against white invaders
    D. provide a context for the communication of ancient knowledge

65. The Pueblo Indians of the Southwestern U.S. believe in spirits that exercise a supernatural control over the weather. These spirits are known as:
    A. monkalun
    B. hekura
    C. yanomamos
    D. katchinas

Suggested Readings

BARTH, FREDRICK. 1961. *Nomads of South Persia*. New York, NY: Humanities Press.

BASSO, ELLEN B. 1973. *The Kalapalo Indians of Central Brazil*. Prospect Heights, IL: Waveland Press.

BATES, DANIEL AND FRED PLOG. 1990. *Human Adaptive Strategies*. New York, NY: McGraw-Hill.

CHAGNON, NAPOLEON. 1983. *The Yanomamö: The Fierce People*. New York, NY: Holt, Rinehart & Winston.

DOWNS, JAMES F. 1984. *The Navajo*. Prospect Heights, IL: Waveland Press.

DOZIER, EDWARD P. 1983. *The Pueblo Indians of North America*. Prospect Heights, IL: Waveland Press.

EVANS-PRITCHARD, E.E. 1940. *The Nuer*. Oxford: Clarendon Press.

FRIEDL, ERNESTINE. 1975. *Women and Men: An Anthropologist's View*. New York, NY: Holt, Rinehart & Winston.

GLUCKMAN, MAX. 1965. *Politics, Law and Ritual in Tribal Society*. Chicago, IL: Aldine.

GROBSMITH, ELIZABETH S. 1981. *Lakota of the Rosebud: A Contemporary Ethnography*. New York, NY: Holt, Rinehart & Winston.

HAAS, JONATHAN, ed. 1990. *The Anthropology of War*. Cambridge: Cambridge University Press.

HARNER, MICHAEL J. 1972. *The Jivaro: People of the Sacred Waterfall*. Garden City, NY: Natural History Press.

273

HOBBS, JOSEPH J. 1989. *Bedouin Life in the Egyptian Wilderness*. Austin, TX: University of Texas Press.

HOEBEL, E. ADAMSON. 1978. *The Cheyennes: Indians of the Great Plains*. New York, NY: Holt, Rinehart & Winston.

HULTKRANTZ, AKE. 1987. *Native Religions of North America*. New York, NY: Harper/Row.

KEESING, ROGER M. 1971. *Kin Groups and Social Structure*. New York, NY: Holt, Rinehart & Winston.

KHOURY, PHILIP S. AND JOSEPH KOSTINER. *Tribes and State Formation in the Middle East*. Berkely, CA: University of California Press.

KLUCKHOHN, CLYDE. 1967. *Navaho Witchcraft*. Boston, MA: Beardon Press.

LYON, PATRICIA J. 1974. *Native South Americans: Ethnology of the Least Known Continent*. Prospect Heights, IL: Waveland Press.

SAHLINS, MARSHALL D. 1968. *Tribesmen*. Englewood Cliffs, NJ: Prentice Hall.

SERVICE, ELMAN R. 1963. *Profiles in Ethnology*. New York, NY: Harper & Row.

STEARMAN, ALLYN MACLEAN. 1989. *Yaqui: Forest Nomads in a Changing World*. New York, NY: Holt, Rinehart & Winston.

WERNER, DENNIS. 1990. *Amazon Journey: An Anthropologist's First Year Among Brazil's Mekranoti Indians*. Englewood Cliffs, NJ: Prentice Hall.

Answer Key with Page Numbers

1. T 316	23. F 337	45. C 325
2. T 317	24. T 338	46. D 326
3. T 320	25. F 340	47. A 327
4. F 320	26. C 317	48. B 327
5. T 321	27. D 332-319	49. A 328
6. T 321	28. C 319	50. D 328
7. T 322	29. C 319	51. C 329
8. T 322	30. A 319	52. B 329
9. T 323	31. D 319	53. C 329
10. F 324	32. C 320	54. C 330
11. F 324	33. C 319-320	55. B 330
12. T 326	34. A 320	56. D 330
13. T 326	35. C 320	57. B 332
14. T 328	36. B 320	58. B 332
15. T 329	37. B 321	59. B 335
16. F 330	38. D 321	60. C 335
17. F 330	39. D 322	61. C 336
18. T 332	40. C 322	62. C 337
19. F 332	41. A 323	63. C 340
20. T 335	42. D 324	64. B 340
21. T 335	43. A 324	65. D 341
22. F 337	44. C 324	

CHAPTER 17

CHIEFDOMS

Chapter Outline

Law and Religion

Chapter Highlights

A **chiefdom** is a form of social organization with a **centralized political authority** presiding over a **regional population** numbering in the thousands or tens of thousands. Chiefdoms differ from tribes with respect to the existence of leadership in the form of a permanent **institution** represented by the **chief**. Chiefs manage economic production and contacts with other groups. They have special access to luxury goods which they can **redistribute** in order to create **cooperative alliances**. The most important difference between chiefdoms and either bands or tribes is the fact that economic and political power are concentrated in the **office** of the chief. This centralized structure makes chiefdoms capable of organizing materials and labor in significant ways. However, it also makes them vulnerable to external influences. Most modern chiefdoms have been dissolved as a result of Western imperialism and colonial practices.

Chiefdoms have economies based on agricultural production and the accumulation of **surplus**. For this reason, they tend to be located in areas with rich and abundant resources. Ancient chiefdoms existed on rich alluvial lands of the Mississippi Valley. Modern chiefdoms were found in Polynesia, sub-Saharan Africa, and the Northwest Coast of North America. With the exception of Northwest Coast chiefdoms, whose subsistence was based on fishing and hunting sea mammals, all of them had economies based on **horticultural intensification** - labor-intensive agriculture designed to produce a surplus. Each also took advantage of **regional symbiosis**, the interchange of products produced by groups living in different resource areas.

The ability to produce, store, and redistribute food is an important aspect of the economy of chiefdoms. Accumulation and management of a surplus is a factor in the emergence of social differentiation between descent groups and individuals. Property ownership in chiefdoms is closely tied to kinship, and the emergence of wealthy and powerful **descent groups** is an important factor in the origin of chiefs. There are a number of theories on the origins of chiefdoms. **Elman Service** suggested that regional symbiosis played a major role, as different descent groups gained control over the procurement and exchange of specific resources. **Timothy Earle** feels that control over land and especially labor was more important.

Two basic types of exchange in chiefdoms are **reciprocity** and **redistribution**. Reciprocity (**reciprocal exchange**) is based on the transfer of goods of equal value (**balanced reciprocity**) or unequal value (**unbalanced reciprocity**) between groups or individuals. An example of this was the *kula* exchange as practiced by Trobriand Islanders, in which ritual exchanges of status objects provided a context for **barter** in other goods. Redistribution is the centralized allocation of accumulated goods. The classic example of this type of exchange is the *potlatch* of Northwest Coast chiefdoms. In a *potlatch*, an individual gains power by giving away large quantities of possessions and creating a sense of indebtedness among the beneficiaries of his generosity.

The social order of chiefdoms is based on the existence of a **hierarchy, or rankings** of unequal descent groups and individuals. Rank is often indicated by **status symbols**, such as special jewelry, costumes, or possessions. Interactions between members of differing social status are governed by **sumptuary rules** of behavior. The typical social organization of a chiefdom is the **conical clan**, a large descent group with a common ancestor. Rank is determined by an individual's kinship distance from this ancestor. Marriage within chiefdoms was usually conditioned by social rank. **Endogamy** refers to marrying within one's social group. Powerful individuals, especially chiefs, often practiced **polygyny** - having more than one wife.

Legal and religious institutions are more formal in chiefdoms than in bands or tribes. Both were usually centered on the office of the chief, who served as both supreme judge and high priest. Hawaiian chiefdoms, for example, have been referred to as **theocracies** because the power of chiefs derived from their place in a moral and sacred order.

Chiefdoms were rarely peaceful. Because of the need to defend and sometimes increase political authority and access to agricultural land or other property, chiefdoms were frequently engaged in **warfare**. **Slavery** and **human sacrifice** were often the result of these conflicts, although the latter was also undertaken in other ritual contexts.

Surplus production, social hierarchies, and complex **ideological systems** promoted a high level of quality and expressiveness in rituals and material culture. Control of labor led to the creation of **monumental architecture**, fine craft items, and extensive use of valuable and imported materials. Chiefdoms are characterized by elaborate rituals, with music, dancing, and exuberant costumes.

Terms and Concepts You Should Know

chiefdom (345):

chief (345):

intensive horticulture (347):

regional symbiosis (349):

reciprocal exchange (351):

kula (351):

barter (351):

kitomu (352):

redistributional exchange (352):

potlatch (352):

hierarchical society (354):

office (354):

rank (356):

sumptuary rules (356):

conical clan (356):

stinkard (356):

endogamy (357):

polygyny (357):

cultural hegemony (358):

adjudication (359):

tabu (360):

mana (360):

Makahiki (360):

moai (361):

totem poles (361):

fakaniua (362):

People to Know About

Jacques Maquet (347):

Elman Service (350):

Timothy Earle (350):

Bronislaw Malinowski (351):

Ruth Benedict (352):

Annette Weiner (353):

Marvin Harris (353):

Robert Carneiro (355):

Cultures to Know About

Tahitians (347):

Central African societies (347):

Mississippians (347):

Northwest Coast societies (348):

Kpelle (350):

Trobriand Islanders (351):

Kwakiutl (352):

Hawaiians (354):

Natchez (356):

Easter Island (361):

Cahokia (361):

Thinking About What You Have Read

The following questions or problems may be of help to you in studying the material presented in both the text and in your class. You may want to write out the answers to these questions (writing something down always seems to help solidify it in one's mind) or just think about them.

1. What role did kinship and rules of descent and inheritance play in the social structure of a chiefdom? What are some of the theoretical models for the kinship structure of this type of society? Draw a diagram of a conical clan and explain what is meant by this term.

2. Compare and contrast the social organization of chiefdom societies with the social organization of bands and tribes. Be specific with regard to characteristics of family organization and kinship, marriage and residence rules, gender relations, and the status of the elderly.

3. What theories have been proposed for the origins of chiefdoms? What social processes result in and perpetuate economic inequality and social stratification? What factors may have been involved in this evolution or change? Present a hypothetical scenario for how a chiefdom might emerge over time.

4. What are the principal reasons that Northwest Coast societies are characterized as chiefdoms and not tribes or bands? How do they differ from Polynesian chiefdoms?

5. Did religion and belief systems play a significant role in legitimizing the power of the chief? If so, discuss some specific examples of how chiefly authority is related to religious beliefs. If not, discuss the specific ways in which religion will affect the characteristics of a chiefdom.

6. If you were an archaeologist investigating an ancient society, what are the unique characteristics of houses, burials, artifacts, artwork, etc. that might lead you to identify it as a chiefdom?

7. How did the practices of reciprocity and redistribution differ in chiefdoms from the way they functioned in bands and tribes? Why do you think that these differences exist? What factors affected the way exchanges took place?

8. What was the role of the *kula* for members of Trobriand Island society? Describe how the *kula* worked and the specific activities associated with it.

9. What are the ways that a person could become chief in a chiefdom? What were the responsibilities of a chief? What were the limitations to a chief's power?

10. What forms does marriage take in chiefdom societies? What are the effects of endogamy and polygyny on the political structure of chiefdoms?

11. Describe the methods used to resolve disputes in chiefdoms. What kinds of legal systems are found in chiefdom societies? What is the role of the chief in resolving conflicts?

12. What is meant by the term "shamanism"? What is a shaman, and what role did the shaman play in the administration of chiefly authority?

CHECKING YOUR UNDERSTANDING: PRACTICE EXAMINATION

We suggest that you take this practice exam and then check your answers against the key provided at the end of this section. Use the questions that you got wrong as a guide to further study. Try to learn why specific answers are right and wrong. You may even want to take the practice exam a second time to review what you have learned.

True-False Questions

1. All societies that have "chiefs" are considered to be "chiefdoms."

2. Chiefdom societies are very similar to one another no matter where they are found.

3. Archaeologists have successfully documented the emergence of chiefdoms from prior forms of society in a large number of cases.

4. Most chiefdom societies have occupied ecological regions that contain abundant resources.

5. The Tahitians practiced intensive horticulture.

6. Chiefdom societies in Liberia, Zaire, and central Africa were able to produce surpluses of sorghum, rice, and millet.

7. The ancient cultures of the Mississippi Valley included chiefdom societies.

8. Northwest Coast chiefdoms subsisted primarily off the cultivation of maize, beans, and squash.

9. In order for chiefdoms to exist, natural resources had to be plentiful and seasonal, and the people needed to have the knowledge and means of preserving and storing those resources.

10. Elman Service theorized that the key factor in the evolution of chiefdoms was regional symbiosis.

11. The *kula* is an example of redistributional exchange.

12. In a *potlatch*, an individual achieves power and status by destroying or giving away large quantities of food and valuables.

13. All individuals in chiefdom societies have equal rank and status.

14. Rules of endogamy in Hawaiian chiefdoms actually resulted in sibling marriages.

15. In chiefdoms, the children of the chief always marry individuals of equal or higher status.

16. Polygyny, or the practice of one chief having many wives, was rare in chiefdom societies because it diluted the power of a single ruling lineage.

17. An example of an endogamous marriage would be the marriage of a chief's son to a woman captured from another chiefdom.

18. In chiefdom societies, gender relations were unequal, with males exercising political and economic control over females.

19. In Polynesia, a powerful chief would have been considered by other members of his culture to have more *mana* than a commoner.

20. The ancient chiefs of Hawaii often sought to legitimize their authority through ritual human sacrifice.

Multiple Choice Questions

21. A chiefdom is a political economy that organizes regional populations of _____ of people.
    A. groups numbering in the dozens
    B. hundreds and hundreds
    C. thousands or tens of thousands
    D. several millions

22. Archaeologists and historians have found that most chiefdom societies
    A. occupied areas that were rich in natural resources and conducive to producing a surplus.
    B. were located in marginal lands that demanded intensive irrigation and plow agriculture.
    C. were based on intensive foraging, supplemented by occasional hunting and fishing.
    D. relied on herd animals as the basis of their subsistence economy.
    E. were composed of two or more hunting-gathering bands that were integrated by strong patrilineal kin ties.

23. Among the most important agricultural products for Tahitian chiefdoms were:
    A. maize and beans
    B. sorghum and millet
    C. wheat and barley
    D. yams and sweet potatoes

24. Native American societies of the Northwest Coast such as the Bella Coola, Haida, and Tlingit are usually categorized as chiefdoms. However, they are atypical of chiefdom societies because:
    A. they cultivated taro, yams, and sweet potatoes
    B. they were governed by tribal councils
    C. they were hunters and gatherers and did not practice agriculture
    D. they had no urban centers

25. To maintain adequate resources, chiefdom societies:
    A. give certain individuals the power to organize the accumulation of surplus
    B. engage in frequent warfare for the purpose of obtaining elite craft items
    C. fission into smaller tribal units in times of shortage
    D. devote a significant part of their productive capacity to religious activities

26. In Hawaii, Cahokia, and Northwest Coast chiefdoms, the residence of the chief and his family was:
    A. modest and inconspicuous
    B. elaborate, spacious, and highly decorated
    C. shared by individuals of lower social status
    D. indistinguishable from houses of other families

27. Food storage can directly affect political economy because:
    A. accumulation of surplus within households results in differences in social status
    B. storage reduced the need to be economically productive
    C. it is essential for the survival of foraging societies dependent upon unreliable resources
    D. food was a principal commodity in long-distance exchange

28. The status of an individual chief is closely linked to:
    A. the size of his tribe
    B. the prestige of his descent group
    C. his skills as a hunter
    D. the seasonality of resource availability

29. According to Timothy Earle, the key factor in the evolution of chiefdoms was the ability of the chief to control:
    A. warfare
    B. labor
    C. tribute
    D. regional symbiosis

30. The *kula* was a ceremonial exchange of:
    A. specially prepared seafood delicacies
    B. spears, arrows, and projectile points
    C. unmarried women and girls
    D. necklaces and armbands made of shell

31. The *kula* is an example of what type of exchange?
    A. redistribution
    B. balanced reciprocity
    C. hypergamy
    D. market exchange
    E. silent trade

32. *Kula* exchanges were important because they provided a context for:
    A. barter in utilitarian goods
    B. cooperation in military activities
    C. cross-cousin marriages
    D. deep-sea fishing

33. The predominant form of economic exchange in chiefdom societies is:
    A. negative reciprocity
    B. redistribution
    C. free market capitalism
    D. long-distance tribute

34. During a *potlatch*, a Northwest Coast chief:
    A. gave away or destroyed food and craft items
    B. received goods and tribute from his subjects
    C. sacrificed slaves and captives
    D. traded women with neighboring societies

35. Which of the following might be interpreted as a modern example of the potlatch?
    A. A local politician gives away hundreds of frozen turkeys at a campaign rally.
    B. A special interest group pays the salary and expenses of a lobbyist.
    C. A former president makes speeches in favor of his party's new candidate.
    D. Delegates at a national convention trade buttons and other campaign memorabilia.

36. A major difference between redistributional and reciprocal economies is that:
    A. reciprocal economies are more common in societies with inequalities in social status
    B. redistributional economies tend to make certain individuals wealthier than others
    C. reciprocal economies always involve the exchange of a recognized form of currency
    D. only redistributional economies involve transfers of goods among related villagers

37. According to anthropologist Annette Weiner, the significance of the *kula* was that it:
    A. accompanied economic competition, in which participants sought to accumulate profits
    B. represented a system of balanced reciprocity that emphasized notions of equality
    C. was the only possible means of carrying out long-distance trade between islands
    D. symbolized the hereditary power of rulers on Pacific islands

38. The system of leadership in chiefdoms differed markedly from the big-man system found in some tribes in that:
    A. chiefdoms had no hereditary rules of succession
    B. tribal societies were led by warriors
    C. the leader of a chiefdom usually inherited his position
    D. big-man societies had no status differentiation

39. One of the most important characteristics of Trobriand chieftancy was:
    A. religious devotion
    B. generosity
    C. thrift
    D. boastfulness

40. The rule of primogeniture in the succession of political authority
    A. provided for continuity for the political system and avoided a power struggle when the chief died.
    B. enhanced the prestige of the king.
    C. usually caused a power struggle within the central chiefly hierarchy.
    D. often generated regional warfare that was tied to the symbiosis of the area.
    E. rarely occurred since succession was closely linked to the matrilineal descent rules.

41. Anthropologist Robert Carneiro viewed _____ as one of the decisive factors in the evolution of chiefdoms.
    A. warfare
    B. long-distance trade
    C. theocracy
    D. ancestor worship

42. Cultural norms and practices used to differentiate the higher-status groups from the rest of society are known as:
    A. rights to succession
    B. sumptuary rules
    C. social strata
    D. taboos

43. Among the Natchez Indians of the Mississippi region, marriage provided a systematic form of:
    A. social mobility
    B. wealth differentiation
    C. surplus redistribution
    D. cross-cousin exchange

44. Among chiefdom societies, the typical family form was the:
    A. matrilineage
    B. nuclear family
    C. extended family
    D. moiety

45. In most chiefdom societies:
    A. men were considered to be superior to women
    B. women were considered to be superior to men
    C. both sexes were considered to be equal
    D. gender status was dependent upon kinship

46. The authority structure in chiefdoms:
    A. restricted the power of political leaders to matters concerning their own kinship units
    B. gave chiefs the power to sanction certain behaviors above the interests of specific kin groupings
    C. delegated power to the heads of several different lineages
    D. favored mediation over adjudication

47. Hawaiian chiefdoms have been referred to as:
    A. gerontocracies
    B. oligarchies
    C. democracies
    D. theocracies

48. The funerary ritual of the Great Sun, leader of the Natchez Indians, was accompanied by:
    A. a potlatch
    B. the sacrifice of his wives, guards, and attendants
    C. intertribal wife exchange
    D. barter and exchange of basic utilitarian goods

49. The term *shaman* is used to designate:
    A. an individual who had the ability to sicken and to cure, and who often served as spiritual guide to chiefs
    B. a cosmic power that can be increased through brave deeds, diminished through illness, and passed from a chief to his sons
    C. the New Year's festival in ancient Hawaii, at which human sacrifices were practiced
    D. the principal ancestor in a conical clan

50. The most prominent feature of the site of the Cahokian chiefdom in western Illinois is:
    A. the wall of a thousand year old masonry temple
    B. a 100 foot high, flat-topped mound of earth
    C. the carving of a chief in war regalia on local limestone
    D. an elaborate burial containing over 400 gold beads

Suggested Readings

BENEDICT, RUTH. 1934. *Patterns of Culture*. Boston: Houghton Mifflin.

CARNEIRO, ROBERT. 1970. "A theory of the origin of the state." *Science* 169:733-738.

DUMOND, DON E. 1972. "Population growth and political centralization." In Brian Spooner, ed., *Population Growth: Anthropological Implications*. Cambridge, MA: MIT Press.

DRUCKER, PHILIP. 1965. *Cultures of the North Pacific*. San Francisco: Chandler.

EARLE, TIMOTHY K. 1977. "A reappraisal of redistribution: Complex Hawaiian chiefdoms." In T. Earle & J. Ericson, eds. *Exchange Systems in Prehistory*. New York: Academic Press.

_____. 1987. "Chiefdoms in archaeological and ethnohistorical perspective." *Annual Review of Anthropology* 16:279-308.

FRIED, MORTON. 1967. *The Evolution of Political Society: An Essay in Political Anthropology*. New York: Random House.

HARDING, THOMAS G., & BEN J. WALLACE, eds. 1970. *Cultures of the Pacific*. Garden City, NY: Free Press.

HARRIS, MARVIN. 1977. *Cannibals and Kings: The Origins of Cultures*. New York: Random House.

JOHNSON, ALLEN & TIMOTHY EARLE. 1987. *The Evolution of Human Societies: From Foraging Group to Agrarian State*. Stanford, CA: Stanford University Press.

KIPP, RITA SMITH, & SCHORTMAN, EDWARD M. 1989. "The political impact of trade in chiefdoms." *American Anthropologist* 91(2):370-385.

KIRCH, PATRICK V. 1984. *The Evolution of the Polynesian Chiefdoms*. Cambridge: Cambridge University Press.

MALINOWSKI, BRONISLAW. 1922. *Argonauts of the Western Pacific*. New York: Dutton.

_____. [1926] 1959. *Crime and Custom in Savage Society*. Paterson, NJ: Littlefield, Adams.

SAHLINS, MARSHALL D. 1958. *Social Stratification in Polynesia*. Seattle: University of Washington Press.

_____. 1968. *Tribesmen*. Englewood Cliffs, NJ: Prentice Hall

SERVICE, ELMAN. [1962] 1971. *Primitive Social Organization: An Evolutionary Perspective*. New York: Random House.

_____. 1975. *Origins of the State and Civilization: The Process of Cultural Evolution*. New York: W.W. Norton & Co., Inc.

SERVICE, ELMAN, & MARSHALL SAHLINS. 1960. *Evolution and Culture*. Ann Arbor: University of Michigan Press.

WEINER, ANNETTE B. 1987. *The Trobrianders of Papua New Guinea*. New York: Holt, Rinehart & Winston.

Answer Key with Page Numbers

1. F 345	18. T 358	35. A 352
2. F 345	19. T 360	36. B 352
3. F 346	20. T 360	37. A 353
4. T 346	21. C 345	38. C 354
5. T 347	22. A 348	39. B 354
6. T 347	23. D 347	40. A 354
7. T 347	24. C 348	41. A 355
8. F 348	25. A 349	42. B 356
9. T 349	26. B 349	43. A 356
10. T 350	27. A 349	44. C 358
11. F 360	28. B 349	45. B 358
12. T 352	29. B 350	46. B 359
13. F 354	30. D 351	47. D 360
14. T 355	31. B 351	48. B 360
15. F 356	32. A 351	49. A 360
16. F 357	33. B 352	50. B 361
17. F 357	34. A 352	

CHAPTER 18

AGRICULTURAL STATES

Law

Mediation and Self-Help

A CASE STUDY: LAW IN CHINA

Warfare

Religion

Ecclesiastical Religions

Universalistic Religions

Divine Rulers, Priest, and Religious Texts

Art and Architecture

Near Eastern and European Monuments

Monuments in the Americas

Chapter Highlights

This chapter and the next one examine **state societies**. The structural hallmark of state societies is a bureaucratic organization or government. With the intensification of agriculture in different regions of the world, **agricultural state** societies emerged.

The origins of food production have been a subject of debate by anthropologists for years. Theories often cite population pressure as a factor intrinsic to the origin of domestication. David Rindos (an archaeologist) recently argued that humans unintentionally hastened domestication of plants by such activities as weeding, irrigating, storing, and burning fields. This unintentional manipulation or selection of certain plants and specific characteristics eventually lead to domestication. Other archaeologists argue that culturally patterned behaviors (learning, cognition, and conscious processes) are equally important in understanding the origins of domestication. Most anthropologists argue that the process of domestication was complex, involving the **coevolution** of plants, animals, the physical environment, and humans. Whatever the exact processes, this phenomenon, and the later agricultural intensification, took place in a number of regions of the world.

Domestication occurred independently in the Near East, eastern Asia, and the Americas. As a consequence of changes that took place during the **Neolithic**, numerous cultures eventually developed **intensive agriculture** (the use of permanent fields and the cultivation of crops using irrigation and fertilizers). This intensification led to the rise of **agricultural states** in such regions as Mesopotamia, Egypt, China, South America, and Mesoamerica.

The rise of mortality rates, along with increases in fertility rates, were among the demographic conditions that are part of an agricultural or agrarian society. High fertility rates were sometimes encouraged by agricultural states in order to raise population levels for a variety of political purposes. Metallurgy, shipbuilding, paper making, printing, and many scientific ideas are only some of the dramatic innovations in agrarian society's technology.

Agricultural states showed great regional variation in their political economies. Large-scale bureaucratic empires with centralized governments emerged in the Near East, China, and the Americas. In Africa (called **segmentary states**), India, and Southeast Asia (called **theater states**) less centralized and less encompassing state societies arose. A type of decentralized political economy, known as **feudalism**, resulted from the breakup of large-scale centralized states at various times in Japan and Europe.

Increased food production, storage, and a rise in population numbers freed a number of individuals from full-time agricultural activities, thus allowing them to pursue specialized functions and occupations (e.g., potters, weavers, traders). Two types of property ownership occurred depending upon the organization of the agricultural state. In **centralized states**, property was owned and administered by governments. In contrast, in **feudal states**, lords and nobles owned and controlled estates that were inherited through family lines. In both types of states long-distance trade and government-regulated monetary exchange systems developed. Within this context, both merchants and markets developed. In some cases a **moral economy** emerged among the **peasantry** in which labor and resources were exchanged at the community level.

The complexity of agricultural states made it difficult for individuals to rely solely upon kinship organizations. Such things as occupation and land ownership became important in organizing the society. Family and kinship, however, remained an integral part of agricultural states. The **extended family** predominated in both rural and urban areas. **Patrilineal** and **bilateral** kin groups were found in 90% of the agricultural civilizations, while only 9% were comprised of **matrilineal** groupings. An example of a matrilineal grouping was the **Nayar** family in southern India. **Marriages** were arranged and based on political and economic considerations. In contrast to prestate societies, **polygyny** and **bridewealth** were rare. **Monogamy** and **dowry exchanges** were major patterns found in agricultural states. **Divorce** was uncommon because of the **corporate nature** of the extended family and need for cooperative agricultural labor.

Agricultural states were more **patriarchal** than bands, tribes, or chiefdoms. In fact, Martin and Voorhies have suggested that as women's role in agricultural production decreases so does their social status. Women's roles became confined to the domestic arena, while men were allowed to engage in public activities. The restricted role of women was revealed in practices such as *purdah*. Obviously the role of women varied from area to area, and in some regions women were accorded relatively equal status with men.

Agricultural states are usually considered **closed societies** by anthropologists because social status is **ascribed** rather than **achieved**. Class, **caste**, slavery, and both racial and ethnic stratification were the basis of social status and stratification in these agrarian societies. Social mobility was limited.

Many agricultural states developed writing systems for political, economic, and religious record keeping. **Ideographic, hieroglyphic, syllabic,** and **alphabetic** writing systems developed. Formalized legal systems with **codified laws** developed. The first recognized codified laws were the **Laws of Hammurabi** (the Babylonian code of law). **Self-help** and **mediation** still remained as ways to resolve disputes.

The religious traditions that developed in many agricultural states are known as **ecclesiastical religions** (no separation between state and religious authority). These religions had religious texts, full-time priests, and the conception of the divinity of rules. In the Near East and southern Asia other religious traditions emerged that are termed **universalistic religions**. In these religions the spiritual messages apply to all of humanity, not just to the culture where the religion originated.

Agrarian society art and architecture included **monuments** such as the pyramids of the Old and New Worlds. Some **diffusionists** have claimed that the occurrence of these monumental structures and other features provides evidence of the connection between the Old and New World civilizations. Most anthropologists dismiss these grandiose diffusionist schemes and view these structures and developments as indigenous to each area.

Terms and Concepts You Should Know

state (365):

artificial selection (365):

coevolution (366):

Levant (366):

Fertile Crescent (366):

Mesopotamia (366,368):

intensive agriculture (367):

civilization (367):

feudalism (370):

command economy (371):

peasants (371):

moral economy (371):

dowry (374):

purdah (375):

closed society (376):

caste (376):

ethnicity (377):

pictographs (377):

idiographic writing (377):

hieroglyphic writing (377):

syllabic writing (378):

alphabetic writing (378):

ecclesiastical religions (380):

universalistic religions (380):

rites of legitimation (381):

People to Know About

David Rindos (366):

8Ester Boserup (365,374):

Jack Goody (374,376,377):

Kay Martin & Barbara Voorhies (373,375):

Cultures and Sites to Know About

Nayar (373-374):

Han Dynasty (379):

Aztec (377,382):

Olmec (382,384):

Maya (384):

Jericho (366):

Thinking About What You Have Read

The following questions or problems may be of help to you in studying the material presented in both the text and in your class. You may want to write out the answers to these questions (writing something down always seems to help solidify it in one's mind) or just think about them.

1. What is a state as understood by anthropologists? Explain the major structural differences between state and prestate societies.

2. What factors were responsible for the development of societies that produced food. That is, when, where, and how did the domestication of plants and animals take place?

3. Explain, compare, and contrast the demography and technology in agricultural states with those of your own society or culture.

4. Describe the variations in political economy found in agricultural states. Why do you think these variations exist? What are segmentary states and theater states, and how do they differ from feudalism?

5. What is the division of labor in agricultural states? Describe the form property rights took in agricultural societies.

6. Two forms of property ownership predominated in agricultural states. What were these, and what were the ramifications?

7. How does a command economy differ from a moral economy?

8. Who and what are peasants?

9. Describe the structure and patterns of trade, monetary exchange, merchants, and peripheral markets in agricultural states. What forms do they take? Do you see any parallels in the U.S.?

10. Describe the social organization of agricultural societies. Have some of the kinship functions and kinship grouping that were found in band, tribe, and chiefdom societies been replaced by other groups, entities, or organizations?

11. Describe the family structure of the Nayar of southern India. How does it differ from your family structure? Does the Nayar family perform the same functions as your family?

12. What forms does marriage take in agricultural states?

13. Describe dowry and bridewealth. In what sorts of societies do we find each of these practices? Why the differences?

14. Why was (is) polygyny rare in agricultural states? What form of marriage is the most frequent?

15. Why is divorce rare in agricultural civilizations?

16. How did the transition to intensive agriculture affect the subsistence roles and patterns of both males and females?

17. Describe the forms and extent of female seclusion, patriarchy, status of women, and sexism in agricultural societies. What tends to promote gender equity? Compare and contrast these with those of your own society.

18. What cultural practices reflect highly restricted female roles?

19. What is the status of women in agricultural states? What is a patriarchy?

20. What is slavery? What is the difference between an open form of slavery and a closed form? Why did these two forms develop?

21. Describe the social stratification system of agricultural societies. Compare and contrast these with another system you are familiar with.

22. What is racial and ethnic stratification? Define race and ethnicity. Is there any type of racial or ethnic stratification present in your society?

23. What types of writing systems developed in state societies? Why were these systems invented? What are the differences among the systems?

24. What are codified laws? Where did the first codified laws originate, and what were they called?

25. What are mediation and self-help? Do these forms of redress occur in your society? If so, provide a couple of examples. If not, why do you think this form of redress is missing?

26. How does warfare in agricultural civilizations differ from conflicts found in tribal and chiefdom societies?

27. How does an ecclesiastical religion differ from a universalistic one? Give examples of both types of religion.

28. What are the roles of priest and religious texts in ecclesiastical religions? What are divine rules? How did they become divine, and how do they maintain their divinity?

29. Describe the types of art and architecture found in agricultural states. Do you think there was diffusion of art and architecture from the Old World to the New World? What types of evidence would you need to demonstrate diffusion or contact?

30. Why is Aztec warfare puzzling? What hypothesis or hypotheses do you find the most convincing? Why? Is it incomplete? What types of evidence may help in resolving this puzzle?

CHECKING YOUR UNDERSTANDING: A PRACTICE EXAMINATION

We suggest that you take this practice exam and then check your answers against the key provided at the end of this section. Use the questions that you got wrong as a guide to further study. Try to learn why specific answers are right and wrong. You might even consider taking this practice test more than once, several days apart.

1. According to your text, the earliest evidence of domestication in the Americas comes from Mesoamerica and is dated to between 10,000 and 7,000 years ago.

2. The transition from foraging to food production was accomplished in one area of the world, and then this innovation diffused to the rest of the world.

3. A major factor associated with the rise of agricultural states was the development of more sophisticated technology.

4. High infant morality rates and the view that children are future assets who can care for their parents in old age encouraged individuals in agricultural states to have only one or two children so that special care could be accorded each child.

5. An egalitarian agricultural state society emerges once land is owned and controlled by certain individuals.

6. A decentralized form of political economy based on landed estates in which autonomous patrons who owned the land demanded tribute from their serfs or peasants is called a homage state.

7. Individuals who cultivate land for their basic subsistence while paying tribute to a ruling elite are known as slaves.

8. In agricultural states a tributary mode of production replaces the kin-ordered mode of production found in forager and tribal societies.

9. The production of agricultural surpluses and luxury items made it possible for individuals and governments to become involved in internal and external trade.

10. The majority of agricultural states have either matrilineal or ambilineal kin

11. Bridewealth exchanges were restricted to the elite in agricultural states, whereas dowries were limited to the peasantry.

12. Goods and wealth paid by the bride's family to the groom's family is known as a dowry.

13. Monogamy is the primary form of marriage in most agricultural states.

14. Divorce was rare in agricultural states.

15. With the rise of agricultural states women were finally accorded equal status to men.

16. Closed societies are ones in which social status is achieved, not ascribed.

17. An open system of slavery provided no opportunities for upward mobility or incorporation into kin groups.

18. One of the strongest cultural forces that helped unite the Chinese civilization was the idiographic writing system since Chinese who spoke different dialects (Mandarin, Cantonese, or Hakka) could read the text without any difficulty.

19. The frequency and intensity of warfare and conquest decreased from foragers to agricultural states through tribal societies and chiefdoms.

20. Judaism, Christianity, Islam, Hinduism, and Buddhism are considered ecclesiastical religions.

21. It has been suggested that the Aztec practice of human sacrifice was linked to the fact that, since fat and protein were scarce, some people were able to supplement their nutritional requirements by consuming human flesh.

22. Humans can unintentionally and unconsciously improve the genetic characteristics of plants in their environment.

23. Archaeological studies indicate that life expectancy initially decreased with the development of intensive agriculture

24. The populations of tribal societies grow faster than those of agricultural states.

25. One of the most significant changes in demographic patterns with the rise of the agricultural state was that the average family decreased in size.

Multiple Choice Questions

26. The process whereby a human population consciously modifies plants or animals in order to improve their productive capacity and utility is known as:
    A. material selection
    B. artificial selection
    C. agricultural revolution
    D. coevolution

27. Although it is unclear whether this occurred before or after humans increased their food supply through domestication, archaeologists agree that human populations _____ at the end of the Ice Age.
    A. increased
    B. decreased
    C. stayed the same

28. The gradual emergence of sedentary, agricultural communities occurred as a result of the _____ of human, plant, and animal populations.
    A. irradiation
    B. migration
    C. coevolution
    D. independence

29. The Fertile Crescent is a term sometimes used to refer to a region of early farming communities in:
    A. Egypt
    B. the Middle East
    C. China
    D. North America

30. The Natufian communities of the Levant date to approximately _____ years ago.
    A. 1,200,000
    B. 120,000
    C. 12,000
    D. 1,200

31. Among the tools associated with Natufian lifeways are:
    A. mortars and pestles
    B. bronze daggers
    C. pottery vessels
    D. plows

32. Obsidian, a volcanic glass found at Neolithic sites in the Middle East, is used by archaeologists to infer the existence of:
    A. agriculture
    B. religious rituals
    C. warfare
    D. long-distance trade

33. Archaeological evidence indicates that rice was under cultivation in regions of southern China by:
    A. 500,000 B.C.
    B. 50,000 B.C.
    C. 15,000 B.C.
    D. 5,000 B.C.

34. Spirit Cave and Khok Phanom Di are two sites that have yielded evidence for early farming practices in:
    A. the Fertile Crescent
    B. Southeast Asia
    C. Mesoamerica
    D. East Africa

35. Maize, chili peppers, and avocados were among the earliest domesticated plants in:
    A. Iran
    B. Thailand
    C. Africa
    D. Mexico

36. The term "intensive agriculture" refers specifically to the use of technology such as:
    A. domesticated animals
    B. irrigation and fertilizers
    C. permanent settlements
    D. storage facilities

37. Mortality rates of agricultural states are _____ those of bands and tribes.
    A. higher than
    B. lower than
    C. about the same as

38. The term "division of labor" refers to the:
    A. strategy used to conquer new lands and extract tribute
    B. partition of a given project into discrete stages of work
    C. emergence of multiple professions, including farming, craftworking, government, and religious specialists
    D. invention of new technologies that accompanied the evolution of civilization

39. Agricultural states in which rulers are the heads of specific lineages but exercise only symbolic or ritual power over outlying regions are known as _____ states.
    A. feudal
    B. theater
    C. segmentary
    D. intensive

40. Knights and *samurai* are two examples of:
    A. centralized authorities
    B. theatrical rule
    C. feudal lords
    D. emperors

41. According to anthropologist Eric Wolf, the tributary mode of production replaced one in which economic exchanges were based on:
    A. long-distance trade
    B. feudal markets
    C. kinship-based reciprocity
    D. agricultural surplus

42. In horticultural societies, which practice occurs more frequently?
    A. dowry
    B. bride service
    C. bridewealth
    D. primogeniture

43. In agricultural societies (agrarian societies), the primary form of marriage was:
    A. polygamy
    B. polyandry
    C. monogamy
    D. polygyny

44. In intensive agricultural societies, which was not a primary task of women?
    A. cooking
    B. child rearing
    C. caring for domesticated animals
    D. working in the fields

45. *Purdah* is the practice of
    A. foot binding among women
    B. confining women to the house
    C. female inheritance of property
    D. gift exchange during the marriage ceremony
    E. economic exchange between competing clans

46. Which writing system consists of having a sign for each sound of the language?
    A. hieroglyphic writing
    B. syllabic writing
    C. ideographic writing
    D. alphabet writing

47. Which writing system simplifies a picture into a symbol, which has a direct relationship to the sound of a word?
    A. hieroglyphic writing
    B. syllabic writing
    C. ideographic writing
    D. alphabet writing

48. Which writing system has characters that express nothing but a sequence of sounds?
    A. hieroglyphic writing
    B. syllabic writing
    C. ideographic writing
    D. alphabet writing

49. The first codified laws were called the
    A. Ten Commandments
    B. Code of Ptah-en-Thoth
    C. Han Dynasty Codes
    D. Laws of Hammurabi

50. The characteristic religious system of agricultural societies is
    A. communal religions
    B. ecclesiastical religions
    C. shamanistic religions
    D. individualistic religions
    E. reflective religions

Suggested Readings

ADAMS, ROBERT MCC. 1966. *The Evolution of Urban Society: Early Mesopotamia and Prehispanic Mexico*. Chicago, IL: Aldine.

BIBBY, GEOFFREY. 1962. *Four Thousand Years Ago: A Panorama of Life in the Second Millennium B.C.* New York, NY: Penguin.

BRODA, JOHANNA CARRASCO AND EDUARDO MATOS MOCTEZUMA. 1988. *The Great Temple of Tenochtitlan: Center and Periphery in the Aztec World*. Berkeley, CA: University of California Press.

CARRASCO, DAVID. 1990. *Religions of Mesoamerica*. New York, NY: Harper-Row.

CASO, ALFONSO. 1988. *The Aztecs: People of the Sun*. Norman, OK: University of Oklahoma Press.

COE, MICHAEL. 1990. *Mexico*. New York, NY: Thames.

GOODY, JACK. 1971. *Technology, Tradition and the State in Africa*. London: Oxford University Press.

LAMBERG-KARLOVSKY, C.C. AND JEREMY A. SABLOFF. 1985. *Ancient Civilizations: The Near East and Mesoamerica*. Prospect Heights, IL: Waveland Press.

LEON-PORTILLA, MIGUEL. 1990. *Aztec Thought and Culture: A Study of the Ancient 2Nahuatl Mind*. Norman, OK: University of Oklahoma Press.

MacNEISH, RICHARD S. 1991. *The Origins of Agriculture and Settled Life*. Norman, OK: Univesity of Oklahoma Press.

OLIVER, PAUL. 1987. *Dwellings: The House Across the World*. Austin, TX: University of Texas Press.

READER, JOHN. 1988. *Man on Earth*. Austin, TX: University of Texas Press.

SABLOFF, JEREMY A. 1990. *The Cities of Ancient Mexico: Reconstructing a Lost World*. New York, NY: Thames and Hudson.

SERVICE, ELMAN. 1975. *Origins of the State and Civilization: The Process of Cultural Evolution*. New York, NY: Norton.

WHITEHOUSE, RUTH AND JOHN WILKINS. 1987. *The Making of Civilization: History Discovered Through Archaeology*. New York, NY: McGraw-Hill.

Answer Key with Page Numbers

1. T 367	18. T 378-379	35. D 367
2. F 368-369	19. F 379	36. B 367
3. T 369	20. F 380	37. A 368
4. F 369	21. T 382	38. C 368
5. F 370	22. T 366	39. C 370
6. F 370	23. T 368	40. C 370
7. F 371	24. F 369	41. C 371
8. T 371	25. F 369	42. C 374
9. T 372	26. B 365	43. C 374
10. F 373	27. A 366	44. D 375
11. F 374	28. C 366	45. B 375
12. T 374	29. B 366	46. D 378
13. T 374	30. C 366	47. A 378
14. T 375	31. A 366	48. B 378
15. F 375	32. D 366	49. D 378
16. F 376	33. D 367	50. B 380
17. F 377	34. B 367	

CHAPTER 19

INDUSTRIAL STATES

Chapter Outline

The Commercial, Scientific, and Industrial Revolution
Modernization
Environment and Energy Use
Demographic Change
The Demographic Transition
Urbanization
Technology and Economic Change
Technology and Work
The Division of Labor
Economic Exchange
    MARKET ECONOMIES
Perspectives on Market Economies
    CAPITALISM
        Capitalism in the United States
        Capitalism in Japan
    SOCIALISM
        Socialism in the Former Soviet Union
    HYBRID ECONOMIC SYSTEMS
The Evolution of Economic Organizations
    MULTINATIONAL CORPORATIONS
Social Structure
Kinship
Family
Marriage
    DIVORCE
Gender
    GENDER AND THE DIVISION OF LABOR
    FEMALE STATUS IN INDUSTRIAL SOCIETIES
    FEMINISM
Age
Social Stratification
The British Class System
Class in the United States
Class in Japan and the Former Soviet Union
Ethnic and Racial Stratification

Political Organization
Political Organization in Socialist States
Industrialism and State Bureaucracy
Law
Japanese Law
Warfare and Industrial Technology
Religion
Religion in Socialist States
Religion in Japan

Chapter Highlights

Chapter 19 focuses on cultures that have developed since the **Industrial Revolution** of the late eighteenth century into modern **industrial societies**. Along with technological advances in the mechanical production of goods and services, these societies experienced changes in economic and political organization that resulted in the formation of **nation-states**. These are defined as political communities with well-defined territorial boundaries, formalized legal systems, and centralized governments.

The emergence of industrialized societies is closely linked to trade and commerce. Long-distance trade and government-managed **mercantilism** permitted the accumulation of vast wealth in the hands of powerful citizens and centralized governments. Mercantile competition resulted in the formation of state-sponsored trading companies that accelerated global exploration. The **scientific revolution**, together with economic interests, produced **industrialization** - the large-scale transformation of raw materials into consumer goods.

The Industrial Revolution initiated a long process of **modernization**, characterized by the drive for capital accumulation, technological innovation, and investment for the production of wealth. Modernization and industrialization have resulted in profound changes in cosmologies and social attitudes as well as in the natural and cultural environment. They have also led to vast differences between **low-energy** preindustrial societies and **high-energy** industrial cultures.

Population increase accompanied the Industrial Revolution, mostly due to improved nutrition and health care. A **demographic transition**, defined by a decline in birth and death rates, changed family size. Population density also increased dramatically, especially as a result of urbanization.

Labor conditions in industrialized societies were transformed by technology. The **division of labor** is more complex than in preindustrialized societies. It can be divided at a general level into three sectors: the extraction of energy and raw materials (**primary sector**), factory production of goods (**secondary sector**), and service industries like education, finance, distribution, and sales (**tertiary sector**). Economies in which the majority of people are employed in the **service sector** are characteristic of **postindustrial** societies.

Industrial societies have a **market economy**, in which values of goods and services are determined by supply and demand. Land, labor, and capital have monetary values and are freely bought and sold. Unlike the situation in preindustrial societies, market forces supersede kinship and centralized leadership in the process of economic exchange.

Two models for the growth of industrial society have been predominant: the market economy of **capitalism** described by **Adam Smith** and state-supervised economy of **socialism** described by **Karl Marx**. In capitalism, both natural resources and the **means of production** and distribution (factories and stores) are privately owned. Private property and the right to free competition on the open market are fundamental to its success, so government intervention is discouraged. Drawbacks to the capitalist system are that it promotes vast economic differences between the rich and poor and does little to protect the general public from exploitation. In socialism, the government seeks to protect individuals from the exploitation that accompanies capitalism. Private ownership of wealth-generating property is discouraged, and both prices and wages are controlled by the state. Socialism is guided by the concept that meeting the basic needs of the population is more important than guaranteeing individual freedom to accumulate wealth. A drawback to the socialist system is that government bureaucracies, however well intentioned, tend to be inefficient and corrupt. They also must, of necessity, limit individual freedom. The governments of most industrialized societies today are **hybrid economic systems**, combining elements of both capitalism and socialism. This is known as **democratic socialism**.

Economic organizations evolve over time. In capitalist societies, wealthy corporations absorb smaller competitors to produce **oligopolies** in which a few major corporations control production. **Monopoly capitalism**, in which large corporations reduce free competition, results in private control of the market. In socialist societies, state-owned corporations had the same effect. One result of vast capital accumulation is the **multinational corporation**, an economic organization that operates in several different societies. **Alvin Wolfe** has proposed that multinational corporations are evolving into **supranational** organizations that will surpass nation-states in power. All of these processes transform industrialized societies.

Kinship and the family are far less important in industrialized than in preindustrialized societies. Geographical mobility reduces the role of the extended family, although the strength of **kinship networks** remains strong in ethnic groups that derive economic and social support from them. Divorce rates tend to be higher in industrialized societies, but there is greater gender equality in employment. **Feminism** is a movement that has helped women to move closer to equal rights and opportunities, although **patriarchy** still persists in all industrialized societies.

The role of the elderly diminishes with industrialization. As the rate of technological change increases, knowledge rapidly becomes obsolete. The result is a dramatic decrease in status for older citizens. This is less true in societies like Japan and Russia, where traditional respect for the elderly remains strong.

Industrialized societies are highly **stratified** with respect to social class. However, as open societies, social mobility is greater than in the closed societies of chiefdoms and agricultural states. Economic restructuring produces structural mobility, in which new occupational opportunities help individuals to change social status. The U.S. differs from Great Britain in the absence of a titled **aristocracy**, but it still has distinct social classes. Members of the upper class and upper middle class, representing about 15% of the population, have a far higher standard of living and many more opportunities than the majority of the population. Class divisions and conflicts are also evident in Japan and the former Soviet Union.

Most industrial states also have stratification on the basis of race or ethnicity. In the U.S., social mobility varies widely among people of European, African, Asian, and Latin American ancestry. This type of stratification has increased in European countries due to immigration from former colonies. Strong ethnic divisions exist in the former Soviet Union. In Japan, despite high social homogeneity, there is widespread discrimination against people of *burukamin* and Korean ancestry.

The political organization of industrialized societies is guided by concepts like **popular sovereignty**, government by the people, and **nationalism**, a loyalty to the nation-state. The former was given strongest support by classes that benefited directly from government policies. The latter was strengthened by mass media and the creation of an "**imagined community**," an allegiance to a nation-state that is far removed from local concerns. These two concepts are predominant in both capitalist and socialist societies. However, in the former Soviet Union, Stalinist nationalism led to **totalitarian** rule and extreme repression.

Complex legal systems are also characteristic of industrialized states. These have a proliferation of **administrative law**, reflecting bureaucratic control and technical requirements. The legal system becomes the most important means of social change, as in civil rights legislation. In Japan, the legal system is influenced by traditional values for group harmony. Mediation, through a *nakado*, is more common than **adjudication** through the courts and there is little concern for absolute justice.

Secularization, the declining role of religion in society, is more extreme in industrialized than in preindustrial societies. This is largely due to the importance of scientific explanations, rational thought, and the free expression of ideas. However, religion remains a powerful force in modern nation-states. It plays a critical role in the definition of individual and group identity, and helps people to cope with the changes that accompany industrialization.

Terms and Concepts You Should Know

industrial society (387):

nation-state (387):

mercantilism (388):

scientific revolution (388):

industrialization (388):

modernization (388):

demographic transition (390):

urbanization (390):

primary sector (391):

secondary sector (391):

tertiary sector (391):

service sector (391):

postindustrial societies (391):

market economy (391):

capitalism (392):

socialism (393):

mir (394):

czar (394):

democratic socialism (394):

oligopoly (394):

monopoly capitalism (395):

multinational corporations (395):

ie (398):

stem family (398):

dozoku (398):

romantic love (399):

miai (399):

feminism (402):

closed societies (404):

open societies (404):

structural mobility (404):

eta (406):

burakumin (406):

popular sovereignty (407):

nationalism (407):

imagined community (407):

apparatchik (407):

administrative law (408):

nakado (408):

secularization (409):

nihondo (411):

People to Know About

John Bodley (389):

Adam Smith (392):

Julian Orr (396):

Elizabeth Briody (397):

Marietta L. Baba (397):

Steve Barnett (397):

Chia Nakane (400):

Harumi Befu (401):

Rob Steven (406):

Cultures to Know About

United States (393):

Japan (393):

former Soviet Union (394):

Thinking About What You Have Read

The following questions or problems may be of help to you in studying the material presented in both the text and in your class. You may want to write out the answers to these questions (writing something down always seems to help solidify it in one's mind) or just think about them.

316

1. Can anthropologists effectively study industrial states? Are industrial states just too complex for anthropological theory and methodology? Is anthropology best suited for studying less technologically complex non-Western peoples and cultures?

2. Besides the technological differences and the importance of industrial production, what are the principal similarities and most significant differences between industrial states and preindustrial agricultural states?

3. Given what you have learned about the lifestyles of individuals living in preindustrial societies, describe the aspects of your daily life that differ in terms of high energy consumption.

4. What are some of the changes that occurred at the level of households and communities that contributed to the demographic transition accompanying the rise of industrial states?

5. Thinking in terms of primary, secondary, and tertiary sectors of the division of labor in industrial economies, describe the sectors in which your grandparents and parents worked. In which sector will you be employed? What about your children and grandchildren? Can you detect patterns of historical change through your own family's experience?

6. People living in industrial states often take the existence of market economies for granted. What are some of the alternatives to a market economy? How well do these function in industrial states?

7. What were the principal differences between Adam Smith and Karl Marx with respect to their interpretations of capitalism and free market enterprise? Which point of view do you favor, and why?

8. Describe the differences between the growth of capitalist economies in the U.S. and Japan.

9. The stereotypical anthropologist goes to remote locations in order to do ethnographies of primitive peoples. However, anthropology has also been successful in the investigation of industrial corporate culture and practices. What are some of the ways that anthropology has been or could be used to analyze and advise large businesses?

10. Using specific examples, describe the ways that industrialization has affected kinship and family structure in modern societies.

11. What effects has industrialization had on gender roles? Describe some of the differences between gender relations in preindustrial and industrial societies. What have been the benefits and/or drawbacks of the changes associated with industrialization.

12. Define feminism. Do you consider yourself a feminist? What are the goals and methods of the modern feminist movement? What cultural changes do you think they will produce?

13. Do you agree with the assertion that the United States has significant divisions between social classes? What are the principal characteristics that define class in the U.S.? Are there specific privileges and restrictions that accompany social class in the U.S.?

14. What are the principal differences with regard to social stratification due to ethnic affiliation that exist between the United States and Japan?

15. Placing your personal experience in the context of an industrial society, describe the cultural factors that have influenced your decision to pursue a college degree. What effects will a college education have on your social mobility?

CHECKING YOUR UNDERSTANDING: A PRACTICE EXAMINATION

We suggest that you take this practice exam and then check your answers against the key provided at the end of this section. Use the questions that you got wrong as a guide for further study. Try to learn why specific answers are right and wrong. You may even want to take the practice exam a second time to review what you have learned.

True-False Questions

1. Ethnographers have traditionally examined preindustrial societies and have only recently began to focus their attention on industrial societies.

2. Modern industrial states exercise considerable political control over many aspects of the lives of the people through the use of formalized laws and a centralized government.

3. Anthropologists are still trying to understand how the modernization of the whole world was accomplished in less than 15 years.

4. Mercantilism is a system in which the state is controlled by merchants.

5. A market economy is one in which the value of goods is determined by government manipulation and mandate.

6. Anthropologists have predicted that the next phase in the evolution of society that will occur about 2050 A.D. will be termed the postindustrial state in which individuals will revert back to horticulture and foraging.

7. Karl Marx was an ethnographer who studied the !Kung as they transformed their society from one dependent on foraging to one dependent upon a market economy.

8. In a market economy, basic factors of production cannot be assigned a specific monetary value.

9. Capitalism has achieved its ideal of creating an egalitarian society only in two countries, the United States and Japan.

10. Socialist governments seek to create more economic equality and less exploitation of working people.

11. In an attempt to create a more egalitarian society, the Soviet state, under the leadership of Vladimir Lenin, placed the means of production under government control, collectivized agriculture, and regulated prices and wages.

12. An oligopoly is the opposite of a monopoly.

13. In industrial states, kinship and family background have little effect on social mobility.

14. The economic requirements of industrial societies had the effect of dissolving the extended family ties that had become so critical and functional in preindustrial societies.

15. Industrialization in Japan weakened the *ie* and *dozoku*.

16. Romantic love as a basis for marriage is more common in industrial societies than in preindustrial societies.

17. In general, industrialization has undermined patriarchy.

18. Feminism is the belief that women are superior to men.

19. The elderly have more political and social status in industrialized societies than they experienced in preindustrialized societies.

20. Like Great Britain, the United States is considered by anthropologists to be a classless society.

Multiple Choice Questions

21. Most bands, tribes, and chiefdoms have been:
    A. unaffected by global industrialization
    B. directly or indirectly affected by contact with industrial societies
    C. willing participants in global industrialization
    D. organized as preindustrial nation-states

22. A primary feature that separates an industrial society from a preindustrial society is
    A. the fact that all kinship networks, such as kindreds, extended families, lineages, and clans, have been replaced with corporations, businesses, and schools.
    B. that most productive labor in industrial societies involves factory and office work rather than agricultural or foraging activities.
    C. that social stratification decreases, causing a more egalitarian society to develop within industrial states.
    D. a reduction in warfare, conflict, and feuding occurs in industrial states that are based on territory.

23. Industrial societies are organized as:
    A. agricultural states
    B. nation-states
    C. egalitarian societies
    D. democracies

24. Europeans did not engage in systematic relations with non-Europeans until:
    A. 2000 B.C.
    B. the Middle Ages
    C. after A.D. 1500
    D. the nineteenth century

25. The widespread effect of the Industrial Revolution is often referred to as:
    A. modernization
    B. globalization
    C. peripheralization
    D. nationalization

26 A system in which the state government regulates the economy to insure growth, a positive trade balance, and the accumulation of wealth is called
    A. modernization
    B. a circuitous strategy
    C. mercantilism
    D. a market economy
    E. socialism

27. People living in industrial societies on the average consume _____ energy (food, fuel, etc.) than people in tribal or chiefdom societies.
    A. about the same amount of
    B. much less
    C. much more
    D. slightly less

28. The Industrial Revolution was accompanied by a dramatic decrease in:
    A. mortality rates
    B. fertility rates
    C. migration rates
    D. life expectancy

29. The world's largest industrial city is:
    A. Detroit
    B. New York City
    C. Tokyo
    D. Mexico City

30. Karl Marx, in contrast to the views espoused by Adam Smith,
    A. argued that a market exchange and competition would bring prosperity and high wages to all segments of society.
    B. offered a gloomier picture of industrial societies by suggesting that a market economy would bring about misery for millions of people.
    C. suggested that the best way to have a free, democratic, and prosperous society was for the government to take control of the land, resources, and production.
    D. felt that forager, horticulturalist, and pastoralist societies could all be transformed into modern market economy states within 10 to 15 years.

31. The Japanese government developed key industries by:
    A. taxing peasants and subsidizing businesses owned by wealthy families
    B. investing heavily in petroleum production
    C. becoming a major exporter of processed food products
    D. negotiating free trade treaties with the United States and Germany

32. Capitalist societies share three basic ideals. Which of the following is not one of these ideals?
   A. the elements of production are privately owned
   B. companies are free to maximize profits and accumulate wealth
   C. land and resources should be owned and controlled by the state government, while production and services are in the hands of free enterprise
   D. free competition and consumer independence are basic to all economic activities

33. Capitalist societies _____ government regulation of economic affairs.
   A. encourage
   B. discourage
   C. normalize
   D. prohibit

34. Monopoly capitalism:
   A. promotes free market entrepreneurship
   B. decreases free market competition
   C. is a precursor to socialism
   D. is supported by the governments of most industrial states

35. It is estimated that, by the end of the 1990s, over 50 percent of the world's economic production will be controlled by:
   A. developing nation-states
   B. foreign governments
   C. Japan and the United States
   D. multinational corporations

36. Anthropologists who study major corporations such as Xerox and General Motors have found that
   A. the traditional method of participant observation and the use of key informants does not work in this type of setting as it did in small-scale societies.
   B. they must abandon traditional anthropological methods and theories and use exclusively methodologies and theories derived from sociology and psychology.
   C. the traditional methods (e.g., participant observation and the use of key informants) of anthropology provide many insights into the workings and problems of these large corporations.
   D. these corporations are both inflexible and incapable of accepting change that entails manipulation of the social variables of the business.

37. With industrialization the functions of the family changed, and one of the major transformations was the
    A. increase in the frequency of polyandrous marriages, especially those involving brothers.
    B. decrease in the mobility of members of the family since they were all tied to industrial production.
    C. increase in matrilocal residence and a reduction in patrilocal residence.
    D. diminishing importance of the extended family and the emergence of the nuclear family.

38. In Japan, the divorce rate has _____ since industrialization.
    A. increased
    B. decreased
    C. stayed the same
    D. fluctuated wildly

39. As nuclear families replace extended families in industrial societies, older people no longer reside with their adult children. The role of the elderly in retaining and disseminating information has diminished in industrial societies. The elderly have lost much of their economic power. Sociologist Donald O. Cowgill has hypothesized that
    A. the status and role of the elderly in the future will increase because the birth rate has dropped to an all-time low.
    B. there will be an elderly revolution, what he terms the "Silver-Haired Rebellion", which will place much of the lost power and status back into the hands of the older segment of society.
    C. as the rate of technological change accelerates, knowledge quickly becomes obsolete, and this affects (decreases) the status and role of the elderly (they are no longer the storage houses of technological knowledge, libraries and databanks have taken over this role).
    D. in the future there will be a major reorganization of kinship and the family (sort of the "Dan Quaylization" of the family) which will restore the power to the elderly.

40. In industrial states, the most important determinant of social status is:
    A. wealth
    B. kinship
    C. education
    D. intelligence

41. Chiefdoms and agricultural states are classified as _____ because they provide little opportunity for social mobility. Industrial states, on the other hand, are considered _____ because social status can be achieved through individual effort.
    A. oppressive / free
    B. hierarchical / egalitarian
    C. closed societies / open societies
    D. caste cultures / kindred cultures
    E. sedentary societies / nomadic societies

42. Social mobility in Great Britain is:
    A. open (people can move from one class to another)
    B. closed, with social status determined by hereditary descent
    C. a privilege restricted to the upper classes
    D. possible only for white people, and not for people of color

43. In the U.S., children from lower middle class families are _____ to get a college education than children of working class parents.
    A. just as likely
    B. more likely
    C. less likely
    D. less motivated

44. In Japan, the terms *eta* or *burukamin* are used to refer to:
    A. families of the highest social status
    B. descendants of Korean immigrants
    C. American expatriots who have settled there
    D. people of the lowest social class

45. Nationalism is a movement that emphasizes:
    A. the importance of the local community over the industrial state
    B. allegiance to the nation-state and rejection of foreign influence
    C. the dissolution of borders and cultural differences
    D. an embracing of ethnic diversity and religious pluralism

46. Citizens of the former Soviet Union experienced a period of _____ under the government of Joseph Stalin.
    A. unprecedented freedom of expression
    B. capitalist experimentation
    C. extreme repression of individual freedom
    D. *perestroika* and *glasnost*

47. In general, the more complex a society, the _____ its legal system.
    A. less complex
    B. more egalitarian
    C. more complex
    D. less adversarial

48. In Japan, _____ is more common than _____.
    A. mediation/litigation
    B. adjudication/mediation
    C. litigation/adjudication
    D. suing/settling out of court

49. The rise of industries such as airlines, automobiles, petroleum and plastics, and electronics and computers were all directly related to the development of:
    A. socialism
    B. military technology
    C. the United Nations
    D. peripheral societies

50. The decline in the influence of religion in society is called:
    A. de-evolution
    B. secularization
    C. atheism
    D. conservatism
    E. evangelism

Suggested Readings

ANDERSON, BENEDICT. 1983. *Imagined Communities: Reflections on the Origin and Spread of Nationalism.* London: Verso.

BEFU, HARUMI. 1971. *Japan: An Anthropological Introduction.* San Francisco: Chandler.

BERNARD, JESSIE. 1981. *The Female World.* New York: Free Press.

BODLEY, JOHN H. 1985. *Anthropology and Contemporary Human Problems* (2nd ed.). Mountain View, CA: Mayfield Publishing Co.

CHIROT, DANIEL. 1986. *Social Change in the Modern Age.* San Diego, CA: Harcourt Brace Jovanovich.

GOODE, WILLIAM J. 1982. *The Family*, 2nd ed. Englewood Cliffs, NJ: Prentice Hall.

HARRIS, MARVIN. 1981. *America Now: The Anthropology of a Changing Culture*. New York: Simon & Schuster.

HENDRY, JOY. 1987. *Understanding Japanese Society*. London: Croom Helm.

KERBLAY, BASILE. 1983. *Modern Soviet Society*. New York: Pantheon.

LIPSET, SEYMOUR MARTIN, & REINHARD BENDIX. 1967. *Social Mobility in Industrial Society*. Berkeley: University of California Press.

MUMFORD, LEWIS. 1961. *The City in History*. San Diego, CA: Harcourt Brace & World.

NAKANE, CHIA. 1970. *Japanese Society*. Rutland, VT: Charles Tuttle Co.

QUALE, ROBIN G. 1988. *A History of Marriage Systems*. New York: Greenwood Press.

RINER, REED. 1981. "The supranational network of boards of directors." *Current Anthropology* 22(2):167-172.

SCHWARTZ, RICHARD D., & JAMES C. MILLER. 1975. "Legal evolution and societal complexity." In Ronald L. Akers & James C. Miller, eds., *Law and Control in Society*. Englewood Cliffs, NJ: Prentice Hall.

STAVRIANOS, L.S. 1988. *A Global History: From Prehistory to the Present* (4th ed.). Englewood Cliffs, NJ: Prentice Hall.

WOLF, ERIC. 1982. *Europe and the People without History*. Berkeley: University of California Press.

WOLFE, ALVIN. 1986. "The multinational corporation as a form of sociocultural integration above the level of the state." In Hendrick Serrie, ed., *Anthropology and International Business*. Publication No. 28. Williamsburg, VA: Studies in Third World Societies.

1. T 387
2. T 387
3. F 388
4. F 388
5. F 390
6. F 391
7. F 392
8. F 391
9. F 392-393
10. T 393
11. T 394
12. F 394
13. F 395
14. T 398
15. T 398
16. T 399
17. T 402

18. F 402
19. F 403
20. F 404
21. B 387
22. B 387
23. B 387
24. C 387
25. A 388
26. C 388
27. C 389
28. A 390
29. C 390
30. B 392
31. A 393
32. C 392-393
33. B 393
34. B 395

35. D 395
36. C 396-397
37. D 398
38. B 400
39. C 403
40. A 404
41. C 404
42. A 404
43. B 405
44. D 406
45. B 407
46. C 407
47. C 408
48. A 408
49. B 409
50. B 409

CHAPTER 20

GLOBAL INDUSTRIALIZATION

<u>Chapter Outline</u>

Chapter Highlights

As industrial states gained prominence in the world, they affected nonindustrialized societies in numerous ways. This **global industrialization** has been studied by various social scientists in an attempt to understand its dynamics. There are three basic models that have been used to understand the process of this global industrialization and its impact on industrial and nonindustrial societies: (1) modernization theory, (2) dependency theory, and (3) world-systems theory.

Modernization theory provides a basis for understanding social, political, economic, and religious change that accompanies the technological changes inherent in industrialization. Economist W.W. Rostow proposes a five-stage model of the evolution from a preindustrial society to an industrial one. Modernization theorists view **traditionalism** as a retarding element to industrial expansion and social change in underdeveloped societies. Education and changes in cultural values are necessary prerequisites for economic and social development. Modernization theory lumps the world's societies into three categories: The **First World** (modern industrial states), the **Second World** (industrial states with socialist economies), and the **Third World** (premodern agricultural states). Modernization theory has been criticized in a number of ways. A major criticism is the fact that the **applied model** did not give the desired results it was supposed to in the Third World. It is also considered by some to be **ethnocentric** in its nature. Others critics see it placing blame for lack of change on the preindustrial societies themselves.

Dependency theory developed as a critique of modernization theory. Dependency theorists (e.g., Andre Gunder Frank) view global change as the consequence of interrelationships between the First and the Third Worlds. The spread of capitalism and the political domination (**imperialism** and the establishment of **colonies**) of the Third World by First World nations is the focus of study for these theorists and model builders. This approach shows that no society evolves in total isolation. Critics feel that dependency theory is too pessimistic and neglects the internal features of many Third World countries.

World-systems theory, as developed by sociologist Immanuel Wallerstein, emerged as a response to both modernization and dependency theories. This theory divides the world, based on economic criteria, into **core**, **peripheral**, and **semiperipheral societies**. This theory has been criticized for focusing almost solely on economics while ignoring other cultural features.

These three theories have stimulated ethnographic research and have provided models for anthropologists to use and criticize while examining the dynamics of societal change across the world.

Nonstate societies or **Fourth World** peoples have been affected by **global industrialization**. Foragers, tribes, and chiefdoms have undergone rapid changes ever since Western capitalist expansion began. Some of the consequences of these globally induced changes have been depopulation, **deculturation**, the disintegration of communities, **ethnocide**, and even **genocide**. The author of your text examines the impact of global industrialization on five **forager societies**: the !Kung San, Dobe !Kung, Mbuti Pygmies, Ik, and Siriono.

329

Pastoralists and horticulturalists have also been adversely affected by global industrialization. Native North Americans and South American horticulturalists have felt the impact of industrial nations in numerous ways ranging from subtle social changes to forced cultural change to relocation or even to massacre. Examples include the **Yanomamö**, **Bedouins**, and **Qashqai**.

Some **chiefdom societies** appeared to fare a bit better than other nonstate societies because being more centrally organized, they could adapt and develop state organizations themselves after contact with industrial nations. Examples in the text include the Polynesian chiefdoms in Tahiti and Hawaii.

As nonstate peoples were confronted by the industrialized nations, they developed means of resistance called **revitalization movements**. The **Ghost Dance** and **Peyote Cult** in North America and the **cargo cults** of Melanesia represent attempts at reinstituting traditional cultural values and patterns.

The disappearance of nonstate societies and their culture leads to the loss of beneficial knowledge. It is in our interest that these populations remain healthy and vibrant rather than declining and disappearing. Some anthropologists have focused their attention on trying to give Fourth World inhabitants a choice of preserving their **cultural heritage**. As time goes on, Fourth World peoples are becoming politically aware and active in demanding their autonomy and human rights.

Terms and Concepts You Should Know

global industrialization (414):

modernization theory (414-415):

First World (415):

Second World (415):

Third World (415):

underdeveloped society (416):

dependency theory (416-417):

imperialism (417):

colony (417):

world-systems theory (417-418):

core societies (417-418):

peripheral societies (418):

semiperipheral societies (418):

Fourth World (418, 420):

ethnocide (420):

genocide (420):

Kalahari Desert (420):

Ituri Forest (422):

deculturation (423):

revitalization movement (430):

Ghost Dance (430):

Peyote Cult (430-431):

cargo cults (431):

indigenous (433):

People You Should Know

W. W. Rostow (414-415):

Andre Frank (416):

Immanuel Wallerstein (417-418):

Eric Wolf (418, 421):

Richard Lee (420-422):

Colin Turnbull (422):

Allan Holmberg (423):

Barry Isaac (423):

Donald Cole (428):

Lois Beck (428):

Jack Weatherford (432):

Cultures You Should Know

!Kung San (420-422):

Mbuti Pygmies (422):

Ik (422):

Siriono (423):

Yanomamö (425-427):

Bedouins (428):

Oashqai (428):

Thinking About What You Have Read

The following questions or problems may be of help to you in studying the material presented in both the text and in your class. You may want to write out the answers to these questions (writing something down always seems to help solidify it in one's mind) or just think about them.

1. Describe, explain, and evaluate the modernization theory of global industrialization. How has this theory been criticized? Are the criticisms valid or not?

2. What are the five stages of W.W. Rostow's modernization theory? What are the First, Second, and Third Worlds?

3. What is the dependency theory of global industrialism? Make sure you incorporate and discuss imperialism and colonies when answering this question. Has dependency theory been criticized?

4. What is the world-systems theory of global industrialism? How does it differ from modernization and dependency theories? Discuss core, peripheral, and semiperipheral societies. Has world-systems theory been criticized?

5. What is the anthropological contribution to studies of global industrialization? If you were studying global industrialism, which theory would you use?

6. What is a Fourth World society? What has the expansion of industrialism done to Fourth World groups? Discuss ethnocide, genocide, and deculturation within this context. Are you familiar with any of these types of changes?

7. Describe the way of life and the changes that occurred due to industrialism on the following foragers: !Kung San, Dobe !Kung, Mbuti Pygmies, Ik, and Siriono. Do you see any parallels or not?

8. Have horticulturalist and pastoralist societies been affected by global industrialism? If so, in what ways?

9. How have chiefdom societies fared in the process of global industrialism? Are all indigenous groups affected the same way, or are there differences? Compare and contrast the effects among foragers, horticulturalists, pastoralists, and chiefdom societies.

10. What are revitalization (revivalist, nativistic, and millenarian) movements? Compare and contrast the Ghost Dance, Peyote Cult, and cargo cults.

11. What is being done to preserve indigenous societies if anything? Should we just let these cultures die and be replaced by global industrialism?

12. Can we assume that "What is good for us is good for them" when we look at the rest of the world? Why or why not? Is this an ethnocentric view? Give one example to support your opinion and one example which supports the opposite viewpoint.

13. "Industrialization and urbanization are mixed blessings, and within each blessing is a curse." Explain this statement. Do you agree with this statement or not? Why? Give examples to support you answer.

14. What price do indigenous peoples have to pay to become part of the industrialized global network? What types of changes and modifications have occurred among peoples and cultures of the industrialized and nonindustrialized worlds? What has progress brought?

15. What are some of the advantages and disadvantages of prestate and industrialized societies?

16. How can you accommodate traditional cultural patterns in the modern industrial world?

17. Briefly describe the factors responsible for problems such as poverty and alcoholism in communities of Mbuti pygmies.

CHECKING YOUR UNDERSTANDING: A PRACTICE EXAMINATION

We suggest that you take this practice exam and then check your answers against the key provided at the end of this section. Use the questions that you got wrong as a guide for further study. Try to learn why specific answers are right and wrong. You may even want to take the practice exam a second time to review what you have learned.

True-False Questions

1. According to modernization theorists, the primary impediments to economic development are poor nutrition and lack of health care facilities.

2. The term "Second World" refers to premodern agricultural states.

3. The final stage of modernization is mass production and consumption of material goods and services.

4. Theorist David McClelland has argued that the most important variable for producing the process of modernization is the Protestant work ethic.

5. A principal criticism of modernization theory is that it posits that Western industrial-capitalist society is superior to all others.

6. Dependency theory states that underdevelopment results from lack of formal education, which prevents modernization.

7. In dependency theory, the term "metropole" refers to "First World" societies.

8. The world systems theory proposed by Wallerstein classifies all countries within the categories of dominant, predominant, and submissive.

9. The term "Fourth World" refers to modern, industrial nations such as Japan and Great Britain.

10. The !Kung San are a horticulturalist group that live in the tropical rainforests of South America.

11. The destruction of a traditional society's language, customs, and way of life is known as pacification.

12. Resettlement of Mbuti Pygmies on plantations outside of the rainforest by the government of Zaire has resulted in their contribution to the nation's economy through taxation.

13. Anthropologist Colin Turnbull worked among the Ik.

14. Deculturation is the loss of traditional patterns of culture.

15. Conflict between the Iroquois and other indigenous tribal groups in the 1600s was primarily due to the introduction of guns and ammunition by the French.

16. The displacement of Native Americans from their tribal lands in the U.S. in order to make the land available to white settlers was a myth invented by radical American Indian activists.

17. The discovery of gold within Yanomamö territory has led to unprecedented economic prosperity for these horticulturalists.

18. Contacts with outsiders have led to a dramatic increase in infectious diseases among the Yanomamö of the Amazonian rainforest.

19. Before 1934, Native Americans were considered to be "wards of the state" by the U.S. government.

20. The political autonomy of the Qashqai pastoralist tribe in Iran has decreased in the years since the Iranian Revolution.

21. The Al-Murrah Bedouins, who traditionally made their living from a caravan trade and the care of camels, are now replacing camels with all terrain vehicles and motorcycles.

22. Christian missionaries to the Hawaiian Islands in the nineteenth century taught native children that their traditional way of life was barbaric and uncivilized.

23. Two examples of indigenous chiefdoms that were transformed through contact with the West are the Aztec and Inca.

24. Revitalization movements are attempts by Western nations to accelerate economic and social change within indigenous Third World societies.

25. Tribal peoples in Papua New Guinea who believed that Western goods were generated by spirits rather than being manufactured in factories developed rituals called cargo cults that were based on interpretations of the behavior of foreigners.

Multiple Choice Questions

26. In Rostow's formulation of modernization theory, traditionalism refers to:
    A. conservative reinvestment strategies
    B. an emphasis on maintaining family and community relationships
    C. achievement of a high standard of living
    D. preservation of strongly religious attitudes

27. "Premodern" societies are societies that:
    A. subsist on hunting and gathering
    B. have no formal systems of education
    C. are characterized by attitudes that inhibit individual initiative and incentive
    D. existed prior to 1950

28. The best way to eliminate traditionalism is believed to be through:
    A. democracy
    B. long-distance trade
    C. improved health care
    D. mass education

29. Whether a nation is considered to be developed or underdeveloped is based on:
    A. literacy
    B. gross national product (GNP)
    C. infant mortality
    D. life expectancy

30. Dependency theorists attribute the poverty of Third World countries to:
    A. corrupt governments
    B. traditionalism
    C. economic imperialism
    D. trade barriers

31. Neoimperialism refers to:
    A. economic colonization of Third World countries by multinational corporations
    B. the effects of socialist and communist ideologies on Third World countries
    C. relationships between Second World and Third World societies
    D. democratic processes instituted after World War II

32. In world systems theory, nonindustrialized societies that have little control over their own economies are classified as:
    A. dependent
    B. codependent
    C. colonial
    D. peripheral

33. Wallerstein acknowledged that underdeveloped countries could develop economically as a result of:
    A. education
    B. modernization
    C. specific historical circumstances
    D. balance of trade

34. In studying processes of global industrialization, modern anthropologists favor models from:
    A. modernization theory
    B. dependency theory
    C. world systems theory
    D. ethnological research

35. One of the principal causes of alcoholism among !Kung San has been:
    A. the cultivation of maize, melons, sorghum, and tobacco
    B. participation in government work projects such as road construction
    C. introduction of a cash economy through wage labor
    D. recruitment by the South American military

36. Participation in activities of the South African military has led to an increase in _____ among the !Kung San.
    A. voter registration
    B. violence
    C. political activism
    D. fertility

37. In 1972, the "only governing principle" among the Ik of Uganda was:
    A. reciprocity
    B. responsibility to family and lineage
    C. respect for the elderly
    D. individual survival

38. Colin Turnbull noted that the Ik of Uganda, a group of foragers resettled in arid mountain areas so they could become farmers, forced children out of their parents' homes at the age of:
    A. 3
    B. 6
    C. 12
    D. 15

39. The abandonment of traditional horticultural subsistence systems by the Iroquois was brought about chiefly through:
    A. decimation of the population by European diseases
    B. trading furs to the French for guns, ammunition, and liquor
    C. the introduction of the horse by Spanish explorers
    D. intermarriage of Iroquois women and European settlers

40. The development of a system of reservations for Native Americans in the U.S. was a policy developed for the purpose of:
    A. preserving Native American rights to tribal lands
    B. resettling Indian groups to make land available to white settlers
    C. permitting unlimited use of traditional hunting grounds
    D. encouraging the growth of Native American populations

41. It has been estimated that the Native American population declined from a high of between 1.2 to 2.6 million at the time of initial European contact to around _____ in 1890.
    A. one million
    B. 500,000
    C. 250,000
    D. 20,000

42. Large corporations that have sought to use land on Native American reservations for garbage landfills and toxic waste dumps have:
    A. split communities into factions both for and against these projects
    B. encountered universal resistance from Native American leaders
    C. been able to carry out their projects without any resistance
    D. always been motivated to act in the interest of Native Americans

43. The principal *modus operandi* of Christian missionaries to indigenous peoples of the South American rainforest regions has been to teach the Indians that their traditional culture, values, and beliefs are:
    A. misguided
    B. sacred
    C. invaluable
    D. adaptational

44. In most of South America, to be called *indio* is:
    A. no big deal
    B. purely descriptive
    C. insulting
    D. a compliment

45. The traditional territory of the Yanomamö Indians is located in what are now:
    A. Bolivia and Argentina
    B. Peru and Chile
    C. Brazil and Venezuela
    D. Colombia and Ecuador

46. Anthropologist Jason Clay has sought to improve the economic conditions of rainforest peoples through:
    A. large-scale literacy campaigns
    B. promoting the benefits of cattle ranching and beef consumption
    C. international marketing of renewable rainforest products
    D. government entitlement programs

47. It is likely that the Yanomamö will survive as a people only if they can develop an economy based on:
    A. hunting and gathering
    B. trade in manufactured products
    C. nomadic pastoralism
    D. agricultural production

48. The Ghost Dance was a revitalization movement that occurred in:
    A. Hawaii
    B. Papua New Guinea
    C. the United States
    D. Mexico

49. The Peyote Cult is a blend of _____ religious traditions.
    A. Aztec, Toltec, and Maya
    B. Hopi, Buddhist, and Shinto
    C. Navajo and New Age
    D. Christian, Comanche, and Kiowa Apache

50. Since the 1970s, most peoples of the Fourth World have become _____ in their respective countries.
    A. politically aware
    B. culturally extinct
    C. more numerous
    D. ethnic majorities

Suggested Readings

BERNARD, RUSSELL AND PERTTI J. PELTO. 1986. *Technology and Social Change.* Prospect Heights, IL: Waveland Press.

BODLEY, JOHN H. 1985. *Anthropology and Contemporary Human Problems.* Mountain View, CA: Mayfield.

_____. 1988. *Tribal Peoples and Development Issues: A Global Overview.* Mountain View, CA: Mayfield.

_____. 1990. *Victims of Progress.* Mountain View, CA: Mayfield.

BROKENSHA, DAVID W. AND PETER D. LITTLE. 1988. *Anthropology of Development and Change in East Africa.* Boulder, CO: Westview Press.

CHIROT, DANIEL. 1986. *Social Change in the Modern Era.* Orlando, FL: Harcourt Brace Jovanovich.

DOWNING, THEODORE E. AND GILBERT KUSHNER. 1988. *Human Rights and Anthropology.* Cambridge, MA: Cultural Survival.

GUGLER, JOSEF. 1988. *The Urbanization of the Third World.* New York, NY: Oxford University Press.

HOROWITZ, MICHAEL M. AND THOMAS M. PAINTER. 1986. *Anthropology and Rural Development in West Africa.* Boulder, CO: Westview Press.

JOSEPHY, ALVIN M., JR. 1976. *The Patriot Chiefs: A Chronicle of American Indian Resistance.* New York, NY: Penguin Books.

LITTLE, PETER D. AND MICHAEL D. HOROWITZ WITH ENDRE NYERGES. 1987. *Lands at Risk in the Third World: Local-Level Perspectives.* Boulder, CO: Westview Press.

MCNICKLE, D'ARCY. 1982. *Wind From an Enemy Sky.* Albuquerque, NM: University of New Mexico Press.

MILLER, FRANK C. 1990. *Old Villages and a New Town: Industrialization in Mexico.* Prospect Heights, IL: Waveland Press.

PODOLEFSKY, AARON AND PETER J. BROWN. 1991. *Applying Cultural Anthropology.* Mountain View, CA: Mayfield.

RECK, GREGORY G. 1986. *In the Shadow of Tlaloc: Life in a Mexican Village.* Prospect Heights, IL: Waveland Press.

RICHARDSON, MILES E. 1986. *San Pedro, Colombia: Small Town in a Developing Society.* Prospect Heights, IL: Waveland Press.

ROMANN, MICHAEL AND ALEX WEINGROD. 1990. *Living Together Separately: Arabs and Jews in Contemporary Jerusalem.* Princeton, NJ: Princeton University Press.

SHOSTAK, MARJORIE. 1983. *Nisa: The Life and Words of a !Kung Woman.* New York, NY: Vintage Books.

SPINDLER, LOUISE S. 1985. *Culture Change and Modernization: Mini-Models and Case Studies.* Prospect Heights, IL: Waveland Press.

STERMAN, ALLYN MACLEAN. 1989. *Yuqui: Forest Nomads in a Changing World.* New York, NY: Holt, Rinehart and Winston.

TRUNBULL, COLIN M. 1962. *The Lonely African.* New York, NY: Simon & Schuster.

TURNER, B. L. AND STEPHEN B. BRUSH. 1987. *Comparative Farming Systems.* New York, NY: Guilford Press.

WEYLER, REX. 1982. *Blood of the Land: The Government and Corporate War Against the American Indian* Movement. New York, NY: Vintage Books.

Answer Key with Page Numbers

1. F 415	18. T 425	35. C 420
2. F 415	19. T 425	36. B 421
3. T 415	20. T 428	37. D 422
4. F 415	21. F 428	38. A 423
5. T 416	22. T 429	39. B 423
6. F 416	23. F 429	40. B 424
7. T 417	24. F 430	41. C 425
8. F 417-418	25. T 431	42. A 425
9. F 418	26. B 415	43. A 425
10. F 420	27. C 415	44. C 425
11. F 420	28. D 415	45. C 425
12. F 422	29. B 416	46. C 426
13. T 422	30. C 417	47. D 427
14. T 423	31. A 417	48. C 430
15. T 424	32. D 418	49. D 431
16. F 424	33. C 418	50. A 433
17. F 425	34. D 418	

CHAPTER 21

LATIN AMERICA AND THE CARIBBEAN

Chapter Highlights

Chapter 21 presents a broad introduction to the anthropology of Latin America and the Caribbean. The cultures of this part of the world are a complex blend of **indigenous** traditions and new ones introduced as a result of the **conquest** and **colonization** of the New World by Europeans. Massive migrations of people of Spanish and Portuguese descent and the importation of African slaves contributed to the diversity of a social landscape that was already highly varied in **pre-Columbian** (before Columbus) times. More recent migrations have included large numbers of people from South and East Asia as well as other European countries, and the modern **world system** has had a profound effect on the legacy of indigenous and colonial economies.

Preindustrial societies of the New World ranged from band societies to major agricultural states. In **Mesoamerica**, the **Olmec, Maya, Teotihuacán**, and **Aztec** cultures were among the most complex societies. The earliest urban center was **Teotihuacán**, which became the sixth largest city in the world by A.D. 600. The Aztec **empire**, based in the **Valley of Mexico**, controlled over 25 million people before its destruction at the hands of Spanish *conquistadores*. In South America, the **Inca** civilization was preceded by several millennia of cultural development, including the empires of **Huari** and **Tiahuanaco**. The Inca empire was a highly organized militaristic government that administrated most of the **Andean region** before it also fell to Spanish domination.

The **Spanish Conquest**, driven by the desire to accumulate wealth, brought most of Latin America under the control of the Spanish crown. Exceptions were Brazil, colonized by the Portuguese, and Haiti, a French colony. **Colonization** had a dramatic effect on the population of Latin America. Epidemic diseases and colonial policies resulted in the loss of tens of millions of **Native Americans**, and large numbers of slaves were imported from Africa to provide labor for plantations. The colonial economy was extractive, using mines and plantations to export precious metals and agricultural products like sugar. Systems of *encomienda* and *hacienda* and policies like *congregacion* and *ejido* were aimed at getting the maximum amount of labor from rural **peasants**.

The Catholic Church played a key role in the transformation of Latin American society. **Missionaries** brought Western culture to indigenous populations, although this often resulted in a **syncretism** of Christian and traditional belief systems.

The **heterogeneity** of Latin American populations produced new social categories based on ethnicity. These included *indios*, creoles, *mestizos*, mulattoes, and *ladinos*. Relationships between these groups have been fraught with conflicts stemming from racial prejudice and discriminatory practices.

Colonial landscapes were transformed through wars of **independence** and social **revolutions**. Among the principal accomplishments of revolutions was the redistribution of land from colonial *haciendas*, but **land tenure** in Latin America remains far from equitable.

The modern economic development of Latin America varies widely from country to country. Venezuela and Mexico have become **semiperipheral** societies due to petroleum production and investments by multinational corporations. Unfortunately, social reforms are hampered by enormous **international debt**. Most countries remain **peripheral** societies, with economies based on the export of raw materials and unprocessed agricultural goods.

Ethnographic studies in Latin America have concentrated on studies of peasant communities. These have provided information on the structure of traditional systems such as **closed corporate communities** that focus on the production of subsistence goods as well as **open peasant communities** that are dependent upon world markets. Among the most interesting structures is the *cargo* system of Mexico and Guatemala, in which individuals gain status by committing effort and large amounts personal property to community service. Other institutions include relations of fictive kinship, such as the **dyadic contract** of *compadrazgo*.

Latin American ethnography has also extended to urban areas, where studies have concentrated on the culture of the urban poor. Anthropologist **Oscar Lewis** hypothesized the existence of a **culture of poverty** characterized by attitudes of hopelessness, but his theory has been challenged by more recent fieldwork that indicates this "culture" does not exist when there are real economic opportunities. Other studies have shown how Indians who migrate to the cities for work maintain effective **networks** with their home villages that help them to survive.

Terms and Concepts You Should Know

intensive horticulture (436):

chinampas (437):

corvée labor (438):

346

conquistador (439):

depopulation (441):

encomienda (441):

mita (442):

hacienda (*haciendado*): (442):

fazenda (442):

peon (442):

ejido (442):

congregaciónes (442):

pueblos (444):

cabildos (444):

caciques (444):

synchretism (445):

peninsulares (446):

mestizo (446):

mulatto (446):

creole (446):

indio (446):

revolution (446):

rising expectations (447):

relative deprivation (447):

silicosis (448):

International Monetary Fund (IMF): (448):

maquiladora (449):

export platforms (449):

hierarchy (450):

coca (450):

peasant (452):

closed corporate community (452):

open peasant community (452):

plural society (453):

ladino (453):

cofradía (453):

cargo system (453):

principal (453):

leveling mechanism (453):

fictive kinship ties (455):

dyadic contract (455):

patron-client ties (455):

compadrazgo (455-6):

padrino/madrina (456):

compadre/comadre (456):

machismo (456):

squatter settlement (457):

culture of poverty (457):

arrimado network (458):

People to Know About

Hernando Cortés (440):

Francisco Pizarro (440):

Sydney Mintz (443):

Virgin of Guadalupe (445):

Emiliano Zapata (447):

United Fruit Company (450):

Phillipe Bourgois (450):

Catherine Allen (450):

David Strug (451):

Robert Redfield (452):

Oscar Lewis (452, 457):

Laura Nader (454):

Frank Cancian (455):

Robert Van Kemper (458):

Places to Know About

Teotihuacán (437):

Tenochtitlán (438):

Tiahuanaco (438):

Hispañola (440):

Bocas del Toro (450):

Tepoztlán (452):

Chan Kom (452):

Tzintzuntzan (458):

Cultures to Know About

Olmec (436):

Maya (436):

Teotihuacán (437):

Aztec (438):

Moche (438):

Huari (438):

Tiahuanaco (438):

Inca (438):

Iberians (439):

ladinos (453):

Zapotecs (454):

Thinking About What You Have Read

The following questions or problems may be of help to you in studying the material presented in both the text and in your class. You may want to write out the answers to these questions (writing something down always seems to help solidify it in one's mind) or just think about them.

1. What are some of the ways that the ancient civilizations of Latin America have affected the nature of contemporary cultures?

2. What were the principal motivations for the Spanish Conquest of the Americas and how did these motivations affect the development of colonial policy toward native peoples?

3. Define the colonial institutions of *encomienda* and *congregacion*. What are the most significant effects that these institutions would have had on the lives of indigenous peoples? How might these institutions have affected demography, public health, and nutrition?

4. How did the *hacienda* system work? What were its principal goals and achievements? How did *haciendas* and *fazendas* affect the distribution of wealth and land in Latin America?

5. Besides autonomy from European governments, independence movements in Latin America had the objective of eliminating the *casta*, or social categories of the colonial period. What were these categories and how did they affect public policy and social relations in colonial Latin America? Were independence movements successful in eliminating these categories?

6. What is meant by the terms "rising expectations" and "relative deprivation"? What were the effects of rising expectations and relative deprivation on political movements in Latin America?

7. How did the countries of Mexico and Venezuela make the transition from peripheral to semiperipheral societies? What would need to happen in these nation-states before they were considered to be core societies?

8. What impact have multinational corporations had on Mexican society? How did this come about? Do you think the presence of multinational corporations in Mexico is good or bad for the society as a whole? Why?

9. Describe the labor policies of United Fruit Company plantations in Central America. What strategies did the United Fruit Company use to avoid unionization? What were the social impacts of United Fruit Company policies?

10. How has cocaine use in the U.S. affected the lives of South American farmers? How have they been affected by the "War on Drugs"?

11. According to what you have read, how would you characterize economic activities in Latin American peasant villages? Would you expect to find competition between entrepreneurial individuals or widespread cooperation and communal projects? Use specific examples to illustrate your points.

12. What is meant by the term "closed corporate community"? Who lives in these communities? How do they differ from open peasant communities?

13. Describe how the *cargo* system works. What are its costs and benefits both to individuals and to the community as a whole?

14. Give an example of a dyadic contract and the kinds of interactions that would accompany it. What are the motivations for entering into such a contract? What benefits does it provide and at what costs?

15. With regard to the notion of a "culture of poverty," do you agree with its proponent Oscar Lewis or with his critics? Why do you support one view over the other?

CHECKING YOUR UNDERSTANDING - A PRACTICE EXAMINATION

We suggest that you take this practice exam and then check your answers against the key provided at the end of this section. Use the questions that you got wrong as a guide to further study. Try to learn why specific answers are right and wrong. You may even want to take the practice exam a second time to review what you have learned.

True - False Questions

1. Because of its homogenous Spanish culture, Latin America has relatively little cultural diversity.

2. The major indigenous civilizations of Mesoamerica were based on economies of rice, beans, and wheat products.

3. *Chinampas* were terraces built to create horizontal land and prevent erosion.

4. There were no real urban areas in Mexico until after the period of initial Spanish colonization.

5. Wool production was an important part of the ancient Andean economy.

6. The term "Iberian" is used to refer to both the Portuguese and the Spanish cultures.

7. Guatemala and Honduras were colonized by the Portuguese.

8. The Spanish made extensive use of forced labor from indigenous peoples.

9. On *haciendas*, Spanish soldiers were the main source of manual labor.

10. Research conducted by anthropologist Sydney Mintz has focused on bananas, the first commercialized crop in Latin America.

11. As a rule, the *haciendas* were inefficient and agricultural production was secondary to the maintenance of status divisions.

12. Native customs that included human sacrifice made it easier for indigenous people to accept the story of the Crucifixion.

13. The Virgin of Guadalupe has special significance for the indigenous people of Mexico because she reportedly first appeared to an Indian convert to Christianity.

14. Individuals born to couples of mixed European and African descent were referred to as *mestizos*.

15. One of the principal accomplishments of the Mexican Revolution was eradication of Indian cultural practices.

16. The petroleum industry in Mexico is owned and controlled by multinational corporations.

17. El Salvador and Bolivia are considered to be peripheral societies.

18. Workers on United Fruit Company plantations were classified on the basis of racial stereotypes.

19. A "closed corporate community" is one in which peasants produce agricultural goods primarily for local subsistence.

20. A major criticism of Oscar Lewis' "culture of poverty" theory is that it places the blame for continued conditions of poverty on the middle class.

Multiple Choice Questions

21. The largest pyramid in pre-Columbian America was constructed in:
    A. Mexico
    B. Peru
    C. Bolivia
    D. Brazil

22. The Aztec empire flourished in the culture area known as:
    A. Mesopotamia
    B. the Andes
    C. Mesoamerica
    D. the Pampas

23. The Inca Empire was preceded in the Andes region by an earlier empire known as:
    A. Aztec
    B. Maya
    C. Teotihuacán
    D. Huari

24. Hernando Cortés first confronted the Aztec empire in Mexico in the year:
    A. 1492
    B. 1519
    C. 1776
    D. 1812

25. The gold and silver of the Aztec and Inca empires was used to:
    A. create an enormous welfare state
    B. improve the living conditions of Native Americans
    C. purchase the Louisiana Territory
    D. enrich the Spanish nobility

26. Archaeologists have estimated that Indian populations in Mesoamerica at the time of the Conquest numbered over 25 million. Within two hundred years the indigenous population of Mesoamerica numbered:
    A. 1.5 million
    B. 5 million
    C. 15 million
    D. 50 million

27. One of the principal industries to make use of indigenous labor in the Spanish colonies was:
    A. manufacturing
    B. shipbuilding
    C. mining
    D. agroforestry

28. Manual labor in the *haciendas* was performed principally by:
    A. slaves
    B. peons
    C. colonists
    D. soldiers

29. The Spanish colonial policy of Indian resettlement was known as:
    A. *encomienda*
    B. *hacienda*
    C. *congregación*
    D. *mestizaje*

30. The Indian leaders of indigenous communities in Latin America were known to the Spanish as:
    A. *caciques*
    B. *haciendados*
    C. *peones*
    D. *congregaciones*

31. The process of religious syncretism is one in which:
    A. ancient belief systems are adjusted to modern society
    B. two distinct religious traditions are blended into one
    C. one religion grows by gaining converts from another
    D. a multiethnic society becomes a society with only one religion

32. The Virgin of Guadalupe has special significance for the indigenous people of Mexico because:
    A. she reportedly first appeared to an Indian convert to Christianity
    B. her home is believed to be on top of a volcano in Central America
    C. she has become a powerful symbol of armed rebellion
    D. her image was created prior to the Spanish Conquest

33. People of European descent born in Latin America were labeled:
    A. creoles
    B. mulattoes
    C. mestizos
    D. Cajuns

34. Development projects in Mexico have been hindered primarily by:
    A. revolutionary bandits
    B. high international debt
    C. difficult topography
    D. language barriers

35. Current economic conditions suggest that the number of *maquiladoras* in Mexico will:
    A. increase
    B. decrease
    C. stay the same

36. Both Mexico and Venezuela have been successful at producing large quantities of:
    A. steel
    B. rubber
    C. coal
    D. petroleum

37. Which of the following economic trends are most likely to benefit both Mexico and Venezuela?
    A. rising prices for oil
    B. falling prices for oil
    C. rising prices for basic agricultural goods
    D. falling prices for basic agricultural goods

38. Anthropologist William Roseberry has characterized modern Venezuela as a/an _____ society.
    A. urbanized, nonindustrial
    B. industrialized, rural
    C. rural, nonindustrial
    D. urbanized, industrial

39. The principal export of Venezuela in the nineteenth century was:
    A. petroleum
    B. slaves
    C. coffee
    D. rubber

40. One of the strategies United Fruit Company management reportedly used to prevent the organization of workers into labor unions was:
    A. providing comprehensive health care to all workers
    B. encouraging membership in the Communist Party
    C. segregating ethnic groups into distinct occupational categories
    D. using democratic elections to determine who served in management positions

41. Among the effects of chewing coca is:
    A. suppression of fatigue
    B. drunken behavior
    C. vivid hallucinations
    D. episodes of violent behavior

357

42. Latin ethnographers felt that anthropologist Robert Redfield was wrong in his interpretation of Mexican peasant communities as:
    A. harmonious and noncompetitive
    B. divided into competitive political factions
    C. differentiated and heterogeneous
    D. hotbeds of highly individualistic villagers

43. A "plural society" is one which is:
    A. composed of a single ethnic groups
    B. characterized by two competing ethnic groups
    C. made up of several different ethnic groups
    D. hostile to ethnic minorities

44. A Latin American of indigenous or *mestizo* ancestry is most likely to be identified as *ladino* if he or she:
    A. crosses the border to work in southern California
    B. speaks Quiché, a highland Maya language
    C. works in a Coca-Cola bottling plant in Guatemala
    D. goes to the market wearing traditional Maya clothing

45. The *cargo* system is most similar to:
    A. *kula*
    B. *potlatch*
    C. *mita*
    D. *mana*

46. Ethnologist Kay Warren has pointed out that the *cargo* system can also be interpreted as a means of maintaining Indians' position of _____ relative to *ladinos*.
    A. dominance
    B. equality
    C. subordination
    D. economic superiority

47. *Machismo* is an unwritten code of behavior for Latin American:
    A. men
    B. women
    C. children
    D. adolescents

48. The term "culture of poverty" refers primarily to characteristics of _____ that inhibit individuals from pursuing economic opportunities.
    A. technology
    B. kinship organization
    C. values systems
    D. family health

49. A main criticism of Oscar Lewis' "culture of poverty" theory is that it places the blame for continued conditions of poverty on:
    A. government agencies
    B. poor people
    C. violence and crime
    D. the middle class

50. Although long-term success is dependent on personal initiative and hard work, studies like those of Robert Van Kemper indicate that initial adjustment to urban life by rural peasants is facilitated by the existence of:
    A. networks of friends and relatives
    B. the *hacienda* system
    C. multilingual radio and TV broadcasts
    D. religious pluralism

Suggested Readings

ALLEN, CATHERINE J. 1988. *The Hold Life Has: Coca and Cultural Identity in an Andean Community*. Washington, DC: Smithsonian Institution Press.

FOSTER, GEORGE M. 1967. *Tzintzuntzan: Mexican Peasants in a Changing World*. Boston: Little, Brown.

INGHAM, JOHN M. 1986. *Mary, Michael, and Lucifer: Folk Catholicism in Central Mexico*. Austin: University of Texas Press.

KOTTAK, CONRAD. 1983. *Assault on Paradise: Social Change in a Brazilian Village*. New York: Random House.

LEWIS, OSCAR. 1959. *Five Families: Mexican Case Studies in the Culture of Poverty*. New York: Wiley.

_____. 1961. *The Children of Sanchez*. New York: Random House.

MINTZ, SYDNEY. 1985. *Sweetness and Power*. New York: Viking Penguin.

PACINI, DEBORAH, & CHRISTINE FRANQUEMONT, eds. 1986. "Coca and Cocaine: Effects on People and Policy in Latin America." *Cultural Survival Report* 23. Cambridge, MA: Cultural Survival Inc., and Latin American Studies Program. Cornell University.

REDFIELD, ROBERT. 1930. *Tepotzlan, A Mexican Village: A Study of Folk Life*. Chicago: University of Chicago Press.

REDFIELD, ROBERT, & ALFONSO VILLA ROJAS. 1934. *Chan Kom, a Maya Village*. Washington, DC: Carnegie Institute.

SMITH, CAROL, ed. 1990. *Guatemalan Indians and the State: 1540-1988*. Austin: University of Texas Press.

VAN KEMPER, ROBERT. 1980. "Migration and adaptation: Tzuntzuntzeños in Mexico City." In Geogre Gmelch & Walter P. Zenner, eds., *Urban Life: Readings in Urban Anthropology*. New York: St. Martin's Press.

WARREN, KAY B. 1989. *The Symbolism of Subordination: Indian Identity in a Guatemalan Town*. Austin: University of Texas Press.

WOLF, ERIC. 1955. "Closed corporate communities in Mesoamerica and Java." *Southwestern Journal of Anthropology* 13(1):1-18.

_____. 1958. "The Virgin of Guadalupe: A Mexican national symbol." *Journal of American Folklore* 72:34-39.

_____. 1959. *Sons of the Shaking Earth*. Chicago: University of Chicago Press.

_____. 1966. *Peasants*. Englewood Cliffs, NJ: Prentice Hall.

WOLF, E.R., & S. MINTZ. 1950. "An analysis of ritual co-parenthood (compadrazgo)." *Southwestern Journal of Anthropology* 6. (Reprinted in Jack A. Potter, May Diaz, & George Foster, eds., *Peasant Society: A Reader* [pp. 174-199]. Boston: Little, Brown, 1967.)

Answer Key with Page Numbers

1. F 436	18. T 450	35. A 449
2. F 436	19. T 452	36. D 449
3. F 437	20. F 457	37. A 449
4. F 437	21. A 437	38. A 449
5. T 438	22. C 438	39. C 449
6. T 439	23. D 438	40. C 450
7. F 440	24. B 440	41. A 450
8. T 440	25. D 441	42. A 452
9. F 442	26. A 441	43. C 453
10. F 443	27. C 441	44. C 453
11. T 444	28. B 442	45. B 454
12. T 445	29. C 442	46. C 455
13. T 445	30. A 444	47. A 456
14. F 446	31. B 445	48. C 457
15. F 447	32. A 445	49. B 457
16. F 448	33. A 446	50. A 458
17. T 448	34. B 448	

CHAPTER 22

AFRICA

Chapter Highlights

Sub-Saharan Africa is a very diverse biome with many different societies and ways of life. Prior to contact with Western populations, many complex agricultural states existed in Africa. These included large urban civilizations that thrived in Mali, Ghana, and Zimbabwe. One of the largest urban centers is known as **Great Zimbabwe**, located in southeastern Africa. In West Africa the **Yoruba** built a number of large urban centers, including the city of **Ife** which was a political and ceremonial center. As a result of long-distance trade, these agrarian states had contact with Mediterranean, East Indian, and Middle Eastern societies to the north. Consequently, Islam and Islamic culture spread to some of the sub-Saharan African societies.

Although Africa had "open" forms of slavery (see Chapter 11) prior to contact with the West, the development of Western mercantilism gave rise to what we know as the African slave trade. This system was a "closed" form of slavery where slaves were classified as property, with no personal rights. In order to provide labor for the plantation systems of the New World, millions of Africans were uprooted and sent as slaves to the Americas. It has been estimated that between 1440 and 1870 that as many as 40 million Africans were captured, and 12 million were forcibly sent to the New World. The slave trade not only had a demographic impact on Africa by decimating indigenous populations, but it also disrupted agricultural production and economic exchange and led to the expansion of some coastal empires.

Africa was dramatically changed by Western **imperialism** and **colonialism**. Europeans divided up the regions of Africa for their own economic and political purposes, paying little or no attention to traditional boundaries or the wishes of the indigenous peoples. Africans were forced by colonial regimes to produce cash crops or participate in mining ventures. These changes resulted in a decline in agricultural production and a rise in wage labor. Eventually global economics began to shape the sociocultural systems throughout Africa. European endeavors also affected the traditional political structures in Africa,

With the introduction of formalized education, new African elites emerged within the colonial regimes. These individuals became involved in the new economics and politics of colonization. Colonization also brought missionaries and the introduction of Christianity. In many cases missionaries treated Africans paternalistically by trying to protect them from the ills of colonization while at the same time providing schooling and medical treatment. Missionaries also attempted to repress traditional religious belief systems and practices. In many cases this **ethnocentric** perspective had devastating consequences for Africans.

Colonial rule in Africa declined after World War II and by the 1970s 31 former European colonies had gained their independence. The first colony to become independent was Ghana (1957). In some cases the transition to independence was relatively easy and peaceful, but in other cases the move was very costly. For example, the *Mau Mau* uprisings in Kenya resulted in the deaths and imprisonment of thousands of Africans. Kenya eventually became independent in 1963 under the leadership of Jomo Kenyatta.

In South Africa colonization and independence produced a system of racial stratification called **apartheid**. Apartheid is a system that assigns varying statuses and rights, both social and political, to groups of individuals based on **racial** criteria. The concept of apartheid is based on the idea that white culture and values are superior to nonwhite African culture and values thus making Africans inferior economically, politically, and socially   Opposition to apartheid lead to resistance movements, the major one being the **African National Congress (ANC)**. During the 1980s and 1990s international attention forced the government of South Africa to institute some reforms and in 1991 racial registration laws were abolished. In 1994 all South Africans were permitted, for the first time, to vote in a national election. **Nelson Mandela's** ANC received a solid majority of the votes, and Mandela was elected president. He will share power with whites during a five-year transition period.

All African countries, with the exception of South Africa, are considered **peripheral nations**. Even countries such as Nigeria, with its vast oil reserves and other raw materials, remains a peripheral nation. Inflation, ambitious expansion schemes, and the decline of agricultural production have contributed to the economic problems of Nigeria. South Africa, in contrast, has been able to maintain a diversified economy, a good communication network, and an extensive transportation system. In fact, the gross national product (GNP) of South Africa alone makes up 20% to the total GNP for the continent.

Anthropological research in Africa prior to World War II was focused on tribal societies in sub-Saharan Africa. For example, the work of E.E. Evans-Pritchard on the Nuer is considered a classic. After WW II anthropologists changed their focus and started to examine the cultural transitions that were occurring due to independence movements. Thus, **ethnologists** began to examine complex agricultural states that were being affected by the **core nations**. In-depth studies of societies such as the **Bunyoro** and **Swazi** detailed how traditional kingdoms responded to colonialism and to the global economy. The classical study of the Bunyoro was conducted by **John Beattie**. Beattie focused on the political economy and how it was adapting to colonial demands. He also used the **comparative method**, contrasting the Bunyoro kingdom to the feudal states of medieval Europe. The Swazi were studied by anthropologist **Hilda Kuper**, who detailed the traditional political and economic structure of this kingdom and the changes that occurred during the colonial period and later independence.

Other anthropological studies have focused on **ethnicity**. Herbert Lewis estimates that there are about 1000 distinct ethnic groups (different language groups) divided among the 50 African countries. Many individuals hoped that as independence from colonial control occurred that the new African nations would develop into **pluralist societies**. Pluralism, however, has not been the norm. As an example of ethnic differentiation, the authors of your text examine Nigeria and it three major ethnic divisions, the **Yoruba**, **Hausa**, and **Igbo**.

In general, African social organization centers around **lineages** and **extended families**. It is predicted by some that as industrialization and agricultural commercialization spread throughout Africa that social organization will also change. Anthropologist **Niara Sudarkasa** has challenged the idea that all families in the world will eventually become **nuclear families**. She argues that the nuclear family in Africa is not the basic building block of social organization since it is not the unit of production, consumption, socialization, and emotional support. Not all anthropologists agree, but they do concur that there is much variation in African social organization and the structure and function of the family.

Women are subordinate to men in status since most African societies are **patriarchal**. Women in rural settings provide between 60% and 80% of the household food, they assume major subsistence roles, and are among the poorest people in the world's poorest continent. Urban women are often educated and tend to have more independence than rural women

Urban anthropologists are studying the ways that urban immigrants are adapting to their new environments. For example, **Kenneth Little** examined **voluntary associations** in West African cities and how these organizations helped new immigrants adapt and survive in cities.

Terms and Concepts You Should Know

emirs (462):

imperialism (464):

apartheid (467):

famine (478):

monocropping (478-479):

voluntary associations (480):

People You Should Know About

John Beattie (470-472):

Hilda Kuper (472-473):

M. G. Smith (474):

Victor Uchendu (474):

Niara Sudarkasa (476):

George Murdock (476):

Kenneth Little (480):

Cultures and Sites You Should Know About

Zimbabwe (461):

Bunyoro (470-471):

Swazi (472-473):

Yoruba (474):

Hausa (474):

Igbo (474-475):

Thinking About What You Have Read

The following questions or problems may be of help to you in studying the material presented in both the text and in your class. You may want to write out the answers to these questions (writing something down always seems to help solidify it in one's mind) or just think about them.

1. What were some of the early political states and kingdoms in Africa before Western contact? Where were they located?

2. What impact did long-distance trade have on Africa?

3. How are mercantilism and the slave trade related? What were the consequences of the slave trade (demographic, sociocultural)?

4. Describe the imperialism and colonization of Western and Central Africa and Eastern and Southern Africa. What were the consequences of imperialism and the politics of colonialism?

5. How did the indigenous elite fare under colonialism, and what effect did Christianity have on the peoples?

6. Describe the process of nationalism and independence following World War II. Given the various migrations of peoples within Africa and from outside Africa into Africa, how long should a people be in an area before they also have a historical right to be there? Why?

7. What is apartheid? What is the role of apartheid in South Africa? Has there been any resistance to apartheid?

8. Describe Africa in the world system using Nigeria (a peripheral nation) and South Africa (a nonperipheral nation).

9. What type of ethnological studies were conducted in Africa before World War II? What happened after World War II?

10. Using ethnographic studies of change, describe the Bunyoro and the changes they have made over time. Compare this to the Swazi, paying particular attention to the political organization.

11. How ethnically complex is Africa? Using Nigeria as an example, discuss ethnic differentiation, its problems, and it resolution. Do you see any parallels in your own society?

12. Using Nigerian ethnic differentiation as a model, how would you evaluate the multicultural diversity in the U.S.? Does the emphasis on ethnic "rights" and the increasing refusal to assimilate or mainstream mean that the U.S. is losing its identity and unity? Will the U.S. experience some severe ethnic differentiation problems in the future?

13. Describe the cultures of the Yoruba, Hausa, and Igbo. How do (did) these groups get along in Nigeria? Do you see any parallels in your society?

14. Do you think it is valid to compare the problems in Nigeria, Somalia, Rwanda, Yugoslavia (or what used to be Yugoslavia), and parts of the former Soviet Union? Do you see any parallels?

15. What are the role and structure of the family in Africa? What is the role of women in Africa, in both urban and nonurban settings? Are generalizations of these types possible, or is the cultural diversity in Africa too great to characterize African women and the family?

16. What did Niara Sudarkasa find when she studied African families?

17. What has urban anthropology found in Africa? What are voluntary associations and how do they function?

18. What is a famine? How can anthropologists apply their knowledge to famine problems in Africa?

CHECKING YOUR UNDERSTANDING - A PRACTICE EXAMINATION

We suggest that you take this practice exam and then check your answers against the key provided at the end of this section. Use the questions that you got wrong as a guide to further study. Try to learn why specific answers are right and wrong. You may even want to take the practice exam a second time to review what you have learned.

True-False Questions

1. According to archaeologists, the site of Zimbabwe was the home to a tribal society

2. The first organized religion to spread through sub-Saharan Africa was Christianity.

3. "Open" forms of slavery means that slaves could be bought and sold on the open market.

4. It has been estimated that about 90 million Africans were imported to the New World as slaves.

5. Two of the principal factors discouraging European colonization of the African interior was the presence of cannibals and dangerous animals.

6. The Hottentots were a tribal people of South Africa.

7. French colonial policies in Africa were directed at collecting taxes through appointed African leaders.

8. Mission schools and Christian education taught Africans to be ashamed of their traditional culture.

9. A difficult transition to independence in Kenya was caused by violent conflicts among the Kikuyu tribe, Zulus, and Hottentots.

10. The only African country that is not considered a peripheral society is Rwanda.

11. In 1993, the average per capita income in Nigeria was $25,000.

12. The Bunyoro kingdom was studied by anthropologist Napoleon Chagnon.

13. The *Mukana*, or king, of the Bunyoro polity received most of his wealth from military conquest of neighboring kingdoms.

14. The eight years of Idi Amin's rule in Uganda were characterized by unprecedented economic and social growth.

15. The Swazi state is based on a Marxist-Leninist ruling junta.

16. The principal ethnic divisions residing in Nigeria are the Boer, Afrikaner, and Zulu.

17. Prior to the colonial period, most Yoruba were subsistence peasant farmers.

18. Anthropologist Niara Sudarkasa has challenged the idea that the typical African family has a nuclear structure.

19. African women in urban regions are more likely to have multiple husbands and large families than rural women.

20. Most African societies are matriarchal, placing women in a subordinate status.

21. A famine is defined by the existence of food shortages and outbreaks of smallpox and AIDS.

22. Urban African women without formal education who lack the support of extended families and village communities are especially vulnerable to exploitation and alienation.

23. To resolve food crises, some Africans have called for increased regional trade within Africa and less reliance on the world market and global economy.

24. Ethnological research has recently focused on strategies used by urban immigrants to adapt to their new surrounding.

25. Since all associations and clubs in African societies are controlled by males, voluntary associations are not open to women.

Multiple Choice Questions

26. The principal enclosure at the site of Great Zimbabwe was constructed of:
    A. mud and mud brick
    B. reeds and thatch
    C. stone masonry
    D. hardwood logs

27. The first Europeans to develop extensive trade contacts with peoples of sub-Saharan Africa were the:
    A. Germans
    B. Italians
    C. French
    D. Portuguese

28. Historians have estimated that as many as _____ Africans were captured for slavery between 1440 and 1870.
    A. one million
    B. five million
    C. fifteen million
    D. forty million

29. The slave trade had a/an _____ effect on native African industries such as iron smelting and cloth manufacture.
    A. stimulating
    B. insignificant
    C. disruptive
    D. commercializing

30. Between 1885 and 1908, a brutal colony was established in the Congo by the government of:
    A. Portugal
    B. Belgium
    C. Austria
    D. Poland

31. The Boers and Afrikaners of South Africa came from:
    A. England
    B. Holland
    C. Germany
    D. France

32. Boer settlers had their most intense conflicts with indigenous Africans of a culture called the:
    A. Yoruba
    B. !Kung
    C. Maasai
    D. Zulus

33. The present-day political boundaries of African states reflect:
    A. traditional tribal homelands of the 15th century
    B. the limits of 17th century African chiefdoms
    C. European interests of the late 19th century
    D. needs of 20th century independent African republics

34. The first African colony to gain independence from a European state did so in:
    A. 1782
    B. 1883
    C. 1917
    D. 1957

35. The political independence of West African nations was achieved primarily as a result of:
    A. international pressure
    B. violent revolutions
    C. peaceful nationalist movements
    D. colonization

36. Apartheid is a system in which social and political rights are based on an individual's:
    A. education
    B. economic status
    C. religious beliefs
    D. physical characteristics

37. By the late 1980s, petroleum production in Nigeria had:
    A. contributed to the decline of agricultural production
    B. provided revenues that were used to subsidize large scale farming
    C. helped Nigeria to become what Wallerstein terms a "core society"
    D. led to a dramatic growth in the industrial sector

38. After World War II, the majority of ethnological research in sub-Saharan Africa shifted from _____ to _____.
    A. tribal societies, agricultural states
    B. agricultural states, hunting and gathering societies
    C. rural villages, urban areas
    D. tribal societies, band-level societies

39. Beattie compared the Bunyoro kingdom to:
    A. feudal states of medieval Europe
    B. the ancient empire of the Aztecs
    C. Hawaiian chiefdoms
    D. nomadic Bedouin tribes

40. Idi Amin, who seized power in Uganda in 1971, tried to make Uganda:
    A. self sufficient and independent from the world economy
    B. a Hong Kong-like center for international commerce
    C. dependent on trade with the U.S., England, and France
    D. an export economy based on government-subsidized cash cropping

41. Most of the residents of Swaziland are:
    A. employed in the petroleum industry
    B. white Boer settlers
    C. agricultural peasants and subsistence farmers
    D. Communists

42. Over 90% of the irrigated land and most of the heavy industry in Swaziland is owned by:
    A. white settlers
    B. the royal family
    C. village cooperatives
    D. tribal chiefs

43. The traditional territory of the Hausa people is:
    A. savanna
    B. rainforest
    C. desert
    D. coast

44. Ethnologist Abner Cohen's research in Ibadan, Nigeria emphasized:
    A. the use of ethnic distinctions and cultural symbols to mobilize economic behavior
    B. the importance of inter-ethnic collaboration in the resolution of crises
    C. the failure of tribal networks to mobilize political behavior
    D. how insignificant ethnic distinctions became in the absence of whites

45. The typical Yoruba head of household will be:
    A. polygynous
    B. female
    C. unmarried
    D. absent

46. Most African societies are:
    A. patriarchal
    B. matriarchal
    C. egalitarian
    D. pastoral

47. A common factor that exacerbates the impact of famine in Africa is the practice of:
    A. growing a single crop
    B. diversifying agricultural production
    C. using pesticides to combat insects
    D. increased regional trade

48. One of the principal causes of deforestation in Africa has been:
    A. agroforestry by multinational corporations
    B. the Greenhouse Effect
    C. global warming
    D. cooking with firewood

49. Among the long-term solutions to the food crisis in Africa is:
    A. diversifying plant species to improve productive capacity of the land
    B. concentrating on intensive production of wheat and corn
    C. opening more land to cattle ranching
    D. using foreign investments to become more industrialized

50. _____ include political, religious, recreational, and occupational groups that provide an intermediate form of social group between tribal affiliations and urban society that functioned as a mutual-aid organization during early phases of adjusting to urban life.
    A. Moieties
    B. Clans
    C. Secret cults
    D. Voluntary associations
    E. Ethnic gatherings

Suggested Readings

BARNARD, ALAN. 1992. *Hunters and Herders of Southern Africa: A Comparative Ehtnography of the Khoisan Peoples.* New York, NY: Cambridge University Press.

BEATTIE, JOHN. 1988. *Bunyoro: An African Kingdom.* New York, NY: Holt, Rinehart and Winston.

COMAROFF, JEAN. 1985. *Body of Power, Spirit of Resistance.* Chicago, IL: University of Chicago Press.

CRAPANZANO, VINCENT. 1986. *Waiting: The Whites of South Africa.* New York, NY: Random House.

DWYER, KEVIN. 1986. *Moroccan Dialogues: Anthropology in Question.* Prospect Heights, IL: Waveland Press.

FAKHOURI, HANI. 1987. *Kafr El-Elow: Continuity and Change in an Egyptian Community.* Prospect Heights, IL: Waveland Press.

FERNEA, ELIZABETH WARNOCK WITH ALEYA ROUCHDY. 1985. *Nubian Ethnographies.* Prospect Heights, IL: Waveland Press.

FRY, PETER. 1992. "Anthropology in Southern Africa". *Current Anthropology* 33(2): 230.

GIBBS, JAMES L., JR. ed. 1965. *Peoples of Africa.* New York, NY: Holt, Rinehart & Winston.

GLAZER, ILSA. 1979. *New Women of Lusaka.* Mountain View, CA: Mayfield.

RAMSEY, JEFFRESS. 1993. *Africa.* Guildord, CT: Dushkin.

SAIFOFI, TEPILIT OLE. 1986. *The Worlds of a Maasai Warrior.* Berkeley, CA: University of Califoria Press.

SALEM-MURDOCK, MUNEERA AND MICHAEL M. HOROAWITZ, eds. 1990. *Anthropology and Development in North Africa and the Middle East.* Boulder, CO: Westview Press.

SCHAFFER, MATT AND CHRISTINE COOPER. 1980. *Mandinko: The Ethnography of a West African Holy Land.* Prospect Heights, IL: Waveland Press.

SHOSTAK, VALENE L. 1983. *Nisa: The Life and Words of a !Kung Woman.* New York, NY: Vintage Books.

SPINDEL, CAROL. 1989. *In the Shadow of the Scared Grove.* New York, NY: Vintage Books.

STOLLER, PAUL. 1989. *Fusion of the Worlds: An Ethnography of Possession Among the Songhay of Niger.* Chicago, IL: University of Chicago Press.

THOMAS, ELIZABETH MARSHALL. *The Harmless People.* New York, NY: Vintage Books.

TURNBULL, COLIN. 1962. *The Lonely African.* New York, NY: Simon & Schuster.

TURNER, EDITH. 1987. *The Spirit and the Drum: A Memoir of Africa.* Tucson, AZ: University of Arizona Press.

UCHENDU, VICTOR C. 1965. *The Igbo of Southeast Nigeria.* New York, NY: Holt, Rinehart and Winston.

Answer Key with Page Numbers

1. F 461	18. T 476	35. C 467
2. F 462	19. F 477	36. D 467
3. F 463	20. F 477	37. A 469
4. F 464	21. F 478	38. A 470
5. F 464	22. T 478	39. A 471
6. T 465	23. T 479	40. A 471
7. F 466	24. T 480	41. C 472
8. T 466	25. F 480	42. A 473
9. F 467	26. C 462	43. A 474
10. F 469	27. D 463	44. A 475
11. F 469	28. D 464	45. A 476
12. F 470	29. C 464	46. A 477
13. F 471	30. B 464	47. A 478
14. F 471	31. B 465	48. D 479
15. F 472	32. D 465	49. A 479
16. F 474	33. C 465	50. D 480
17. T 474	34. D 466	

CHAPTER 23

THE MIDDLE EAST

Chapter Highlights

The Middle East, which includes areas of northern Africa and southwestern Asia, is a region of great ethnic diversity. Cultures share ancient traditions that date back to before the world's earliest agricultural villages, which appeared here during the **Neolithic** period and were followed by the emergence of urban societies such as those of the **Sumerians, Babylonians,** and **Assyrians** in **Mesopotamia** and the ancient **Egyptians** in the **Nile Valley.** These cultures laid the foundations for **Judaism, Christianity,** and **Islam.** Although all three religions remain powerful forces in the region, the modern Middle East is characterized by the predominance of the **Islamic tradition.** As with Latin America and Africa, the Middle East was profoundly affected by European **colonization.** Participation in the **world system,** and reactions against it, have helped shape the culture of the region as it exists today.

In order to understand the culture of the Middle East, it is essential to know the history of Islam. **Muhammad,** believed to be a prophet of **Allah** (God), received revelations recorded in the text known as the **Qur'an** (Koran). These provide a code of moral behavior, spiritual guidance, and insights into the nature of the universe. Muhammad established the center of a **Muslim** empire at **Mecca,** a focal point of Islam. After Muhammad's death in 632, ideological differences split Muslims into two distinct divisions - the **Sunni** and the **Shi'a.** The Sunni emphasize the ability of an individual to communicate with Allah. The Shi'a believe that an *imam*, a descendant of Muhammad, must act as an intermediary between the human and the divine worlds. All Muslims recognize a codified legal system known as the **Sharia** that, together with the Qur'an, has become the basis for political governance in Islamic states.

Relations between the Middle East and Europe can be traced back to **Byzantine** times, when Christianity was spread westward by the **Holy Roman Empire** to become the dominant European religion. After the fall of the Roman Empire, Christians occupying the **Holy Land** were defeated by expanding Islamic empires. During the **Medieval** period, European lords sponsored the **Crusades** in an unsuccessful attempt to capture the Holy Land and gain access to Eastern trade routes. It was not until the fifteenth century that the Portuguese opened Middle Eastern **ports of trade.**

The modern history of the Middle East begins with the establishment of the **Ottoman Empire,** an Islamic state based in **Istanbul** that controlled most of the region under a dynastic succession of sultans from the fifteenth through the early twentieth centuries. When the empire weakened, the French moved in to control North Africa, Lebanon, and Syria; Russia occupied central Asia and northern **Persia** (Iran); and the British colonized Egypt, Iraq, Palestine and southern Iran. Most of these colonies lasted until after World War II and some persisted until the dissolution of the U.S.S.R. in the 1990s.

European colonization of the Middle East was aimed at converting traditional economies to agricultural production for the world market. It was accompanied by secular forms of education and the creation of new, Westernized social classes. Muslim reactions to Christian domination resulted in **nationalist and independence movements** that achieved independence for most Middle Eastern nations by the 1960s. **Palestine** gained independence as the state of Israel in 1948, serving as a homeland for Jewish refugees.

The contemporary Middle East has been affected in profound ways by petroleum revenues and Islamic **revivalist movements**. Ethnologists have studied processes of demographic change, **urbanization**, and the transformation of peasant communities by **global industrialization**. **Kafr el-Elow**, Egypt, and **Demirciler**, Turkey provide case studies of the effects of industrialization on rural communities.

Kinship, marriage, and **gender relations** have been prominent topics of investigation. These include studies of the *hamula*, a **patrilineal clan** led by a **sheik** that coordinates economic, political, and ceremonial activities. Marriage, mandated by Islam, includes both **polygyny** and *bint amm*, a form of **parallel-cousin marriage**. Arranged marriages are common, as is the *mahr*, or **bridewealth** payment. Gender relations in Islamic countries are highly complex, and it is wrong to assume that the wearing of veils, traditional dress, and observation of *purdah* can be explained simply as male domination of women.

The issues that affect cultures of the Middle East are best interpreted through case studies of social change. One of these is the **Islamic Revolution** in Iran that occurred in the 1970s when a Westernized dictatorship was replaced by religious totalitarianism. Conflicts between Islamic sects, majority governments and ethnic minorities, Christians and Muslims, and Jews and Palestinians have also been the subjects of anthropological investigations.

Terms and Concepts You Should Know

agricultural empire (483):

ziggurat (483):

Islam (484):

Qur'an (485):

Shi'a (485):

Sunni (485):

caliph (485):

imam (485):

Allah (485):

Five Pillars of Islam (486):

Sharia (486):

sultan (486):

ulama (486):

Crusades (487):

Zionism (488):

reformist movements (489):

Holocaust (490):

Oil Crisis of 1973-81 (490):

OPEC (490):

fellaheen (492):

hamula (493):

bint amm (494):

mahr (495):

purdah (497):

urban-folk model (497):

doctrine of the imamate (498):

mullah (498):

mujtahid (498):

ayatollah (498):

Sufism (498):

tariqa (498):

marabout (498):

Islamic fundamentalism (498):

shah (499):

White Revolution (499):

Hizbollah (501):

People to Know About

Abraham (484):

Muhammad (484):

Hani Fakhouri (491):

Joe Pierce (492):

Ali (497):

Husayn (498):

Muhammad Reza Pahlavi (499):

Khomeini (500):

Yasser Arafat (502):

Places to Know About

Ur (483):

Babylon (483):

Assyria (483):

Memphis (484):

Thebes (484):

Mecca (484):

Medina (485):

Suez Canal (487):

Persia (488):

Palestine (489):

Kafr el-Elow (491):

Demirciler (492):

Cultures to Know About

Sumerians (484):

ancient Egyptians (484):

Bedouins (484):

Ottoman Empire (486):

Shi'a

Sufism

Iran (499):

Thinking About What You Have Read

The following questions or problems may be of help to you in studying the material presented in both the text and in your class. You may want to write out the answers to these questions (writing something down always seems to help solidify it in one's mind) or just think about them.

1. What are some of the differences between the early civilizations of the Middle East and those of Mesoamerica and the Andean regions?

2. Describe the origins of the Islamic tradition. By what means was it spread throughout the Middle Eastern region? How has the practice of modern Islam been affected by its particular history?

3. Characterize the nature of the relationship between Europe and the Middle East from medieval times up to the present day. How successful have Europeans been at introducing Western culture and values to the Middle East?

4. What were the principal countries involved in the colonization of the Middle East during the latter half of the nineteenth century? How did each differ from the others in terms of its style of colonial administration?

5. Discuss the principal motivations behind reformist, nationalist, and independence movements in the Middle East. How successful have these been at achieving their goals?

6. Provide a brief history of the state of Israel and its relationships with other Middle Eastern nations. What are the roots of the conflict between Palestinians and Israelis? How was this conflict affected by the activities of Europeans?

7. What have been the main effects of petroleum production on Middle Eastern nations? How have oil revenues affected demographics, economic investment, and social structure in petroleum-producing nations?

8. Discuss the effects of industrialization on rural villages like Kafr el-Elow, Egypt and Demirciler, Turkey. Do you think that the changes resulting from industrialization in these communities have been mostly positive or mostly negative? Why?

9. What is the traditional structure of kinship in Islamic communities? How has this structure been affected by colonization and industrialization?

10. Describe marriage customs typical of Middle Eastern societies. What is meant by a *bint amm* marriage and what function does it serve? What is *mahr*?

11. What is the status of women in traditional Islamic societies? How does Islamic law affect the rights and privileges of women? Which do you think is more important, honoring religious traditions or rejecting them in favor of gender equality? Why?

12. What are the differences between Sunni and Shi'a Muslims? How did these differences originate and what has been the effect of this division on the modern practice of Islam?

13. What are the principal goals of Islamic fundamentalism in the Middle East? What are the supporters of these goals doing to achieve them? Do you think that Islamic fundamentalism is good or bad for nation-states in the Middle East? Why?

14. The Islamic Revolution in Iran was one of the most significant social revolutions of the past two decades. Summarize the events leading up to this revolution and the effects that it has had on Iranian society.

15. How have ethnic and religious diversity within Middle Eastern nation-states been addressed by their governments? What are some specific examples of situations in which ethnic and religious differences have led to violent conflict? How might such conflicts be resolved?

CHECKING YOUR UNDERSTANDING - A PRACTICE EXAMINATION

We suggest that you take this practice exam and then check your answers against the key provided at the end of this section. Use the questions that you got wrong as a guide to further study. Try to learn why specific answers are right and wrong. You may even want to take the practice exam a second time to review what you have learned.

True-False Questions

1. Arabic is not the language spoken by the majority of people in either Turkey or Iran.

2. Muslims share with Christians and Jews the faith that Abraham was the founder and first prophet of their tradition.

3. European invaders were successful in bringing much of the Middle East under the control of Western governments during the Crusades.

4. To offset British expansion in the Middle East, the Italians built a North African empire in Algeria, Tunisia, and Morocco.

5. Zionism is the name given to a movement that called for the resettlement of Jews into their original homeland.

6. Reformist movements in the Middle East emphasized the importance of adopting Western culture and abandoning traditional Islamic ideology.

7. Nationalism movements in Libya, Kuwait, Saudi Arabia, and Iraq were successful in taking the controlling interests in petroleum production away from multinational corporations.

8. The *per capita* incomes of some Middle Eastern countries surpass those of many core countries.

9. Middle Eastern countries with relatively small populations but large oil revenues have adopted policies that encourage population growth.

10. The case study of the village of Kafr el-Elow demonstrates that the standard of living in rural communities declines rapidly as a result of industrialization.

11. Introduction of a money-based economic system to the village of Demirciler, Turkey was unsuccessful due to the importance of networks of reciprocity.

12. The *hamula* has always been a source of pride and loyalty within rural Arab communities.

13. Polygyny is prohibited by Islamic law.

14. First-cousin marriages are common in Arab societies.

15. According to the *Qur'an*, men are in charge of women.

16. Despite the notion that women should be subordinate to men, the *Sharia* (Islamic law) grants women equal legal status.

17. *Purdah* reinforces the separation between the domestic private sphere of women and the male-dominated public sphere.

18. The Islamic Revolution in Iran was motivated by the desire to establish a Western-style democracy.

19. According to most Muslims, one's religious life should be separate from one's economic, social, and political affairs.

20. All Arabs are Muslims.

Multiple Choice Questions

21. The Persian civilization flourished in what is now known as:
    A. Iran
    B. Israel
    C. Egypt
    D. Iraq

22. The world's first written legal codes are found in:
    A. Mesoamerica
    B. Egypt
    C. Mesopotamia
    D. China

23. Caravan routes that transported goods from port cities to inland centers were managed by a group of people known as:
    A. Bedouins
    B. Marsh Arabs
    C. Phoenicians
    D. Crusaders

24. The founder and first prophet of the Islamic tradition was:
    A. Moses
    B. Jesus
    C. Abraham
    D. Muhammad

25. After receiving religious revelations, Muhammad began to preach about a universal deity known as:
    A. Allah
    B. Jehovah
    C. Osiris
    D. the Holy Spirit

26. In addition to being a religious leader, Muhammad was a:
    A. physician
    B. carpenter
    C. warrior
    D. fisherman

27. Rulers of the Ottoman Empire were given the title of:
    A. pharaoh
    B. sultan
    C. imam
    D. caliph

28. Military expeditions undertaken by European rulers for the purpose of ending Islamic control of the Holy Land were known as:
    A. the Crusades
    B. *jihad*
    C. the Diaspora
    D. vendettas

29. Trade with India and China was taken over from the Muslims by the:
    A. Portuguese
    B. British
    C. Germans
    D. French

30. Egypt briefly came under French rule in:
    A. 1576
    B. 1621
    C. 1798
    D. 1882

31. Western forms of education introduced to Middle Eastern countries were more
    _____ than traditional schools of the region.
    A. religious
    B. secular
    C. quantitative
    D. rigorous

32. In the Middle East, global industrialism has resulted in greater economic
    _____.
    A. equality
    B. inequality
    C. accountability
    D. control

33. Which of the following ideas would have been supported by nationalist leaders
    such as Gamal Nasser?
    A. establishment of a pan-Arab socialist government
    B. close economic alliances with Western nations
    C. British control of the Suez canal
    D. mandatory education in English and French

34. As nationalism movements spread in the Middle East, multinational
    corporations that were producing oil for the international market:
    A. received strong support from oil-producing nations
    B. reaped enormous "windfall profits" from oil use in regional conflicts
    C. saw the value of their product fall dramatically
    D. lost their controlling interests in the region's economy and politics

35. The high fertility rates of Islamic countries are most readily explained by:
    A. the value of large families in agricultural economies
    B. Islamic religious beliefs
    C. high infant mortality rates
    D. poor education and high rates of illiteracy

36. The appearance of new socioeconomic classes in villages like Kafr el-Elow can be attributed to:
   A. industrialization
   B. high fertility rates
   C. government welfare projects
   D. oil production

37. The office of a sheik is based on:
   A. wealth
   B. political power
   C. kinship
   D. religious knowledge

38. In the Middle East, the nuclear family is becoming:
   A. more important than the extended family
   B. less important than the extended family
   C. most prevalent among rural peasants
   D. most prevalent among the urban poor

39. The practice of *bint amm* marriages is probably closely tied to:
   A. Islamic religious beliefs
   B. political relationships between distant lineages
   C. specific economic relationships
   D. a nomadic existence

40. Islamic tradition requires:
   A. payments made by the family of the bride to the family of the groom
   B. payments made by the family of the groom to the family of the bride
   C. payments made by the groom to the bride
   D. payments made by the bride to the groom

41. In countries like Saudi Arabia and Egypt, attempts to reform the status of women are often:
   A. perceived as Western assaults on Islamic morality
   B. initiated and supported by fundamentalist Islamic leaders
   C. considered to be part of the agenda of nationalist movements
   D. interpreted as the only way to achieve peace in the region

42. The degree of gender equality that exists in Middle Eastern countries is directly related to:
   A. oil revenues
   B. degree of Western influence
   C. importance of rural vs. urban production
   D. distance from the Mediterranean

43. The Shi'a Muslims believe that:
    A. Islam should be governed by descendants of Ali
    B. the Islamic homeland is located in Iraq
    C. imams do not have special supernatural powers
    D. all Muslims should be Arabs

44. Traditional Shi'a theology, based on the doctrine of the imamate:
    A. does not distinguish between religion and politics
    B. draws a firm line separating Islamic beliefs and secular governments
    C. guarantees religious freedom for all
    D. has become the basis for the monarchy of Saudi Arabia

45. The Hizbollah, based in Lebanon, is:
    A. a radical, fundamentalist Shi'a group favoring theocratic rule
    B. a progressive political party encouraging Western values
    C. an ancient Christian sect that advocates pacifism
    D. an extremist Jewish organization seeking justice for Israel

46. Palestinian Arabs believe they are entitled to a national territory in lands currently controlled by:
    A. Israel
    B. Libya
    C. Iraq
    D. Turkey

47. It is probably fair to say that most of the terrorist activity in the Middle East has been based on:
    A. economic injustices deriving from colonialism
    B. racial inequality
    C. competition for international trade
    D. religious beliefs and ideology

48. The most knowledgeable scholars and religious specialists in the tradition of the Shi'a Muslims are known as:
    A. ayatollahs
    B. rabbis
    C. imams
    D. hamulas

49. Mystical Islamic practices in North Africa are based on relationships between:
    A. patriarchs and extended families
    B. the mullah and his congregation
    C. marabouts or sheiks and their followers
    D. churches and public schools

50. The Kurds are a group located in:
    A. desert regions of Saudi Arabia
    B. hill country between Syria and Lebanon
    C. mountainous regions of Turkey, Iran, and Iraq
    D. the southern Nile Valley

Suggested Readings

ABU-LUGHOD, JANET. 1961. "Migrant adjustment to city life: The Egyptian case." *The American Journal of Sociology* 62:22-32.

AL-THAKEB, FAHAD. 1985. "The Arab family and modernity: Evidence from Kuwait." *Current Anthropology* 26(5):575-580.

BATES, DANIEL G., & AMAL RASSAM. 1983. *Peoples and Cultures of the Middle East*. Englewood Cliffs, NJ: Prentice Hall.

BECK, LOIS, & NIKKI KEDDIE, eds. 1978. *Women in the Muslim World*. Cambridge, MA: Harvard University Press.

CHIROT, DANIEL. 1986. *Social Change in the Modern Age*. San Diego: Harcourt Brace Jovanovich.

EICKELMAN, DALE F. 1976. "Moroccan Islam: Tradition and Society in a Pilgrimage Center." *Modern Middle East Series*, No. 1. Austin: University of Texas Press.

_____. 1989. *The Middle East: An Anthropological Approach*, 2nd ed. Englewood Cliffs, NJ: Prentice Hall.

EL-ZEIN, ABDUL HAMID. 1977. "Beyond ideology and theology: The search for the anthropology of Islam." *Annual Review of Anthropology* 6:227-254.

ESPOSITO, JOHN. 1988. *Islam: The Straight Path*. London: Oxford University Press.

FAKHOURI, HANI. 1972. *Kafr El-Elow: An Egyptian Village in Transition*. New York: Holt, Rinehart & Winston.

FERNEA, ELIZABETH WARNOCK. 1965. *Guests of the Sheik*. Garden City, NY: Doubleday Anchor.

FERNEA, ELIZABETH W., & ROBERT A. FERNEA. 1979. "A look behind the veil." In *Human Nature*. (Reprinted in *Anthropology* 89/90, Guilford, CT: The Dushkin Publishing Group.)

GILSENAN, MICHAEL. 1973. *Saint and Sufi in Modern Egypt*. Oxford: Oxford University Press.

HOURANI, ALBERT. 1991. *A History of the Arab Peoples*. Cambridge, MA: Belknap Press.

KEDDIE, NIKKI R. 1981. *Roots of Revolution: An Interpretive History of Modern Iran*. New Haven, CT: Yale University Press.

MAY, DARLENE. 1980. "Women in Islam: Yesterday and today." In Cyriac Pullapilly, ed., *Islam in the Contemporary World*. Notre Dame, IN: Cross Roads Books.

PIERCE, JOE. 1964. *Life in a Turkish Village*. New York: Holt, Rinehart & Winston.

SPENCER, WILLIAM. 1990. *The Middle East*, 3rd ed. Guilford, CT: Dushkin Publishing Group.

Answer Key with Page Numbers

1. T 483	18. F 500	35. A 491
2. T 484	19. F 501	36. A 492
3. F 487	20. F 501	37. C 493
4. F 487	21. A 484	38. A 493
5. T 488	22. C 484	39. C 494
6. F 489	23. A 484	40. B 495
7. T 490	24. C 484	41. A 496
8. T 490	25. A 485	42. B 496
9. T 491	26. C 485	43. A 497
10. F 492	27. B 486	44. A 499
11. F 493	28. A 486	45. A 501
12. T 493	29. A 487	46. A 502
13. F 494	30. C 487	47. D 502
14. T 494	31. B 488	48. A 498
15. T 495	32. B 489	49. C 498
16. F 496	33. A 489	50. C 501
17. T 497	34. D 490	

CHAPTER 24

ASIA

Chapter Outline

Early Asian Civilizations
Ecclesiastical Religions in Asia
    HINDUISM
    BUDDHISM
    ISLAM
Asia and the West
Colonialism in Asia
    CHINA
    THE DUTCH EMPIRE
    FRENCH INDOCHINA
    THAILAND: AN INDEPENDENT COUNTRY
    THE PHILIPPINES
Consequences of Western Colonialism
    POPULATION GROWTH, AGRICULTURE, AND URBANIZATION
    ECONOMIC CHANGE
Political Change: Nationalism and Independence
    INDIA
    CHINA
        Mao and the Chinese Revolution
    SOUTHEAST ASIA
Asia in the Modern World System
Southern Asia
    INDIA: A DEMOCRATIC PATH TO DEVELOPMENT
    PAKISTAN: A MILITARY STATE
Socialist States in the Periphery
    VIETNAM
Ethnological Research in Southern Asia
The Indian Caste System
    ORIGINS OF THE CASTE SYSTEM
        The *Jatis* and the *Jajmani* System
        Anthropological Explanations of Caste
Social Structure, Family, and the Role of Women in Southern Asia
    THE EXTENDED FAMILY
    THE DOWRY
    GENDER AND STATUS

Ethnological Research in China
  China Since 1970: Red Flag Commune
    REACTIONS TO THE COMMUNE SYSTEM
    THE FAMILY, MARRIAGE, AND KINSHIP IN RED FLAG COMMUNE
  The Status of Women: Change and Continuity
    THE ONE-CHILD POLICY IN CHINA
Ethnological Research in Southeast Asia
  Southeast Asia in the Global Economy
  Island Southeast Asia
Ethnic and Religious Problems
  Sikhs versus Hindus in India
  Tamils and Sinhalese in Sri Lanka

Chapter Highlights

This chapter provides a summary of the history and ethnology of states in Asia, beginning with early agricultural states of the Indus Valley and northern China and ending with contemporary cultures. Important themes of the chapter are the nature of traditional, agricultural village societies and their transformation as a result of **global industrialization**.

The first **agricultural states** and civilizations of Asia appeared in the **Indus River Valley** of Pakistan and in the **Yellow River Valley** of northern China. Early cities of the Indus, dating to around 2500 B.C., were constructed of fired mud brick with elaborate systems of baths and sewers. In China, large cities appeared during the **Shang** dynasty beginning around 1800 B.C. Shang cities were characterized by massive fortification walls, testifying to the importance of warfare and conquest. Agricultural states also thrived, though not at such early dates, in Burma, Thailand, Cambodia, and Indonesia.

Organized religions evolved in conjunction with the emergence of agricultural states. **Confucianism** emphasized the authority of the ruler and stressed rites of legitimation that reinforced the power of Chinese emperors. **Hinduism**, which developed in India, stresses the process of *samsara* (reincarnation). **Buddhism**, also originating in India, teaches a spiritual quest for *nirvana* (enlightenment). **Islam**, diffusing from the Middle East, focuses on the wisdom of the **Qur'an** and **Sharia**.

Despite its ancient heritage, much of Asia experienced the domination of European culture as a result of direct **colonization** in the late nineteenth century. Just as it had sought control of key resources in the Middle East, Great Britain colonized India, Burma, and Malaysia. This resulted in the production of **cash crops** for export and the development of mining enterprises. Colonies were established by the Dutch in Indonesia, the Spanish in the Philippines, and the French in Cambodia, Vietnam, and Laos. China and Thailand were able to resist direct colonization, although the British gained access to China through the **opium trade** and the colonization of Hong Kong.

Western colonialism had dramatic effects on agricultural states of Asia. The control of diseases and improvements in health care led to a population explosion. Production of cash crops could not keep pace with population growth, causing an agricultural involution as land became more scarce. Agricultural economies were transformed by their dependence on global markets, and land, labor, and capital were decoupled from the **moral economy** of village reciprocity.

The response to colonial exploitation was the emergence of **nationalist and independence movements** in the late nineteenth and early twentieth centuries. Much of this was spearheaded by middle classes educated under colonial rule. Individuals like **Mohandas Gandhi** were able to extend nationalist movements to the peasant population and lay the groundwork for India's independence in 1947. In China, early movements for democracy were quashed by a military dictatorship that was in turn ousted by Marxist revolutionaries under the leadership of **Mao Zedong**. The **communist** People's Republic of China was established in 1949. In Southeast Asia, Ho Chi Minh drove the French from Vietnam in 1954, but the establishment of a communist government throughout Vietnam was delayed by U.S. intervention until 1975.

Following independence, Asian countries joined the world system as peripheral societies. Although not direct colonies, these countries were governed by political elites that received military and economic support from core societies. Some, like India and Pakistan, participated in the world **capitalist** economy. Others, like China and Vietnam, became **socialist** states. By the 1980s foreign control of industrialization had been reduced, but most of these societies remained **peripheral** in status.

Ethnological research has revealed many patterns that are particular to Asian societies. Among these is the **caste system** of South Asia. In this system, individuals are identified with *varnas* (**castes**) and *jatis* (**subcastes**) that are hierarchically ranked, endogamous descent groups associated with specific occupations. For example, an members of the hair-cutting *jati* must marry members of other families of haircutters and their children must be haircutters, too. *Jatis* are intimately linked with an economy based on occupational reciprocity, called *jajmani*. In this system, found in rural villages, a dominant caste granted land rights and other privileges in return for services. Members of different *jatis* exchanged goods and services in a type of barter system. Although the *jajmani* system is disappearing in the face of **modernization**, caste-based segregation continues. Explanations of the caste system range from **Louis Dumont**'s argument that it is supported by Hindu cosmology and general consensus to **cultural materialist** explanations that it served to justify inequitable distributions of land and other resources.

In China, ethnological research can be divided into pre-Communist and post-Communist studies. Among the former was a study by **Francis Hsu** grounded in **culture-and-personality theory**. He argued that traditional authoritarian family and clan structures resulted in a competitive and success-oriented male personality type. **Morton Fried** analyzed *kan-ch'ing*, or **patron-client relationships**, between people of different class backgrounds and how connections to the global economy had resulted in hardship for **peasants**. After the formation of the communist People's Republic, **Norman Chance** conducted a study of **Half Moon Village**, a rural commune. His research indicated that communes were not effective at implementing socialist ideals and that traditional kinship relationships persisted in spite of government attempts to alter them. China has also been of interest to demographers. Its **one-child policy**, despite some resistance, has been effective at slowing runaway population growth.

Population migration from Asia is also of interest to anthropologists. **Pamela DeVoe** has been practicing **applied anthropology** among **refugees** from Southeast Asia in the St. Louis area. Among her observations is that refugees lack adequate health care benefits and have trouble adjusting to the culture of health care in the U.S. Other research has extended to refugee camps in different parts of the world.

Ethnological research in Southeast Asia has focused on both village organization and the changes caused by interaction with the global economy. **Clifford Geertz** found that there was a close relationship between religion and social class in Indonesia, where the elites practiced Islam or a combination of Hindu-Buddhist traditions while the majority practiced a **synchretism** of belief systems known as *abangan*. These included *slametan*, a ritual to promote village solidarity. **Robert Hefner** has shown how global trends have resulted in a more widespread practice of Islam in Indonesia.

Ethnic and religious differences have led to conflicts in many parts of Asia. Among these have been tensions between Hindus and Muslims that resulted in the formation of the Islamic state of Pakistan, confrontations between Hindus and **Sikhs** in India that resulted in the assassination of Prime Minister Indira Gandhi, and conflicts between the Buddhist **Sinhalese** of Sri Lanka and a Hindu **Tamil** minority. Many of these problems were exacerbated by colonial practices that defined national boundaries with little regard for ethnic territories or that relocated groups outside of their homelands. Ethnological research plays a major role in helping to understand cultural traditions and the problems that have resulted from colonization and interactions with the global economy.

Terms and Concepts You Should Know

ecclesiastical religion (506):

rite of legitimation (506):

Hinduism (507):

Buddhism (507):

Islam (507):

Kulture-System (508):

agricultural involution (509):

moral economy (509):

Boxer Rebellion (510):

Great Leap Forward (513):

caste system (514-515):

varna (514):

jatis (514):

jajmani (514-515):

Red Flag Commune (519):

Half Moon Village (519-521):

Sikhs (526-527):

Hindus (526-527):

Tamils (527):

Sinhalese (527):

People You Should Know About

Mohandas Gandhi (510):

Mao Zedong (510-511, 513):

Sun Yat-sen (510):

Chiang Kai-shek (510):

Ho Chi Minh (511-512):

Ngo Dinh Diem (511-512):

Jawaharlal Nehru (512):

Indira Gandi (512):

Louis Dumont (515):

Francis Hsu (516):

Marvin Harris (517):

Morton Fried (517):

Nancy Levine (517):

Norman Chance (519-521):

David Banks (523):

Thinking About What You Have Read

The following questions or problems may be of help to you in studying the material presented in both the text and in your class. You may want to write out the answers to these questions (writing something down always seems to help solidify it in one's mind) or just think about them.

1. What were the early Asian civilizations? Where were they located? Describe their ways of life.

2. Describe the ecclesiastical religions of Asia.

3. What were the consequences of Western colonialism in Asia? Examine the demographic, social, economic, political, and agricultural impacts.

4. What were the effects of colonialism on population growth in South and East Asia? What were the principal changes responsible for demographic trends?

5. How did colonial policies affect rural agricultural villages in India and Southeast Asia?

6. As a consequence of colonialism, what political changes occurred in India, China, the Philippines, and southeast Asia?

7. Give two (2) examples of nationalistic movements in Asian countries? What have been the specific results of these movements?

8. How does Asia fit into the modern world system? Compare and contrast India, Pakistan, China, and Vietnam.

9. Discuss the history of communism in China and the effects that it has had on Chinese society. What is the meaning of terms such as the "Great Leap Forward" and the "Cultural Revolution"?

10. What types of ethnological research have been conducted in Asia? What are some of the results of these studies?

11. What is the Indian caste system? How did it originate? Why did it originate? What are the castes (*varnas*) and untouchables (Harijans)? What are the *jatis* and *jajmani* systems?

12. How do anthropologists such as Louis Dumont view and explain castes? What do you think of their analysis?

13. Describe the general social structure, the family, and role of women in southern Asian societies. What is a dowry? Are there any parallels in your culture?

14. What has ethnographic research in China found?

15. Why is the cow sacred in India? What do you think of Marvin Harris' analysis and hypothesis?

16. What did Nancy Levine and other anthropologists find in the Himalayas?

17. Describe the findings of Francis Hsu and Morton Fried. How did Chinese society change after the revolution?

18. What is the status of women in China? What did Norman Chance find out about women in his ethnographic work in Half Moon Village?

19. What measures has China taken to control population growth? To what extent have these measures been successful? Do you think these measures would be effective in other countries where population growth is a problem? Why or why not?

20. What is the one-child policy in China? How is it working?

21. Describe the role(s) of southeast Asia in the global economy.

22. Who is David Banks, and what did he do?

23. What did Clifford Geertz find out in the island area of southeast Asia? Compare the work of Geertz to the findings of Robert Hefner.

24. Describe and evaluate the problems of Sikhs versus Hindus in India. How would you solve the problems? Describe the problems between the Tamils and Sinhalese in Sri Lanka. Could you solve their problems? Are there any similarities between these factions?

CHECKING YOUR UNDERSTANDING - A PRACTICE EXAMINATION

We suggest that you take this practice exam and then check your answers against the key provided at the end of this section. Use the questions that you got wrong as a guide to further study. Try to learn why specific answers are right and wrong. You may even want to take the practice exam a second time to review what you have learned.

True-False Questions

1. Two of Asia's largest cities, Harappa and Mohenjo-Daro, developed on the Yellow River in what today is the country of China.

2. Wet-rice cultivation and extensive irrigation projects provided the basis for large state societies such as the Pagan dynasty of Burma, the Khmer empire of Cambodia, and the Majapahit kingdom in Indonesia.

3. The ritual activities associated with Confucianism were rites of passage that reinforced the rule of the Chinese emperors.

4. Hinduism is a major world religion that developed in China.

5. Buddhists accept many Hindu concepts, including samsara, karma, and moksha or nirvana; yet, Buddhists have evolved into two major branches in different geographic regions.

6. In the nineteenth century, India became a colony of Britain.

7. The British eventually gained access to China by dealing in addictive drugs.

8. The Philippines were first colonized by Spain.

9. Western expansion and colonialism in Asia brought diseases and increased mortality rates, leading to dramatic population decreases.

10. A revolutionary movement by the Muslim population in northern India was crushed by Gandhi's strong military forces, resulting in the formation of a united nation incorporating both Islamic and Hindu traditions.

11. Nationalistic movements in China resulted in accelerated modernization and participation in the global economy.

12. Mao Zedong and his armies gained control of the country and founded the People's Republic of China in 1959.

13. The principal religion in Pakistan is Islam.

14. The government of Pakistan can be classified as a military dictatorship.

15. In the social hierarchy of India, the uppermost class was known as the Sudras.

16. In the social hierarchy of India, the lowermost class was known as the Brahamns.

17. Cultural materialists view Hinduism in India as providing the cultural framework for the caste hierarchy, while French anthropologist Louis Dumont concluded that the caste relationships were based upon prevailing economic and political conditions.

18. Recent ethnographic research has shown that patrilineages and patriclans remain important social groupings in southern India, while no permanent patrilineages or patriclans are evident in northern India.

19. The extended family is the ideal norm for South Asian villages because it provides a corporate structure for landowning, labor, and other functions.

20. American anthropologist Francis Hsu did an ethnographic study of Yunnan to show how personality development is associated with the extended family and clan kinship ties, resulting in a predominant male personality type that is competitive and success-oriented.

21. According to anthropologist Marvin Harris, cows are considered sacred for highly practical reasons such as the use of their manure for both fertilizer and cooking fuel, the use of the oxen they produce to plow the fields, and the non-competitive nature of their food resources.

22. Polyandrous marriages are the norm in Tibet due to the special cultural values given by myths and genealogies that celebrate the unity of family with brothers linked in polyandry, rather than for any environmental or economic reasons.

23. Norman Chance concluded that the status of women had improved under the Communist regime in China because they were no longer being confined to the home, but encouraged to work along with the men in agriculture and industry.

24. Since 1989, family planning policy in China has provided incentives for an urban nuclear family to have a maximum of four people.

25. In rural communities of Southeast Asia, the majority of the population is engaged in the production of cattle and wheat.

Multiple Choice Questions

26. The ancient cities of Harappa and Mohenjo Daro were located on the Indus River in what is today the modern nation of:
    A. Tibet
    B. Afghanistan
    C. Turkey
    D. Pakistan

27. Confucian rituals, some of which were observed by thousands of people at a time, were primarily:
    A. sacrifices to a supreme divine power
    B. rituals of confession and salvation
    C. rites of legitimization for Chinese rulers
    D. celebrations of military victories

28. The belief that an individual's destiny is affected by behaviors in a previous life is known as:
    A. karma
    B. nirvana
    C. Buddha
    D. mañana

29. The Buddhist religion originated in:
    A. India
    B. China
    C. Indonesia
    D. Iran

30. One country in Southeast Asia that was never directly colonized by Europeans was:
    A. Burma
    B. Vietnam
    C. Indonesia
    D. Thailand

31. Population growth in Asia was coupled with:
    A. rapid industrialization
    B. impoverishment of rural peasants
    C. the decline of urban centers
    D. decreased population movement

32. When the U.S. defeated the initial colonial rulers of the Philippines in 1898, they:
    A. granted independence to the island nation
    B. proceeded with a direct colonization of the islands
    C. placed the Philippines under the control of Spanish authority
    D. returned control of the Philippines to China

33. The colonization of Asia and other world areas by European countries and the U.S. is also known as:
    A. Manifest Destiny
    B. global industrialization
    C. the Fourth World
    D. Western imperialism

34. One of the results of British colonialism in India was:
    A. introduction of public education in native languages for rural peasants
    B. elimination of discrimination based on traditional Hindu castes
    C. creation of an English-speaking middle class with Western values
    D. promotion of the concept of democratic government

35. The nation of India is governed by:
    A. religious authority
    B. a monarchy
    C. a democracy
    D. Great Britain

36. An Asian country that has withdrawn from the capitalist world system, prohibiting the entrance of multinational corporations and foreigners, is:
    A. Thailand
    B. Vietnam
    C. Myanmar (Burma)
    D. Pakistan

37. Studies of the *jajmani* system indicate that it:
    A. functioned only for the upper classes
    B. provided all groups with access to goods and services
    C. was utilized only by merchants
    D. functioned only for the poorest peasants

38. Mao Zedong's "Cultural Revolution" succeeded at:
    A. promoting free market enterprise
    B. eliminating the most skilled and educated classes
    C. increasing agricultural and industrial development
    D. opening China to Western influence

39. Vietnam's plan to withdraw from the world economy was based on:
    A. heavy industry using urban labor
    B. resettlement of urban populations into collective farms
    C. an economy oriented toward fishing and other coastal resources
    D. restructuring traditional lineages into matriarchal clans

40. The *jajmani* system of economic relationships is based on:
    A. tribute and taxation
    B. the use of a standardized currency
    C. barter and relationships of reciprocity
    D. potlatch or cargo-style redistribution of goods

41. Early ethnographic research in China focused on:
    A. social consequences of colonialism
    B. the impact of agricultural populations on the natural environment
    C. the role of the extended family and clan in Chinese society
    D. relationships between race and culture

42. Fraternal polyandry refers to the practice of:
    A. one man having several wives
    B. a man marrying his brother's widow
    C. homosexual marriages
    D. brothers sharing a single wife

43. The Chinese Communist Party viewed the traditional family, clan, and patriarchal kinship structure of Chinese villagers as:
    A. a model for the organization of state government
    B. the roots of an egalitarian social system
    C. the undesirable legacy of pre-Communist "feudal" China
    D. a Western-influenced way of life

44. In 1950, the Chinese Communist government passed Marriage Laws that required free choice in marriage by both partners and established a woman's right to divorce without losing custody of her children. At Half Moon village in the 1970s:
    A. women usually chose who would be their husbands
    B. most marriages were arranged by the government
    C. matchmaking and arranged marriages were the norm
    D. divorce was widely approved and occurred in 50% of marriages

45. In modern Chinese villages, women are given chief responsibility for:
    A. household budgets
    B. choosing where to live
    C. employment decisions
    D. family planning

46. The country of Indonesia is made up principally of:
    A. deserts
    B. lake country
    C. islands
    D. savannahs

47. The principal international organization responsible for ensuring that refugee camps maintain minimum standards of health and safety is the:
    A. Red Cross
    B. World Health Organization
    C. Save the Children Foundation
    D. United Nations

48. In the 1960s, Clifford Geertz found that the principal religion of the *abangan*, or rural residents of Indonesia, was:
    A. a local interpretation of Catholicism
    B. a mix of Hinduism and shamanism
    C. Buddhism
    D. a synchretic blend that included animistic religions

49. Sikh separatism was exacerbated by:
    A. policies of the British colonial government
    B. racial differences with neighboring populations
    C. traditional kinship-based reciprocity
    D. American interference during World War II

50. The Tamils and the Sinhalese are two ethnic groups that have been fighting against one another in:
    A. Malaysia
    B. Sri Lanka
    C. India
    D. Thailand

Suggested Readings

BUCK, PEARL. 1973. *The Good Earth.* NY: Washington Square Press.

GEERTZ, CLIFFORD. 1980. *Negara: The Theatre State in Nineteenth-Century Bali.* Princeton, NJ: Princeton University Press.

GEERTZ, HILDRED. 1989. *The Javanese Family: A Study of Kinship and Socialization.* Prospect Heights, IL: Waveland Press.

HEFNER, ROBERT W. 1985. *Hindu Javanese: Tengger Tradition and Islam.* Princeton, NJ: Princeton University Press.

_____.1990. *The Political Economy of Mountain Java: An Interpretive History.* Berkeley: University of California Press.

IMAMURA, ANNE E. 1987. *Urban Japanese Housewives: At Home and in the Community.* Honolulu, HI: University of Hawaii Press.

ISLAM, A.K.M. AMINUL. 1987. *A Bangladesh Village: Political Conflict and Cohesion.* Prospect Heights, IL: Waveland Press.

KEYES, CHARLES. 1987. *Thailand: Buddhist Kingdom as Modern Nation-State.* Boulder, CO: Westview Press.

KIEFER, THOMAS M. 1986. The Tausug: Violence and Law in a Philippine Moslem Society. Prospect Heights, IL: Waveland Press.

NANDA, SERENA. 1990. *Neither Man Nor Woman: The Hijars of India.* Belmont, CA: Wadsworth Publishing Company.

PEACOCK, JAMES. 1978. *Muslim Puritans: Reformist Psychology in Southeast Asian Islam.* Berkeley, CA: University of California Press.

SUTLIVE, VINSON H., JR. 1978. *The Iban of Sarawak: Chronicle of a Vanishing World.* Prospect Heights, IL: Waveland Press.

TAMBIAH, S.J. 1976. *World Conqueror and World Renouncer: A Study of Buddhism and Polity in Thailand Against a Historical Background.* Cambridge: Cambridge University Press.

WOLF, MARGERY. 1968. *The House of Lim.* Englewood Cliffs, NJ: Prentice Hall.

Answer Key With Page Numbers

1. F 505	18. F 515	35. C 512
2. T 505	19. T 515-516	36. C 513
3. F 506	20. T 516-517	37. B 514
4. F 507	21. T 517	38. B 513
5. T 507	22. F 518	39. B 514
6. T 507	23. T 519-520	40. C 514
7. T 508	24. F 521-522	41. C 516
8. B 509	25. F 522	42. D 518
9. F 509	26. D 505	43. C 520
10. F 510	27. C 506	44. C 520
11. F 511	28. A 507	45. D 521
12. F 511	29. A 507	46. C 523
13. T 512	30. D 508	47. D 525
14. T 513	31. B 509	48. D 526
15. F 514	32. B 509	49. A 527
16. F 514	33. D 509	50. B 527
17. F 515	34. C 510	

CHAPTER 25

CONTEMPORARY GLOBAL TRENDS

Chapter Outline

Chapter Highlights

Anthropology provides a perspective on human experience that stretches around the globe and as far back in time as the beginning of humankind. By combining documentation of long-term change with studies of all levels of society in different cultures, anthropologists are especially well qualified to interpret **global trends**. The environment, population density, and technology have all been key variables affecting human culture. The increasing **interdependence** of human societies has resulted in the emergence of a **"global village"** in which all regions are in contact with one another through mass communication, economic networks, and political systems. Just as the lives of people living in a small, traditional village are inextricably connected with one another, so are the destinies of cultures in the modern world.

Since humans first began breaking stones over two million years ago, they have had lasting impacts on the natural environment. However, the impacts of hunting and gathering societies were minor and excruciatingly slow compared to the dramatic and rapid impacts of **industrialized states**. **Pollution** caused by **agribusiness** has linked food production with **environmental degradation**. In this cycle, growing populations cannot be fed without damaging natural resources. **Mechanized agriculture** practiced in both core and peripheral societies as a result of the **Green Revolution** is dependent on the use of fossil fuels and chemical fertilizers, herbicides, and pesticides. These pollute not only the air and water, but also the food that is produced. **Ozone depletion, acid rain**, and the **greenhouse effect** are other global effects of large-scale pollution.

Population growth is another global concern. High fertility rates in agricultural populations, combined with decreasing infant mortality and increasing life expectancy, will increase the world population by more than three billion people in the next fifty years. The **demographic-transition model** suggests that population growth only slows in industrialized nations where values of **individualism, upward mobility**, and **gender equality** provide incentives for reduced family size. Vast natural resources would be necessary to industrialize peripheral societies and effect a spread of this worldview even as the use of these resources accelerates in core societies. A more realistic solution is to use appropriate technology to bring about changes in the social and cultural practices of both core and peripheral societies.

One of the principal problems with modern technology is high **energy consumption**. Industrialized societies consume 80 to 90 percent of the world's nonrenewable energy. Development of **renewable** sources of energy is therefore crucial to continued industrialization. Among the resources being used at rapid rates are tropical **rain forests**, which are repositories of enormous biodiversity. Threatened species of plants and animals, most of them still unknown to science, have the potential to provide essential information about ecology as well as valuable foods, drugs, and useful materials. Human existence was radically transformed when new sources of energy were created by the modification of plants and animals through domestication. **Biodiversity** is necessary if this process is to continue.

Outlooks for the future vary widely. The **Doomsday Model**, based on computer simulations, predicts that the world's natural resources will be exhausted within 100 years. **Julian Simon**, however, argues that natural resources are infinite and that the history of human existence is one of finding solutions to resource problems. Anthropology reveals the problem to be amazingly complex. Ethnological research on the Green Revolution has shown that increases in food production are often accompanied by growth in **social inequality**, the gap between rich and poor. However, in places like **Shahidpur**, India, it has also demonstrated that **government intervention** can be used to temper this trend. **Environmental stress** can be reversed through the implementation of programs, such as **reforestation** in Haiti, that consider long- and short-term benefits together with the needs and concerns of rural peasants.

Archaeological perspectives on the **collapse** of ancient civilizations have provided useful models for interpreting global trends. **Joseph Tainter**, using a **cost-benefit analysis**, argued that the Roman Empire collapsed as a result of **declining marginal returns** on the cost of maintaining a large **imperial** system. He also points out that modern industrial societies cannot collapse in isolation. The only possible collapse is a global one. Faced with this prospect, societies are likely to incur great costs to find solutions to global problems.

Global economic trends condition the way resources are allocated to solving problems. One of the most important trends is the expansion of **multinational corporations**, which some experts feel will eventually assume control of global affairs. Multinational corporations have been attributed with both the improvement and the degradation of Third World countries. Cycles of economic **indebtedness** are seen as **neocolonialism**, increasing the dependency of peripheral societies on investments from core societies. One example of this is the **Potlatch Corporation**, an **agroforestry** company that leased land for timber production in Samoa. Anthropologist **Paul Shankman** noted that this multinational corporation coerced the Samoans into assuming greater risks and receiving fewer benefits than the corporation itself while accepting a relationship of dependency - a common pattern in the Third World.

The dismantling of the former Soviet Union as a result of economic restructuring (*perestroika*) and greater political freedom (*glasnost*) has brought about the independence of non-Russian republics, the **privatization** of industry, and the expansion of a **free-market economy**. Major changes have also occurred with the unification of Germany, the **democratization** of Poland, and the reintegration of Eastern European countries into the world capitalist economy. **Capitalism** - and dependency on the world system--is also increasing in Communist countries like China and Vietnam.

Global industrialization has had profound effects on the economies of core societies like the U.S. and Japan, where the principal trends are for increases in exports and a **postindustrial** emphasis on the service sector. Competition between **core societies** fuels the expansion of multinational corporations. Many previously peripheral societies, like South Korea, Hong Kong, Singapore, and Taiwan, are becoming **semiperipheral** as a result of newly industrializing economies. This has contributed to increasing interdependency within the world system.

Despite increasing interdependency, there are also trends towards increasing divisions within existing societies. Of particular concern to anthropologists are global trends in large-scale **ethnic conflicts**. Theories of ethnicity include the **circumstantialist model**, which emphasizes the situational aspects of ethnic identity, and the **primordialist model**, which asserts that ethnic affiliation is fundamental to individual identity. Conflicts between Serbs, Croatians, and Bosnians in the former Yugoslavia and between Hutus and Tutsis in Rwanda emphasize the importance of finding peaceful ways to resolve inter-ethnic disputes.

Religious attitudes have also fueled both internal and external conflicts. These include increasing **secularization** and increasing **fundamentalism**, both of which can result from the erosion of traditional belief systems by **industrialization** and **modernization**.

Terms and Concepts You Should Know

global village (530):

global industrialism (530):

agribusiness (530):

mechanized agriculture (531):

biotechnology (531):

Green Revolution (531, 536-8):

greenhouse effect (531):

ozone depletion (531):

demographic-transition phase 1 (531):

demographic-transition phase 2 (531):

demographic-transition phase 3 (531):

exponential population growth (533):

doubling time (533):

negative growth rate (533):

ZPG (533):

biodiversity (534):

Doomsday Model (535):

neo-Malthusians (535):

reforestation (538):

cost-benefit analysis (538):

declining marginal returns (538):

power vacuum (539):

global collapse (539):

Earth Summit (539):

multinational corporations (540):

supranational integration (540-541):

neocolonialism (541):

economic diversification (541):

globalized economy (542):

perestroika (543):

glasnost (543):

Solidarity (544):

doi moi (544):

zaibatsu (545):

postindustrial societies (545):

NICs (546):

GATT (546):

ethnic group (548):

circumstantialist model (548):

primordialist model (548):

separatism (549):

secularization (549):

People to Know About

Thomas Robert Malthus (533):

E.O. Wilson (534):

Club of Rome (535):

Julian Simon (535):

Billie DeWalt (537):

Murray Leaf (537):

Gerald Murray (538):

Joseph Tainter (538):

Alvin Wolfe (540):

Paul Shankman (541):

Mikhail Gorbachev (543):

Boris Yeltsin (543):

Lech Walesa (544):

Deng Xiaopeng (544):

Mario Zamora (547):

John Bennett (550):

Places and Cultures to Know About

Shahidpur (537):

Haiti (538):

Roman Empire (539):

Potlatch Corporation (541):

Samoa (541):

Little Dragons (546):

Thinking About What You Have Read

The following questions or problems may be of help to you in studying the material presented in both the text and in your class. You may want to write out the answers to these questions (writing something down always seems to help solidify it in one's mind) or just think about them.

1. What is meant by the term "global village"? What are the processes that can result in the creation of a global village? Do you think that the emergence of global village is a good thing or a bad thing? Why?

2. Describe the three phases of the demographic-transition model. For each, provide an example from the textbook of a society characteristic of that phase. What are the effects of demographic trends on the nature of each of these societies?

3. According to Malthus, populations grow more quickly than the food supply to support them, and as a result constantly experience hunger, warfare, resource scarcity, and poverty. Do you agree with this point of view? Why or why not?

4. What are the tradeoffs between economic development and energy use? Is it possible to attain an ideal level of energy consumption? Why or why not?

5. Discuss the principal concerns for the loss of biodiversity due to habitat destruction. What are the principal reasons for preserving biodiversity?

6. Do you agree or disagree with Julian Simon's assertions: 1) that natural resources are infinite, 2) that creative innovation will provide solutions to problems caused by increasing world population, and 3) that population growth is a stimulus to economic progress? What are the reasons for your positions?

7. What is meant by the Green Revolution? Using specific case studies, discuss the advantages and disadvantages of Green Revolution strategies.

8. Which factors were the most important ones for the success of Green Revolution projects in Shahidpur and Haiti?

9. To what does archaeologist Joseph Tainter attribute the collapse of state societies? Is civilizational collapse possible in the modern world? Why or why not?

10. At the 1993 Earth Summit, representatives of Third World countries outlined several complaints and priorities. Why did the attempt to formulate a legally binding statement that would have prevented developing countries from burning tropical rainforests fail? What is the position of these countries on environmental conservation?

11. Describe the ways that multinational corporations can influence the economies of developing nations. What are the positive and negative aspects of these influences?

12. What is meant by the term "neocolonialism" as applied to multinational corporations? Illustrate your answer with specific examples.

13. How did the policies of *perestroika* and *glasnost* affect the economic organization of the former Soviet Union?

14. How has the globalization of the world economy affected the societies of core nations such as the United States and Japan?

15. Define what is meant by the circumstantialist and the primordialist models for the nature of ethnicity. Which of these models do you prefer, and why?

16. What impact has global industrialization had on the practice of religion in industrialized societies? Do people become more religious or less religious? Why?

CHECKING YOUR UNDERSTANDING: A PRACTICE EXAMINATION

We suggest that you take this practice exam and then check your answers against the key provided at the end of this section. Use the questions that you got wrong as a guide to further study. Try to learn why specific answers are right and wrong. You may even want to take the practice exam a second time to review what you have learned.

True - False Questions

1. As societies have evolved through time, the depletion of natural resources has always been part of the human experience.

2. The "greenhouse effect" results from the depletion of the ozone layer by acid rain.

3. According to the demographic-transition model, populations in advanced industrialized countries will decline.

4. Countries such as Germany and Japan have negative rates of population growth.

5. The typical family in a developing nation will use far more energy than a typical family in a core society.

6. According to Julian Simon, natural resources are not finite but infinite.

7. The Green Revolution has been successful at increasing agricultural production in developing nations.

8. The case study of Shahidipur demonstrates that the adoption of new strains of wheat and irrigation technology by rural peasants had a beneficial effect on local production.

9. In Haiti, Gerald Murray showed that reforestation projects managed by rural peasants are far less successful than those managed by a centralized government.

10. According to Tainter's model, one of the principal factors behind the collapse of the Roman Empire was excessive taxation of productive sectors of the economy.

11. It was apparent at the 1993 Earth Summit that the main priority of many Third World countries is economic development, not environmental conservation.

12. Multinational corporations based in core societies often encourage peripheral societies to incur loans to produce a limited number of export-oriented commodities.

13. The case of the Potlatch Corporation makes it clear that some multinational corporations operate in the best interests of peripheral societies.

14. Anthropologist Marvin Harris, using a cultural-materialist view, has shown how the Persian Gulf War was really a multicorporate venture that attempted to establish a new market for western goods.

15. *Perestroika* is usually translated as "openness."

16. Since the death of Mao Zedong, China has abolished the commune system and reorganized agricultural and industrial production based on individual profits and wages.

17. Japan is dependent upon an export economy to pay for imports of fuel, food, wood, and other raw materials.

18. An individual's ethnicity cannot be changed.

19. According to the primordialist model, ethnic identity is rooted in human biology.

20. The role of religion in modern societies is minimal due to the increasing secularization that accompanies global industrialization.

Multiple Choice Questions

21. The most important factor in the creation of a global village is the existence of a:
    - A. dense and expanding multiethnic population
    - B. worldwide system of instantaneous communication
    - C. readily distributable food surplus
    - D. standard global currency

22. Mechanized agriculture is also referred to as:
    - A. technoculture
    - B. global industrialization
    - C. agribusiness
    - D. biotechnology

23. The greenhouse effect results from:
    - A. increased levels of carbon dioxide
    - B. depletion of the ozone layer
    - C. increased amounts of acid rain
    - D. melting of the polar ice caps

24. The term "Green Revolution" refers to the increased use of _____ to increase food production in Third World countries.
    - A. traditional, organic farming methods that avoid the use of pesticides
    - B. intensive human labor for planting, weeding, and harvesting
    - C. renewable tree- and root-crop products of the tropical rain forests
    - D. mechanized agriculture, genetic engineering, and artificial hybrid crops

25. The combination of high fertility rates and low mortality rates results in:
    A. population growth
    B. population decline
    C. population stabilization
    D. decreased life expectancy

26. Societies in phase 3 of the demographic-transition model experience:
    A. dramatic increases in population growth
    B. high mortality rates
    C. declining rates of population growth
    D. increasing fertility rates

27. A British clergyman and economist named _____ predicted that populations would grow at a very rapid rate (exponential rate) and that the production of food and other vital resources would increase at a much slower rate. As a result, human populations would be subjected to a variety of checks on population growth such as warfare, famine, and disease.
    A. Charles Darwin
    B. E.O. Wilson
    C. Julian Simon
    D. Thomas Malthus

28. Zero population growth means that a population will:
    A. increase
    B. decrease
    C. stay the same

29. Because of human activities and growth, it is estimated that at least one species becomes extinct every day. In fact, biologist E.O. Wilson thinks that with the expansion of industrialism, mechanized agriculture, and deforestation that as many as one-fourth of the world's plant families will become extinct by the end of the next century. The loss of this _____ is a major concern for many individuals since we, as humans, are dependent upon these living organisms for our own survival (for food and medicinal applications).
    A. biodiversity
    B. doubling time
    C. green space
    D. greenhouse effect

30. Which of the following countries is most likely to have the lowest *per capita* energy use?
    A. Mexico
    B. Kuwait
    C. Germany
    D. Bolivia

31. The principal cause of biodiversity loss is:
    A. ozone depletion
    B. water pollution
    C. genetic engineering
    D. deforestation

32. In the 1970s a group of scientists known as the Club of Rome got together to assess global trends and predict the future of the world and the people on it. Using a neo-Malthusian perspective and computer models, they predicted that
    A. there will be an infinite supply of natural resources for hundreds of years to come because biotechnology will make land more productive, and humans will invent new ways of doing things.
    B. the world, as we know it, will end abruptly in 2048 because of the greenhouse effect, coupled with a nuclear winter.
    C. current global trends in population growth, energy consumption, and environmental pollution will exhaust the world's natural resources within the next 100 years.
    D. biodiversity will increase, slowing smothering the world and all its occupants.

33. According to Julian Simon, the natural resources available to human populations are:
    A. going to be used up in the next 100 years
    B. disappearing most rapidly in Third World countries
    C. biodiversity and the productivity of the world's oceans
    D. unlimited

34. One of the most important elements of the Green Revolution is:
    A. improved agricultural technology
    B. intensification of rural labor
    C. environmental activism
    D. the raising of global consciousness

35. Anthropological research may help assess global issues such as population growth, environmental destruction, and technological change by providing a more cautious and analytical approach. This is because anthropology
    A. relies upon the concept of ethical relativism, and it can make major value judgments that other disciplines are incapable of handling or making.
    B. uses the holistic approach, and it has always been concerned with precisely those aspects of human interaction with the environment that are becoming widely recognized by scientists studying global changes in the environment.
    C. has been almost impulsive when studying cultural change and innovation, thus causing anthropologists to be very liberal and impetuous in their recommendations concerning changes in the relationship between human cultures and the physical environment.

36. According to the ethnological research conducted by Murray Leaf, the Green Revolution has been successfully implemented in
    A. Mexico City, Mexico
    B. Shahidpur, India
    C. Rio de Janiero, Brazil
    D. Western Samoa
    E. Turkmenistan and Azerbaijan

37. The case study of Shahidpur indicates that the Green Revolution:
    A. is failing to meet the needs of Third World countries
    B. can be successful when peasants understand the direct benefits of new technologies
    C. only works in situations where the government can retain control of production
    D. only works in small-scale societies

38. Gerald Murray's plan for reforestation in Haiti succeeded because:
    A. peasants realized they would benefit directly from the project
    B. it was profitable to clear land for sugar cane, coffee, and indigo for the international market
    C. traditional land-use patterns had failed
    D. the government assumed ownership of all new trees that were planted

39. According to archaeologist Joseph Tainter, the principal cause for the collapse of societies is:
    A. rising expectations
    B. declining marginal returns
    C. depletion of nonrenewable resources
    D. population growth that exceeds the carrying capacity

40. Tainter's interpretations of the reasons for collapse of complex societies suggest that modern countries:
    A. will never collapse because they are technologically sophisticated
    B. will collapse one-by-one in a "domino effect"
    C. have learned how not to collapse from the mistakes of past civilizations
    D. are so interdependent that any collapse would be global in scope

41. Representatives of Third World countries at the 1992 Earth Summit in Rio de Janeiro made it clear that their number one concern was:
    A. economic survival
    B. environmental conservation
    C. population control
    D. global warming

42. Dependency theorists suggest that multinational corporations are just a new form of neocolonialism that is aimed at supplying the Western world with natural resources and cheap labor. These corporations, rather than helping the populace, actually intensify many of the problems of Third World countries by
    A. making it possible to get cheap food and adequate housing.
    B. creating benefits for a wealthy elite and a small middle class while allowing the vast majority of the population to remain in poverty.
    C. establishing a strong lower class that eventually overthrows the ruling elite in the country.
    D. showing the people all of the riches, modern conveniences, and lifestyles that the majority of the population cannot ever possess.

43. Neocolonialism is term applied to the activities of:
    A. governments of core societies
    B. emergent semiperipheral societies
    C. international banking institutions
    D. multinational corporations

44. Anthropologist Marvin Harris and other cultural materialists stress that _____ play a primary, determinant role in the functioning of a sociocultural system.
    A. ideologies, whether they be primarily religious or primarily political in nature
    B. technological, economic, demographic, and environmental activities directed at sustaining health and well-being
    C. the means of production, representing both capital investments and systems for organizing human labor
    D. the specific histories of a given society and the histories of the various ethnic groups that contribute to its existence

45. The economic restructuring of the former Soviet Union initiated by Mikhail Gorbachev was called:
    A. *balalaika*
    B. *glasnost*
    C. *realpolitik*
    D. *perestroika*

46. Since the 1950s, the production of goods for export in the United States has:
    A. increased
    B. decreased
    C. stayed the same

47. In recent years, a number of countries have been able to transform themselves from peripheral to semiperipheral societies as a result of their "newly industrializing economies" (NICs). Among these have been:
    A. Bolivia, Chile, Peru, and Paraguay
    B. Uganda, Kenya, Zaire, and Tanzania
    C. Afghanistan, Azerbaijan, Turkmenistan, and Uzbekistan
    D. South Korea, Hong Kong, Singapore, and Taiwan

48. Newly industrializing economies (NICs) have changed the context of the world economy through:
    A. low-cost production methods and aggressive marketing
    B. high technology and low-volume sales
    C. the exclusion of multinational corporations
    D. successful Green Revolution strategies

49. The circumstantialist model of ethnicity claims that ethnic identity is:
    A. rooted in biology and heredity
    B. fluid and situational
    C. defined by the dominant majority
    D. an unnecessary political construct

50. The primordialist model views the recognition and assertion of ethnic relation-ships as:
    A. an extension of kin selection
    B. a purely political act
    C. capricious and opportunistic
    D. non-essential to an individual's personal identity

Suggested Readings

BARTH, FREDRIK. 1969. *Ethnic Groups and Boundaries*. Boston: Little, Brown.

BENNETT, JOHN W. 1987. "Anthropology and the emerging world order: The paradigm of culture in an age of interdependence." In Kenneth Moore, ed., *Waymarks: The Notre Dame Inaugural Letters in Anthropology*. Notre Dame, IN: University of Notre Dame Press.

BERNARD, H.R., & P. J. PELTO, eds. 1987. *Technology and Social Change*, 2nd ed. Prospect Heights, IL: Waveland Press.

BODLEY, JOHN H. 1985. *Anthropology and Contemporary Human Problems*, 2nd ed. Palo Alto, CA: Mayfield Press.

BROWN, LESTER R. 1988. "The vulnerability of oil-based farming." *World Watch*. (Reprinted 1990 in Robert Jackson, ed., *Global Issues* 90/91, Guilford, CT: The Dushkin Publishing Group.)

DEWALT, BILLIE. 1984. "Mexico's second green revolution: Food for feed." *Mexican Studies/Estudios Mexicanos* 1:29-60.

FRANKE, RICHARD W. 1974. "Miracle seeds and shattered dreams." *Natural History* 83(1):10.

LEAF, MURRAY. 1984. *Song of Hope: The Green Revolution in a Punjab Village*. New Brunswick, NJ: Rutgers University Press.

MURRAY, GERALD F. 1989. "The domestication of wood in Haiti: A case study of applied evolution." *Anthropological Praxis*. (Reprinted in Aaron Podelfsky & Peter J. Brown, eds., *Applying Anthropology: An Introductory Reader*. Mountain View, CA: Mayfield Publishing Co.)

PIKE, DOUGLAS. 1990. "Change and continuity in Vietnam." *Current History*. 89(545):117-134.

RAYNER, STEVE. 1989. "Fiddling while the globe warms." *Anthropology Today* 5(6):1-2.

SHANKMAN, PAUL. 1975. "A forestry scheme in Samoa." *Natural History* 84(8):60-69.

SIMON, JULIAN L. 1981. *The Ultimate Resource*. Princeton, NJ: Princeton University Press.

TAINTER, JOSEPH. 1990. *The Collapse of Complex Societies*. Cambridge: Cambridge University Press.

U.S. COMMITTEE ON GLOBAL CHANGE. 1988. *Toward an Understanding of Global Change*. Washington, DC: National Academy Press.

VAN DEN BERGHE, PIERRE. 1981. *The Ethnic Phenomenon*. New York: Elsevier Science.

WILSON, E.O., ed. 1989. *Biodiversity*. Washington, DC: National Academy Press.

WOLFE, ALVIN. 1977. "The supranational organization of production: An evolutionary perspective." *Current Anthropology* 18:615-635.

_____. 1986. "The multinational corporation as a form of sociocultural integration above the level of the state." In Hendrick Serrie, ed., *Anthropology and International Business*. Publication No. 28. Williamsburg, VA: Studies in Third World Societies.

WORSLEY, PETER. 1984. *The Three Worlds: Culture and World Development*. Chicago: University of Chicago Press.

Answer Key with Page Numbers

1. T 530	18. F 548	35. B 536
2. F 531	19. T 548	36. B 537
3. T 532	20. F 550	37. B 538
4. T 533	21. B 530	38. A 538
5. F 534	22. C 530	39. B 538
6. T 535	23. A 531	40. D 539
7. T 536	24. D 531	41. A 540
8. T 538	25. A 532	42. B 541
9. F 538	26. C 532	43. D 541
10. T 539	27. D 533	44. B 542
11. T 540	28. C 533	45. D 543
12. T 541	29. A 534	46. A 544
13. F 541	30. D 534	47. D 546
14. F 542	31. D 534	48. A 546
15. F 543	32. C 535	49. B 548
16. T 544	33. D 535	50. A 548
17. T 545	34. A 536	

CHAPTER 26

APPLIED ANTHROPOLOGY

Chapter Outline

The Role of Applied Anthropologists in Planned Change
The Informant Role
The Facilitator Role
The Analyst Role
The Representative Role
The Future of Applied Anthropology
Medical Anthropology
Applied Anthropology and Substance Abuse
Applied Archaeology: Cultural Resource Management
Cultural Relativism and Human Rights
A Resolution to the Problem of Relativism
The Problem of Intervention
Universal Human Rights
The Role of Applied Anthropology

Chapter Highlights

Anthropologists often play different roles. For many years anthropologists have, at times, used their research methods, knowledge, theories, and perspective to solve contemporary problems. In doing such they were engaging in what is called **applied anthropology** (the term **practicing anthropologist** is often used to describe anthropologists who are engaged in this type of work full time). Applied anthropology has grown so rapidly in the past decade or so that many anthropologists are now suggesting that there are not four subfields in anthropology, but five. Applied anthropologists come from all four traditional subfields of anthropology. They research environmental, economic, social, demographic, linguistic, biological, and health-related problems with the goal of finding solutions. They may be employed by governments, private agencies, organizations, or businesses to solve problems or implement changes. Anthropologists are also hired by the people who are affected (or who will be affected) by social, economic, or political change.

There are a number of different ways that one can apply anthropology. The **representative role** is one in which the anthropologist becomes the spokesperson or advocate for the culture or society that is being affected by planned change. This role may be the most difficult since it involves complex moral, political, and ethical judgments. As a **facilitator**, the anthropologist actively implements change within the community or society being studied. The anthropologist may act as an **informant** by transmitting his or her ethnographic knowledge to a government or an agency that plans to promote change in a particular area. This role may involve the production of **social impact statements** that detail the perceived consequences of the planned change. Applied anthropologists can also become involved in the actual development of policy. In doing so, the anthropologist is playing the role of **analyst**. The Vicos Project is an excellent example of this type of application. The fifth role that an anthropologist can assume is one of **a mediator**. In this case the anthropologist becomes an intermediary between differing parties. This may involve mediation among planners, developers, government officials, and the society being affected by the planned changed.

Many applied anthropologists conduct research in medical anthropology. **Medical anthropology** is the study of human health and disease within both an environmental and cultural context. Medical anthropologists deal with health delivery systems, disease processes, cultural theories of disease and disease curing, and medicine. They study such things as traditional medical practices and beliefs, the impact of Western medicine and modern health care on traditional medical systems, and patterns of disease in different cultures.

Anthropologists may also get involved in studying contemporary problems such as substance abuse. Michael Agar's study of heroin addicts and Philippe Bourgois' investigation of crack cocaine usage are excellent examples of how anthropologists can provide information that may be instrumental in solving these types of social problems.

State and federal legislation in the United States requires the preservation of both historic and prehistoric sites and materials. Archaeologists often identify important sites that might be endangered by development (e.g., dam or road construction). They may conduct surveys and excavations in order to preserve data that are important in understanding the cultural heritage of the United States. These applied archaeologists are involved in what is known as **cultural resource management (CRM)**.

Applied anthropologists are acutely aware of the **ethical issues** involved in applying their knowledge to contemporary problems. Ethics in applied anthropology is a complicated and much debated issue. Many ethical questions revolve around the seemingly simple question of: Will the change that is being implemented benefit or harm the people? This is often not an easy question to answer, and in some cases opinions will differ. The applied anthropologist must carefully examine each problem and recommendation.

Early ethnographers who accepted the tenets of **cultural relativism** sometimes embraced **ethical relativism**. Ethical relativism is the idea that a person could not make value judgments about another culture. Most anthropologists now reject ethical relativism because one can understand the worldview of other peoples without accepting or condoning all of their practices or standards. Questions remain, however. Are there universal standards that can be used to evaluate values and harmful cultural practices? What standards should be used? An important task for cross-cultural anthropology is to propose universal standards for making value judgments and to help reduce harmful cultural practices. Hopefully, anthropologists will be able to provide a basis for mutual understanding among the world's people.

Terms and Concepts You Should Know

applied anthropology (553):

practicing anthropologists (553):

representative role (553):

facilitator role (553):

informant role (553):

analyst role (553):

mediator role (554):

social-impact studies (554):

Vicos Project (555):

medical anthropology (556-557):

epidemiology (556-557):

therapeutic pluralism (557):

pot hunters (559):

cultural resource management (559-560):

cultural relativism (561):

ethical relativism (561-562):

metaculture (564):

People You Should Know

Erve Chambers (553):

Thayer Scudder and Elizabeth Colson (554):

Allan Holmberg and Mario Vasquez (555):

David Maybury-Lewis (556):

Michael Agar (558):

Philippe Bourgois (558):

Elvin Hatch (561-562):

John Van Willigen and V.C. Channa (563):

Thinking About What You Have Read

The following questions or problems may be of help to you in studying the material presented in both the text and in your class. You may want to write out the answers to these questions (writing something down always seems to help solidify it in one's mind) or just think about them.

1. What is applied anthropology, and how does it differ from "abstract" anthropology (traditional anthropology)? What roles do applied anthropologist play?

2. What are social-impact statements?

432

3. What is medical anthropology? What is epidemiology? What types of studies are conducted by medical anthropologists?

4. What was the Vicos Project? Was it effective? Do you think the anthropologists should have intervened? What does intervention do to scientific objectivity and detachment?

5. What did Louis Golomb find when he conducted ethnographic research on the curing practices in different ethnic and religious communities in Thailand? How do patients in Thailand use traditional healers and Western-based scientific forms of medicine?

6. What is therapeutic pluralism? Could you become a therapeutic pluralist? Why? Are you one already? Explain how it works.

7. How does applied anthropology contribute to our understanding of substance abuse? What information has been gleaned from these studies? Has it helped? How easy is it to implement change of the type advocated by anthropologists? What other types of social problems do you think applied anthropologists could address?

8. What is cultural resource management? How does it work? Why is it necessary, or is it? Is it necessary or desirable to preserve the past?

9. Define and evaluate the terms cultural relativism and ethical relativism. Do you agree with the critics who charge that anthropologists who believe in cultural relativism do not, cannot, or will not make value judgments concerning norms, values, and practices of specific societies? Why?

10. Do you agree that we live in society that prides itself on a wide range of toleration for other people's ideas, values, and practices? If so, is our society falling into the trap of ethical relativism that anthropology fell into?

11. If all values are relative, subjective, and not objective, then what happens to standards of right and wrong, good and evil? Do you agree that it doesn't matter what you do, just so you are sincere, feel right and good about what you are doing? Why or why not?

12. Have you ever heard government officials in the United States talk about basic human rights? Are there basic human rights? If so, what are they?

13. What is the goal of cultural relativism? What is the goal of ethical relativism? Are these concepts the same? How would an anthropologist, using a cultural relativistic point of view, explain the Nazi's attempt to exterminate the Jews during World War II? Do you think that a cultural relativist point of view could be applied to the problems in what used to be known as Yugoslavia? Could this perspective be fruitfully applied to Somalia or Rwanda?

14. Do you think applied anthropology has a future? Pick a current social problem that exists in your society and show how an applied anthropologist could help understand and solve it.

CHECKING YOUR UNDERSTANDING: A PRACTICE EXAMINATION

We suggest that you take this practice exam and then check your answers against the key provided at the end of this section. Use the questions that you got wrong as a guide for further study. Try to learn why specific answers are right and wrong. You might even consider taking this practice test more than once, several days apart.

True-False Questions

1. Applied anthropologists are often referred to as practicing anthropologists.

2. When an anthropologist becomes a spokesperson for the particular society or group that he or she is studying, the anthropologist assumes the role of "representative".

3. The mediator role involves the applied anthropologist as an intermediary among different interest groups who are participating in a development project.

4. Social impact studies involve in-depth interviews and ethnological studies in local communities to determine how various policies and developments will affect social life in communities about to undergo change.

5. The study by Thayer Scudder and Elizabeth Colson in Zambia found that Dinka, Nuer, and Zulu peoples could easily switch their subsistence pattern from hunting and gathering to sedentary irrigation agriculture.

6. The Vicos Project was an applied anthropological failure because the peasants never became self-sufficient and proud.

7. Michael Agar's applied anthropological study of the forced relocation of Haitian immigrants from Florida to Arizona found that this disruption destroyed the extended family organization and caused extreme mental anguish, often resulting in suicide.

8. Anthropologist Philippe Bourgois found that crack cocaine dealers in Watts were often substituting heroin mixed with methadone for crack.

9. The archaeological record is a renewable resource because we are always creating a new archaeological record.

10. Culture resource management is the evaluation, salvage, and protection of archaeological resources that are threatened with destruction.

11. Unfortunately, current legislation in the United States leaves many archaeological resources unprotected from destruction.

12. Slack Farm is an example of how good cultural resource management projects should be conducted.

13. Cultural relativism and ethical relativism are two terms of the same concept.

14. Cultural relativists argue that no society can claim any superior position over another regarding ethics and morality.

15. Many anthropologists held to a double standard of morality when they criticized large-scale, industrial societies, particularly U.S. society, but were quite reluctant to impose these same standards on prestate societies.

16. All anthropologists doing fieldwork in another culture must accept such practices as infanticide, female subordination, genocide, and sexual abuse.

17. Ethical relativists have argued that because anthropologists have not discovered any universal moral values that each society's values are valid with respect to that society's circumstances and conditions.

18. Elvin Hatch argues that when we understand the values and worldviews of another people, this does not necessarily mean we have to accept all of their practices and standards.

19. John Van Willigen and V.C. Channa found that the increase in dowry deaths was due to a combination of a decrease in the average age of brides and the legalization of abortions in India.

20. The term "metaculture" refers to a worldwide and pluralist culture that emphasizes fundamental human rights and values.

Multiple Choice Questions

21. The use of anthropological data to solve practical problems facing modern-day societies is called:
    A. culturology
    B. megacultural studies
    C. applied anthropology
    D. practical ethnology

22. When an anthropologist actively helps to bring about change in the community being researched, he or she is assuming the role of
    A. facilitator
    B. representative
    C. analyst
    D. informant
    E. mediator

23. Anthropologists who transfer cultural knowledge obtained from ethnological studies to government or other agencies that want to promote change are assuming the
    A. facilitator role
    B. representative role
    C. analyst role
    D. informant role
    E. mediator role

24. Research on possible consequences of change within a community involves
    A. social-impact studies
    B. medical anthropological methodology
    C. ethical anthropologists
    D. moral anthropologists

25. From their research in Zambia, Scudder and Colson concluded that the forced relocation of a rural community due to the construction of a dam would
    A. proceed smoothly without creating any problems or stresses for the people.
    B. make life easier for these people by providing easy fishing.
    C. create extreme stresses that would result in people clinging to familiar traditions and institutions during the period of relocation.
    D. make life much harder for these nomadic foragers because the dam would flood their traditional hunting area.

26. Most of the development work in the 1950s and 1960s sponsored by AID and researched by applied anthropologists
    A. focused on small-scale projects designed to make minimal change in a society or community.
    B. focused on large-scale projects such as hydroelectric dams, industrialization, and mechanized agriculture.
    C. involved Second World peoples who were interested in building Western economic trade networks.
    D. involved the establishment of local health care delivery systems in rural areas of South America.

27. The Vicos Project is an excellent example of an applied anthropology project where the anthropologists played the role of
    A. mediator
    B. informant
    C. facilitator
    D. analyst

28. The study of disease, health-care delivery systems, and theories of disease and curing is known as
    A. epidemiology
    B. social-impact studies
    C. medical anthropology
    D. cultural resource management

29. The study of disease patterns in different societies is known as
    A. diseasology
    B. epidemiology
    C. sickness variation
    D. illness complexity

30. The medical anthropology study of Louis Golomb in Thailand showed that
    A. health care delivery in rural parts of Thailand would be impossible because of the anti-Western sentiments.
    B. people used a combination of ritual, magic, and modern scientific medicine to treat an illness.
    C. visiting nurses would be the best way to institute health care in remote rural areas.
    D. it would be impossible to establish hospitals in urban areas because the people relied upon rural witch doctors and shamans for all their medical needs.

31. The applied study conducted by Philippe Bourgois in Spanish Harlem showed that
    A. older low-income housing projects could be renovated and turned into dormitories for the treatment of drug addicts.
    B. crack dealing was the most realistic route to upward mobility and the attainment of the "American Dream".
    C. heroin used always followed methadone usage among hard-core addicts.
    D. drug dealing and murder were not linked as often as reported in the mass media.

32. Individuals who dig into archaeological sites to retrieve artifacts for collectors while ignoring all the other traces left by these ancient peoples are known as
    A. grave-site robbers
    B. archaeo-bandits
    C. pot hunters
    D. artifact thieves

33. The rate at which archaeological sites are being destroyed is particularly distressing because the archaeological record is considered
    A. a nonrenewable resource.
    B. to be a false record because only select objects are preserved.
    C. a renewable resource because new sites are being created almost daily.
    D. by many applied anthropologists to be a model of how humankind should live and adapt in the future.

34. The evaluation, salvage, and protection of archaeological resources that are threatened with destruction is
    A. epidemiology
    B. social-impact studies
    C. environmental impact studies
    D. cultural resource management

35. Most archaeologists have traditionally found employment teaching at universities or working in museums. Today, many archaeologists are working as _____ evaluating, salvaging, and protecting archaeological resources that are threatened with destruction.
    A. culturologists
    B. zooarchaeologists
    C. applied archaeologists
    D. historians

36. The authors of your text discuss the looting and destruction of an archaeological site in Kentucky. This destroyed archaeological resource is known as the
    A. Cherry Hill site
    B. Blue Grass site
    C. Slack Farm site
    D. Jack Daniel's site

37. The principle that other societies should be understood through their own cultural values, beliefs, norms, and behaviors is
    A. cultural relativism
    B. ethnocentrism
    C. participant observation
    D. objective surveillance

38. The idea that we cannot impose the values of one society on other societies is called:
    A. cultural relativism
    B. ethnosimiliarism
    C. ethical relativism
    D. moral turpitude

39. Ethnologists and applied anthropologists have a role to play in helping define the universal standards for human rights in all societies. The work of John Van Willigen and V.C. Channa in India on the harmful effects of _____ illustrate this perspective and goal.
    A. the caste system
    B. genital mutilation
    C. dowry
    D. forced divorce

40. In India, the practice of dousing a woman with kerosene and burning her to death because the payment of bridewealth from her family was not enough is called _____.
    A. bride disposal
    B. dowry death
    C. money murder
    D. instant divorce

Suggested Readings

BODLEY, JOHN H. 1985. *Anthropology and Contemporary Human Problems.* Mountain View, CA: Mayfield.

_____. 1988. *Tribal Peoples and Development Issues: A Global Overview.* Mountain View, CA: Mayfield.

_____. 1990. *Victims of Progress.* Mountain View, CA: Mayfield.

CHAMBERS, ERVE. 1985. *Applied Anthropology: A Practical GuidE.* Englewood Cliffs, NJ: Prentice Hall.

DESOWITZ, ROBERT S. 1981. *New Guinea Tapeworms and Jewish Grandmothers.* New York, NY: W.W. Norton & Company.

DOWNING, THEODORE E. AND GILBERT KUSHNER. 1988. *Human Rights and Anthropology.* Cambridge, MA: Cultural Survival.

FOSTER, GEORGE AND BARBARA G. ANDERSON. 1978. *Medical Anthropology.* New York: McGraw-Hill.

JOHNSON, RONALD W. AND MICHAEL G. SCHENE. 1987. *Cultural Resource Management.* Malabar, FL: Robert E. Krieger.

KUNITZ, STEPHEN J. 1989. *Disease Change and the Role of Medicine: The Navajo ExperiencE.* Berkley, CA: University of California Press.

LINDENBAUM, SHIRLEY. 1979. *Kuru Sorcery: Disease and Danger in the New Guinea Highlands.* Mountain View, CA: Mayfield.

LANDY, DAVID. 1977. *Culture, Disease, and Healing: Studies in Medical Anthropology.* New York, NY: Macmillan Publishing Co., Inc.

LOGAN, MICHAEL H. AND EDWARD E. HUNT, JR. 1978. *Health and the Human Condition: Perspectives on Medical Anthropology.* North Scituate, MA: Duxbury Press.

MCELROY, ANN AND PATRICIA K. TOWNSEND. 1979. *Medical Anthropology in Ecological PerspectivE.* North Scituate, MA: Duxbury Press.

MOORE, LORAN G. ET AL. 1987. *The Biocultural Basis of Health: Expanding Views of Medical Anthropology.* Prospect Heights, IL: Waveland Press.

PARTRIDGE, WILLIAM, eD. 1984. *Training Manual in Development Anthropology.* Special Publication of the American Anthropological Association and the Society for Applied Anthropology, no. 17.

PODOLEFSKY, AARON AND PETER J. BROWN, eds. 1994. *Applying Anthropology: An Introductory Reader.* Mountain View, CA: Mayfield.

STULL, DONALD D. AND JEAN J. SCHENSUL. 1987. *Culture Change and Modernization: Mini-Models and Case Studies.* Prospect Heights, IL: Waveland.

TRICE, HARRISON M. AND JANICE M. BEYER. 1993. *The Cultures of Work Organizations.* Englewood Cliffs, NJ: Prentice Hall.

TROTTER, ROBERT T., II. 1988. *Anthropology for Tomorrow: Creating Practitioner-Oriented Applied Anthropology Programs.* Washington, DC: American Anthropological Association.

WILLIGEN, JOHN VAN. 1986. *Applied Anthropology: An Introduction.* South Hadley, MA: Bergin and Garvey.

WOOD, CORINNE S. *Human Sickness and Health: A Biocultural View.* Mountain View, CA: Mayfield.

Answer Key With Page Numbers

1. T 553
2. T 553
3. T 554
4. T 554
5. F 554
6. F 555
7. F 558
8. F 558
9. F 559
10. T 559
11. T 560
12. F 560-561
13. F 561
14. F 561
15. T 561
16. F 561
17. T 561
18. T 562
19. F 563-564
20. T 564
21. C 553
22. A 553
23. D 553
24. A 554
25. C 554
26. B 554-555
27. D 555
28. C 556
29. B 556
30. B 557
31. B 558
32. C 559
33. A 559
34. D 560
35. C 560
36. C 560
37. A 561
38. C 561
39. C 563
40. B 563